PRIMARY
FOUNDATIONS

Geography

AGES 7–9

John Corn

CONTENTS

Author
John Corn

Editor
Joel Lane

Assistant Editor
Simon Tomlin

Series Designer
Lynne Joesbury

Designer
Mark Udall

Illustrations
Gary Clifford

Cover photograph
Getty One Stone

ACKNOWLEDGEMENTS

ActionAid for use of material from their Chembakolli Pack, invaluable advice and help in the preparation of material with reference to the website *www.chembakolli.com* (ActionAid Education, Chataway House, Leach Road, Chard TA20 1RR).

Ingleborough Hall Outdoor Education Centre for the use of material and information from their educational pack 'Clapham in the Yorkshire Dales' (Ingleborough Hall, Clapham, North Yorkshire LA2 8EF *www.ingleboro.co.uk*).

Material from the National Curriculum 2000 ©The Queen's Printer and Controller of HMSO. Reproduced under the terms of HMSO Guidance Note 8.

Material from the Programmes of Study and *Geography: A Scheme of work for Key Stages 1 and 2* © Qualifications and Curriculum Authority 1998, 2000.

Every effort has been made to trace copyright holders and the publishers apologize for any inadvertent omissions.

Published by Scholastic Ltd,
Villiers House,
Clarendon Avenue,
Leamington Spa,
Warwickshire
CV32 5PR
Visit our website at
www.scholastic.co.uk

3
Introduction

7
Chapter 1 – Investigating our local area
Living in a village
Living in a town

29
Chapter 2 – Weather and travel
Weather around the world
My weather

54
Chapter 3 – Improving the environment
Improving our school's environment
A case study – Gretton

77
Chapter 4 – Settlers
Village settlers
How towns grow

98
Chapter 5 – Village case studies
Chembakolli: village life in India
Clapham – a village in the Yorkshire Dales

120
Photocopiables

Text © 2000 John Corn; © 2000 Scholastic Ltd
^ ' ⁻ 6 7 8 9 0   ^ ^ ' 5 6 7 8 9

British Library Cataloguing-in-Publication Data
A catalogue record for this book is available from the British Library.

ISBN 0-439-01800-5

Introduction

At the beginning of Key Stage 2, children will have amassed a range of perceptions about the world they live in, and will have a developing knowledge and understanding of it. They will have explored much of their local environment, and will have some experience of more distant places (possibly abroad). When visiting these places, they will have seen physical and human features that are different from those closer to home, and will (subconsciously at least), have made comparisons with features of their own environment.

From these experiences, children have begun to consider the overall nature of the area in which they live. They have developed an increasingly objective understanding of their own environment, especially if they have had opportunities to experience and study others. This knowledge has helped them to develop a 'sense of place': an understanding and appreciation of the character and identity of their own environment, and how it is connected to and affected by nearby environments that may have different characteristics. Formal geographical work in the community has added to their awareness of the distinctive features of their environment and their own place within it.

Children will have had opportunities in Key Stage 1 to consider aspects of environmental change in their locality and beyond, the moral issues that such changes raise, and the responsibility that individuals and groups have for deciding what a community needs. Investigating environmental change involves an understanding of causes and effects and a recognition of the difficulty of making decisions on behalf of others who will be affected by the change.

In their Key Stage 1 geography work, children will have used a range of secondary sources and a variety of enquiry methods in order to gain information about a range of topics.

Geography in Years 3–4 (Primary 4–5)

The National Curriculum states that children should study different places (on different-scale maps) in the UK and abroad, the various people who live in them and how these places are linked to others throughout the world. They should look at the environment they live in and how they might affect it. First-hand observation forms a significant part of this work, and should occur inside the school and in its immediate surroundings. Children should have the opportunity to use various resources in order to pursue their enquiries, including maps, atlases, aerial photographs and ICT.

The learning objectives for geography work in Years 3–4 (Primary 4–5) are:

● To investigate at first hand features of their local environment, including land use and physical and human features. Children should be helped to understand why the settlement in which they live began, and how it has developed into the place it is today.

● To study life and conditions in other parts of the UK and abroad that provide comparisons with their own locality. Through these studies, children should be encouraged to look at how people have used, changed and managed their environment. They should have opportunities to look for similarities and differences in relation to climate, agriculture, industry and human lifestyles. Through this work, they should be encouraged to develop positive attitudes towards others.

● To study the long-term effects of climate and specific weather patterns in the locality of the school and across the world.

● To develop an awareness of the changes taking place in their environment and in other environments, and to appreciate ways in which people's decisions can influence these changes.

● To become aware of how important location is for human activities, and the need for routes and networks to allow the movement of people and goods across a region or country. Children need to be aware that different settlements are connected to others in a variety of ways.

In order to develop a knowledge and understanding of geography, children need to learn certain skills and to be familiar with the basic tools of geographical enquiry. In the early years of Key Stage 2, children need access to Ordnance Survey maps (at a variety of scales) of the locality and more distant places that they may be studying. They should also develop an understanding of the concepts

associated with map work – including plan form, scale, location, direction, height and symbols – so that they can interpret maps fully. They should be encouraged to enjoy maps through having time to explore them, finding places that they know or have heard of (or perhaps that have unusual names), and seeing how particular physical and human features are represented. Games and finding activities are useful ways of helping children to increase their knowledge, understanding and enjoyment of maps. Similarly, they need to become familiar with atlases and globes, and be able to identify physical features (such as oceans, continents, rivers, coasts and areas of highland) and human features (the world's major cities).

Developing enquiry skills

Children need to develop a range of enquiry skills which will help them to increase their knowledge and understanding throughout the Programme of Study for Key Stage 2. These skills need to be developed from the earliest stages in a child's education. In undertaking and developing geographical enquiry, children should be taught to:

● Ask questions such as 'What is it like?', 'How has it changed?' and 'Why is it changing now?', and construct hypotheses to explain features.

● Carry out observations, collecting and recording evidence and communicating it in a variety of ways (for example, through written accounts, oral presentations or displays).

● Access a variety of sources to gain information about their own locality and others, such as the Internet, e-mail, newspapers, holiday brochures, tourist leaflets, aerial photographs and videos.

● Use appropriate fieldwork techniques such as surveys and field sketches, and use instruments such as cameras and wind vanes.

● Make judgements and decisions based on information they have gathered or been given; explain the reasons for their decisions to other children and predict the consequences of their decisions. Children should be able to identify groups of people who may hold a particular view about an issue (such as the building of a bypass road around a village) and say what each view might be.

● Draw plans and maps at a range of scales from photographs and sketches, and label some of the features. Children should develop skills in using and interpreting maps of different kinds and at different scales, including large-scale local maps, OS maps, road atlases, world atlases and globes.

Many enquiry skills are closely related, and any planned activity is likely to involve a combination of them. They are extensions of the experiences children will have had in the early years of their education. In Years 3–4, children will build on these and acquire more specific knowledge and a greater depth of understanding through more detailed investigation of their own locality and a range of others in the UK and beyond.

The local area and beyond

The local area for children in Years 3 and 4 is the locality of the home and school. It is here that they will have had most of their environmental experience through play, visiting nearby friends and relatives, and walking to school. This area is familiar and important to the children, and so it is here that the most useful and relevant work can be undertaken. A preliminary survey of the local environment is important, so that opportunities for fieldwork can be considered and, if necessary, alternatives planned should a survey site prove to be unsuitable or unsafe.

Studies in the local environment require much thought, planning and preparation, but are very rewarding and will provide a firm basis for geographical enquiry into other places. The study of unfamiliar places leads children to look for similarities and differences between their own locality and another in terms of physical and human features, climate and human activities. The QCA scheme for Geography in Key Stage 2 recommends the study of Chembakolli in India, through resources supplied by the charity ActionAid, as a locality in a developing country. Background information and lesson plans in this book promote case studies of Chembakolli and Clapham in the

Yorkshire Dales, encouraging the children to look for similarities and differences between them. The features of these two places should also be compared and contrasted with those of the local environment. In this way, the conditions that make a place unique can be seen and explored, and the myths and stereotypes associated with them exposed.

Detailed exploration of a small place such as a village can offer more than a more general study of a larger place. Children become familiar with smaller places more quickly, understand their characteristics more readily and empathise with the people who live and work there far more easily than when they are studying a larger, more diverse settlement.

Resources for geography in Years 3–4 (Primary 4–5)

Time needs to be spent acquiring and preparing quality resources to enhance the teaching and learning of geography. Specific resources needed to teach particular lesson plans are detailed in this book; but there are many general resources that will be needed throughout, especially when studying the locality of the school:

● Local maps – maps of urban areas at 1:1250, and of rural areas at 1:2500 scale, can be obtained from local planning departments. They can be photocopied, subject to the local education department having a licence that allows schools to do this.

● Base maps – these are simplified extracts, possibly redrawn and enlarged, to focus the children's attention on specific information.

● Ordnance Survey maps – these are produced at a range of scales and cover all areas of the UK. Maps at 1:50 000 scale are essential for meaningful local survey work, and for fieldwork in other sites. Non-local OS maps will need to be purchased from suppliers. Flat maps are easier to use and store than folded maps, which children will find difficult to fold up correctly. Smaller extracts copied from a full map will be easier to manage when working on a smaller area.

● Maps at 1:25 000 and 1:250 000 are also useful. Alternatively, extracts (A3 or A4 size, at 1:50 000 or 1:25 000 scale) that have been used in examinations can be purchased; these are much cheaper, but coverage is patchy and they come without a key. These extracts can be laminated, making them more durable and easier to store than full-sized maps.

● Road atlases are very useful, but the scales, symbols and colours used may vary (however, children are often quite familiar with this type of map). They are easier to use than the more complex OS maps, and give clear locational information – but often, many pages have to be turned when finding a route to a distant place, and this may confuse the children.

● Atlases – a number of similar atlases will be needed, so that groups can have access to the same kind of atlas. Choose atlases that have a good range of maps but do not give too much information, so that the children can understand them. Ensure that some of the atlases contain thematic maps, especially for climate.

● Globes – large political and physical globe maps (not too detailed) are most useful.

● Aerial photographs – try to obtain oblique (rather than vertical) photographs that correspond with the maps being used. Colour photographs will not photocopy as well as black and white; check copyright before copies are made.

Links with other areas of the curriculum

The following is a brief guide to how the lesson plans link with other areas of the curriculum:

● **Literacy** – at all times, pupils should be encouraged to speak accurately and to use the correct geographical vocabulary. Language skills are encouraged throughout the lesson plans in many ways: reading (accounts, reports, brochures and newspapers), writing (newspaper articles, accounts, descriptions, postcards, captions, labels, letters and e-mails), speaking (in group work, plenary sessions, role play, preparing and asking questions) and listening (to the opinions of other individuals, other groups and guest speakers).

- **Numeracy** – many of the lesson plans provide opportunities for children to enhance their numerical skills, including: using scale to calculate distance, drawing and interpreting pie charts and graphs, using the 24-hour clock, ranking, estimating, calculating journey times, making tally charts and tables, reading scales, calculating areas, weighing items and adding up prices.
- **ICT** – word-processing, using a CD-ROM, using graphics packages, databases and desktop publishing techniques, scanning maps and aerial photographs and making spreadsheets.
- **Science** – testing fabrics and conducting a fair test.
- **History** – looking at place name endings, Saxon villages and Victorian houses; comparing old and new maps and photographs; tracing the development of a town over its history.
- **Design and technology** – designing airline meals, menus and logos; making models of typical climatic regions; designing plans for new neighbourhoods and holiday villages; designing posters and symbols.
- **Art** – drawing and painting produce from other countries, making collages.

Programmes of Study

The following chart shows where in the book the various statements in the PoS for Geography at Key Stage 2 can be found:

Geographical enquiry skills:

	1	1a	2	2a	3	3a	4	4a	5	5a
1a) ask geographical questions.	✔	✔	✔	✔	✔	✔	✔	✔	✔	✔
b) collect and record evidence.	✔	✔			✔	✔	✔			
c) analyse evidence and draw conclusions.	✔			✔	✔	✔	✔			
d) identify and explain different views that people, including themselves, hold about topical geographical issues.					✔	✔				
e) communicate in ways appropriate to the task and audience.		✔			✔	✔	✔		✔	
2a) use appropriate geographical vocabulary.	✔	✔	✔	✔	✔	✔	✔	✔	✔	✔
b) use appropriate fieldwork techniques and instruments.	✔	✔			✔	✔		✔		✔	✔
c) use atlases and globes, and maps and plans at a range of scales.	✔		✔	✔	✔	✔	✔	✔	✔	✔
d) use secondary sources of information.	✔	✔	✔	✔	✔	✔	✔	✔	✔	✔
e) draw maps and plans at a variety of scales.		✔			✔		✔		✔	
f) use ICT to help in geographical investigations.		✔			✔			✔	✔	
g) use decision-making skills.					✔	✔	✔			

Knowledge and understanding of places:

	1	1a	2	2a	3	3a	4	4a	5	5a
3a) identify and describe what places are like.	✔	✔	✔		✔		✔	✔	✔	✔
b) locate places studied.	✔	✔	✔		✔	✔	✔	✔	✔	✔
c) describe where places are.	✔				✔			✔	✔	✔
d) explain why places are like they are.		✔			✔				✔	✔
e) describe similarities and differences between places.				✔				✔	✔	✔
f) recognise interdependence between places.	✔		✔	✔		✔	✔	✔	✔	✔

Knowledge and understanding of patterns and processes:

	1	1a	2	2a	3	3a	4	4a	5	5a
4a) explain patterns of physical and human features.		✔		✔		✔	✔		✔	✔
b) explain some physical and human processes and assess their impact.			✔		✔	✔			✔	✔

Knowledge and understanding of environmental change and sustainable development:

	1	1a	2	2a	3	3a	4	4a	5	5a
5a) know how environments can be improved and can affect the quality of life.	✔				✔	✔				
b) know that environments can be sustained, and that they have a role in this.					✔	✔			✔	✔

Investigating our local area

The 'local area' should be considered as including the area around the school where the children live (or the school's catchment area), as well as nearby places that they are familiar with. The local area for children in Years 3–4 (Primary 4–5) may be smaller and less complex than that for older children. Encouraging the children to draw a 'mental map' of their local area (from memory) is a good way of finding out what the local area means to them. It also tells you what places the children are familiar with, and what points of interest there are locally. These are all valuable as starting points and as likely places for field visits. The gaps that the children leave in their maps also make good starting points. Questions such as 'What will I find here?' encourage the children to think carefully about places they are less familiar with.

Mental maps can lead to work on formal mapping, introducing elements such as scale, grid references, direction symbols and plan form. They can be compared with local maps and aerial photographs. They can also be used to focus attention on particular aspects of the local environment, such as shops, roads or types of housing. The children can develop a range of geographical ideas and skills when studying their own locality, and apply them to the study of more distant places.

Through investigation of the local area, the children can collect and analyse information, undertake fieldwork, make and use maps and plans, use secondary source material, identify human and physical features, and examine land use and its environmental impact. A useful tool for fieldwork is the 'base map': a simplified map (based on a printed map) that only shows detail in that area of the map to be studied or surveyed.

Living in a village

The majority of people of working age who live in a village travel each day to another, larger settlement where they work. Years ago this was not the case. Villagers were largely self-sufficient. Most of the things needed by residents were produced or made locally; other items were purchased from traders and tinkers, who would travel between villages selling their goods. The railways (in the nineteenth and early twentieth centuries) and the car (from the mid-twentieth century) have changed the lives of village residents, and the functions and character of the villages themselves.

Nowadays, few people work in villages. Manufacturing is rare in this environment. Those people who are employed there tend to work on the land or in local shops. Most villagers commute to towns, where there are more opportunities and a greater variety of work. The car is the most important mode of transport for villagers, who are often not part of the public transport network of the local town. Personal transport allows flexibility in employment, as well as increased opportunities for leisure. Bus services, when they exist, often do not match the working day or shift.

In order to maintain life in a village, towns are vital. They provide the supermarkets and secondary schools; they are a part of a national (or even international) transport system; and they are a focal point for leisure and recreation. Those people who own a car can combine the advantages of living in a quiet location with the amenities of the town.

Living in a town

Towns have grown up for a variety of reasons: because they were trading centres or industrial centres, or to occupy defensive positions. Later, their populations swelled because of the Industrial Revolution. During the twentieth century, their populations increased slowly; the character of our towns and cities changed with the development of 'housing estates' and suburbs. This growth can be seen on a journey from the outskirts to the centre of most towns and cities: the periods of their history can be seen in the changing types and styles of buildings and different land uses.

Towns are centres of employment and transport. They are a focal point for the provision of goods and services for those living in or near the town (or passing through it). As a result, they are complex places with a wide variety of land uses. They have unique problems, including the loss of public open spaces, increasing pressure on road and rail links, and demands for cheap housing.

Living in a village

The lesson plans that follow should be used as a course of study in one village, rather than as single lessons in different villages. Ideally, a study village needs to be close to the school and be a place that the children know or have heard of. It should have an older village centre and areas of more recent development, exhibiting a range of building types and styles. There may be some facilities in the village, such as a church, post office, shop, school and village hall, and it should have a bus service.

Villages are one kind of settlement. Settlements differ according to their size and the facilities and services they offer. They can be broadly categorised as follows:

● Farmstead – a single working home away from other settlements, with no services.

● Hamlet – a small group of houses with few services, perhaps a telephone kiosk and a post box (some may have a public house).

● Village – a larger settlement with a number of services including some small shops, a village hall, a church, a bus stop and a primary school.

● Town – a complex settlement with a wide range of services including a library, a secondary school, bus and railway stations, department stores and a police station.

● City – offers all kinds of services including colleges and universities, regional hospitals, art galleries and often airports.

Traditionally, to be a city rather than a town, a settlement must have a cathedral. Some cities (such as Ripon, Wells and Ely) are quite small, while some towns (such as Northampton and Huddersfield) are much larger. More generally, population is a determining factor in whether or not a settlement is seen as a city.

Generally speaking, the larger the settlement, the more services (and the greater variety of services) it will offer. Settlements can be seen as a broad-based pyramid or hierarchy, with the more numerous farmsteads at the base and the smaller number of cities at the top.

Villages are no longer self-sufficient communities. The car has meant that although many villagers rely on nearby towns and the amenities that they provide, they can easily combine the advantages of living in a village with the facilities of the town. This has meant that villages have become attractive places to live. House prices have risen to such an extent that many of the people who were born in villages can no longer afford to buy houses there. Many of these people have moved to nearby towns to find work and cheaper housing, while many village houses have been bought by wealthier (usually older) people with no real ties to the village.

The nature of the typical village has thus changed from a distinct community based on family groups to a commuter settlement that is often deserted during the day. Services in villages have generally declined over the years: there is no longer the same need for shops such as grocers, bakers and hairdressers. The changing demands of residents, their increased mobility and the proximity of supermarkets have all accelerated the decline in demand for such services. People without personal transport have become more isolated, and public transport in rural areas tends to be poor and inconvenient.

Villages are small distinct settlements, and so are ideal for case study work. They can be studied in a variety of ways, starting with maps: going from small-scale to large-scale maps will gradually reveal the nature of the village. Aerial photographs can be used to help give the children's image of the village a clearer form, and to reinforce the sense (for young children) of its being a 'real' place. Land use can also be investigated through maps and aerial photographs – but fieldwork is far more rewarding, especially when supported by photographs of each different land use. Fieldwork is also useful for exploring environmental change, and should be used in conjunction with maps and photographs. The lives of village residents can be investigated through the jobs they do and the different services the village provides.

UNIT 1: Living in a Village

Enquiry questions	Learning objectives	Teaching activities	Learning outcomes	Cross-curricular links
What kinds of settlements are there? What features does each have?	• Identify settlement types. • Compare settlements by their size and area.	Work in pairs: tracing settlement boundaries and calculating their areas; finding the shortest journeys between features in a village; recording types and styles of buildings from photographs.	Children: • classify settlements according to their size and features • are becoming familiar with maps • give accurate directions using maps • transfer these skills to the local area	English: writing directions. Maths: calculating area. ICT: word-processing, scanning maps. Design and technology: making mobiles.
What features does a local village have?	• Extract information from secondary sources. • Make deductions from this information.	Individual work: trying to discover where in the village each photograph was taken; comparing the map with the aerial photograph.	• talk about the village using the source material • locate features on the map and aerial photograph	ICT: word-processing, scanning maps and photographs.
How is land in a village used? What is most land used for?	• Use fieldwork to collect evidence. • Interpret a key. • Record information on a map.	Work in pairs: recording land uses on a map; using a colour code.	• talk about land uses in a village and name the most important uses • use a base map to record land uses	ICT: word-processing, using a database, scanning. History: using old maps of the village to look for changes.
Where do people who live in a village work? How do they get there? What services do they need? What can a nearby town offer?	• Use survey sheets to gather information. • Mark places on a map, plot journeys and give directions. • Record information on a chart.	Work in groups: sorting jobs into categories; finding and mapping workplaces and calculating distances travelled; making tally charts based on newspaper advertisements; mapping shortest journeys.	• collect and interpret information • find places and trace journeys • give directions and use a scale	Maths: using a scale, making and using a tally chart; interpreting information on a timetable using the 24-hour clock. ICT: word-processing and desktop publishing.
What changes have taken place in the village?	• Identify and explain changes in the environment. • Understand that different people have different views about environmental changes.	Fieldwork, then group work in the classroom: following a trail; making field sketches; comparing maps and photographs to find evidence of change.	• use fieldwork and secondary sources to gain information • begin to understand about environmental impact.	History: looking at historical maps to identify changes. ICT: word-processing, scanning, adding captions.

Resources
Local OS maps at 1:50 000 scale, A4-sized extracts; tracing paper; cm² graph paper; photographs of different settlements; copies and an OHT version of a map of a local village or extract; a selection of photographs showing the main physical and human features of the village; oblique aerial photographs of the village; large-scale plans of the school and grounds; photographs of different land uses in the village; aerial photographs; a large-scale map of the village; a camera; advertisements for goods and services and for jobs from local newspapers; an environmental change trail; photographs of sites in the village that show change; A4 base maps and historical maps of the village.

Display
Tracings of settlements labelled and arranged in order of size. Village maps and journeys, annotated photographs and mobiles. Annotated photographs linked to the map of the village. Annotated aerial photographs. Completed land use maps of the village with colour codes.

Living in a village

(1 hour) Farm, hamlet, village, town or city?

What you need and preparation

Local Ordnance Survey maps (1:50 000 scale). Most local authorities have agreements with the Ordnance Survey to allow limited photocopying of their maps up to A4 size in both colour and black and white. Larger-sized photocopies can be made, but in black and white only. Schools need to note their LEA's licence number before photocopying. A large-scale road atlas is a suitable alternative – but you need to check the copyright position.

An A4-sized section of the map centred around the school, photocopied and made into an OHT; A4-sized tracing paper to act as an overlay, and some A3-sized tracing paper to cover a greater area of the original map; A4-sized pieces of 1cm^2 graph paper (one per child); a selection of large coloured photographs showing different types of settlements from farms to cities; a large-scale plan of a village, showing the village school.

What to do

(20 mins) Introduction

Ordnance Survey maps of the local area hold a great fascination for children. They are always keen to find towns and other places they have heard of. Give them a few minutes to explore the maps and become familiar with them at their own level and pace.

Introduce the terms *farmstead, hamlet, village, town* and *city*. Describe each one in turn, then ask the children whether they can find a place like that on the map. Ask them to put their fingers on an example of each type of place, then quickly discuss whether they have got it right. Clues that will help them include:

1. Size – single houses next to labelled farms, small groups (hamlets), larger groups (villages) and so on.
2. Functions – these are shown as symbols on the map. Farms have none, hamlets a few (perhaps a public house); villages usually have a public house and a church, perhaps a post office; towns have bus and railway stations; cities have motorway links.

Use the OHT and the A4 map sections to repeat this exercise together, encouraging the children to give many examples. Point out each one that they have found on the OHT, and make a list of place names underneath each 'type of settlement' heading.

Use the photographs to talk about each type of settlement in turn. Ask children to comment specifically on the number, type and size of the buildings in the photograph, and on the land use, services and type of transport that they can see.

(30 mins) Development

The children can work in pairs on these three activities (with each pair trying one activity).
1. Using the A4 section of the 1:50 000 map, or a corresponding area on the full map, trace in pencil the outlines of different settlements on tracing paper and add the name of each settlement. Each pair should trace different places as far as possible. Cut out each shape and draw the outline on a sheet of 1cm^2 graph paper. Add up how many whole squares each settlement takes up (for example, 1, 2–3, 4–5, 6–10, 11–20, 21–30 or 30+). Ask the children what they notice about the chart when it is finished. (Farmhouses and hamlets usually take up 1 square or less, villages 2–3 squares, small towns 4–5 squares, cities from 6 to over 30 squares.)
2. Look at the large-scale map of the village together. Find the school and other places of interest in the village. Now use their fingers to trace the shortest journey from the school to each of the places of interest. Write down the directions for each journey, paying particular attention to the roads and landmarks that are passed on the way.

3. Make a chart of the different settlement types shown in the photographs. On it, record information about the types and styles of buildings, and any other features they can see (services, transport links and so on).

Plenary

10 mins Ask the children what they noticed about the settlement types and the area each took up on the graph paper. Ask them how common each type of settlement is (with reference to the map). Ask them what else a map could tell us about the importance of a settlement (for example, whether it has a hospital or an airport).

Encourage those children using the village map to describe some of their journeys around the village; the other children can try to follow the route described on their outline maps.

Differentiation

More able children could calculate the areas of the settlements more accurately by adding part squares to whole squares. They could look at a larger area of the map, using the A3 extract. They could also be asked to describe routes from the school to other local places, using a local map.

Less able children could tackle the village activity with the help of a structured worksheet, to which they add the missing directions from the school to places of interest. They should concentrate on using correct directional language. Teacher support can be given to assist with map reading.

Assessing learning outcomes

Can the children classify settlements according to their size and features? Do they show an increasing familiarity with maps? Can they give accurate directions using a map? Can they transfer these skills to the locality of the school (using a map)?

ICT opportunities
• Use a word processor to write the settlement categories and list of places.
• Scan maps of different scales to compare how particular local settlements appear on them.

Follow-up activities
• Write about what each type of settlement is like and what it might be like to live there.
• Make a card and string mobile, with the type of settlement written on the front of each card and a picture of how it might look on the back.

What is a village like?
1 hour

What you need and preparation

Copies of a large-scale map of a local village (an A4 section will contain enough information); an OHT of the same map. (See note opposite about copyright.) Your 'master copy' of the map could be marked with arrows (see 'Development' below).

A selection of about ten photographs, taken at ground level, showing different human (or artificial) and physical (or natural) features of the village. These should be taken by a teacher on a preliminary visit. Chemists will produce multiple sets of colour photographs reasonably cheaply.

Copies of an oblique aerial photograph of the village; an OHT of the same photograph. Colour photographs are best for the children to use, but a black and white one will photocopy better. Aerial photographs should be obtainable locally. Choose a photograph that shows a substantial area of the village, including the features already photographed on the teacher's visit. Try to find one that is closely orientated to the village map.

What to do

Introduction
20 mins Give the children copies of the village map. Familiarise them with it by asking a number of questions, such as: *What is opposite the church? On which road is the public house?* Ask them to interpret some of the symbols they can find on the map. Use the map OHT to help with this.

Ask the children to look at the photographs of parts of the village. Talk about each one in turn, and ask the children to describe what they see. Focus their attention on the physical and human features within each photograph: rivers, hills, churches, housing developments and so on.

Learning objectives
• Extract information from large-scale maps, and from aerial and other photographs.
• Make simple deductions from this information.

Lesson organisation
Teacher-led discussion; individual and then paired or small-group activity work; whole-class plenary session.

Vocabulary
map
aerial photograph
physical features
human features

Living in a village

Look at the copies of the aerial photograph and let the children familiarise themselves with this. Again, use an OHT version to help. Ask individual children to find buildings such as the church, a farm or the school, and fields used for grazing animals or for growing crops.

Encourage the children to use the map and the OHT of the aerial photograph to trace the shortest journeys between different places. After a few examples, let them continue with this activity using their own copies of the aerial photograph. Ask them why they think the village has its particular shape, and why it has its particular human and physical characteristics.

25 mins Development

Ask the children (working individually) to write a description of each of the photographs that show human and physical features of the village. At this point, encourage them to speculate as to whereabouts in the village (in general terms) each photograph was taken.

Now ask them to point out exactly where they think each photograph was taken. To simplify this exercise, you could number the photographs and add arrows to the map, pointing to the places photographed. The children can then write in the number of the correct photograph next to each arrow on their own copy of the map.

Finally, working in groups, the children should match the village map to the aerial photograph and, by looking carefully at field boundaries and buildings, examine the different land uses in the village (gardens, allotments, fields, car parks and so on).

15 mins Plenary

Together make a list of vocabulary used that draws together all aspects of the work done during the lesson. Talk about the photographs: what they show and where in the village they were taken. Emphasise how they show features of a village that are different from those of a town.

Differentiation

More able children could be encouraged to explore the map more thoroughly, and to label it using the aerial photograph. They could attempt to locate the places photographed without the help of arrows.

Less able children could look at the photographs and use a single word to describe what they see each time, or annotate a single photograph photocopied onto the middle of a plain sheet of A4 paper.

ICT opportunities
• Use a word processor to write labels and annotations.
• Scan maps and photographs, then place labels and annotations on them.

Follow-up activity
Ask some people from the village to talk to the class about the human and physical features shown in the photographs.

Assessing learning outcomes

Can the children use the resources provided to talk about the main physical and human features of the village? How well can they locate features on the map and the aerial photograph? Can they speculate on the form and functions of the village?

(3 hours) Land use in a village

What you need and preparation

Large-scale plans of the school and its grounds, with different areas marked on it. Photocopiable page 120. A selection of photographs (or a video) taken at ground level, showing a variety of different land uses in the village. Aerial photographs of the village that closely reflect the map or extract to be used.

A large-scale map of the village that shows buildings and field boundaries. If the village is quite large, choose a section that exhibits a variety of different land uses. The map will need to be enlarged and possibly simplified, but based on a large-scale OS map. Each pair of children will need a copy of this map for the fieldwork.

This is a good opportunity to undertake fieldwork and give the children first-hand experience. A camera will be useful for this. A high level of adult supervision will be needed; consult your local LEA guidelines.

What to do

(40 mins) Introduction

Talk about the different ways that land is used in the school (for classrooms, halls, offices and so on) and around the school (for playing fields, car parks and playgrounds). Encourage the children to look at these areas on plans of the school and its grounds. It is important for them to understand that all land is used for something.

Display the village map. Encourage the children to find different places on it and to give directions, so that they become familiar with it.

Give out the photographs and discuss each one in turn (or show the video, stopping regularly to focus on the different ways that land is used). Make a list of all the different land uses found, such as farmland, houses and transport. Ask the children to think about other ways that land might be used in the village, and how all of this information might be recorded on a base map. Together, make a colour-coded land use key showing the uses that they have found. Include such uses as farmland for crops and animals, woodland, roads, churchyard, houses with gardens, shops and allotments.

Explain clearly to the children what will be expected of them on the field trip and how they should keep safe.

(2 hours) Development

At the village, divide the children into pairs. Spend a few minutes looking at different land uses, then finding them on the base map together. Ask each pair to identify land uses within a small area of the village and then to mark the uses on their base map using the colour-coded key. Talk through a few examples with the children: identify a land use in the village, locate it on the map and colour it in the correct colour. Small groups (two or three pairs) can go with an adult to look at different areas of the village.

Back in class, the children will need to copy their land use map (and perhaps their key) out again, as these items tend to suffer in the field. They can present their results using ICT (see below). Talk to the class about photocopiable page 120, then ask them to complete it.

(20 mins) Plenary

Talk about the fieldwork activity and the different land uses found. The children can share their results, producing a complete map of land use in the village. As a class, rank the land uses, starting with the most important (the one that covers the most area) and ending with the least.

Learning objectives
• Use fieldwork to collect evidence about land use.
• Interpret a key.
• Record information on a map.

Lesson organisation
Teacher-led discussion; fieldwork in pairs; whole-class follow-up in school.

Vocabulary
houses and gardens
shops
churches and chapels
roads and paths
farmland
industry and wasteland

Living in a village

Encourage the children to speculate as to how land uses may be different in a town. Think about what new land uses there would be, and which village land uses would not appear in a town.

Differentiation

More able children could tackle a larger area than is shown on the base plan, perhaps using an aerial photograph. They should be encouraged to display the information they have collected using bar graphs and pie charts.

Less able children should complete photocopiable page 120, paying close attention to the sketches for clues. They will need adult support during the fieldwork (particularly in completing their land use map), and with subsequent ICT work.

Assessing learning outcomes

Can the children talk about land use in the village and name the most important uses? Can they understand and interpret a base map and use it to record land use?

1 hour Work, commuting and services

What you need and preparation

Copies of photocopiable page 121. A collection of advertisements for goods and services (for example, restaurants, clothes shops, car repairers) from local newspapers; these need to be selected for the children to use and photocopied onto a sheet. The children can select their own and cut them out, but this tends to be very time-consuming. Try to ensure that most of these advertisements come from the larger towns.

A collection of job advertisements from local newspapers; select these and photocopy them onto a sheet, as above. Copies of local maps (the 1:50 000 OS map is the best for these activities, or a good quality road map can be used); A4-sized tracing paper for use as an overlay.

What to do

10 mins Introduction

Talk to the children about the general kinds of jobs that adults, especially ones living in villages, might do. Refer to 'adults' rather than 'parents' to avoid potential problems. Ask: *Where might adults living in a village find work? How might they get there each working day?*

Discuss other reasons why villagers might want to get to a nearby town during the day. *What services would they need? What could a nearby town offer?* Ask the children where they themselves would go, for example, to buy new shoes, do the weekly food shop or catch a train.

40 mins Development

The class can be divided into six groups, with two groups undertaking each of the following three activities.

1. Two groups can find out what jobs people living in a village do. The children can ask at home, and then a general list can be compiled; or, if they do not live in a village, a prepared list of about 20 jobs can be used. Ask the children to sort the jobs into categories: jobs people do in a village and jobs people do in a town; then jobs in farming, forestry, manufacturing and services.

2. Two groups can ask people where they work, how they travel to work each day and how far their journey is, then make a list showing the different places that people travel to daily in order to

work. Together, mark a selection of these workplaces onto the OS map. Cover the map with tracing paper and encourage the children to trace on it the journey that is made. Some children can then use string and the scale on the map to discover how far the journey is, and check this against any travel information they have. If a survey is not undertaken, use the prepared list with invented travel information.

3. Two groups can make a chart from the collection of advertisements, showing the other settlements to which people who live in a village could travel to buy goods and services. This should be a simple tally chart, recording how many times each settlement is mentioned. Look at the map together. Ask the children if they notice a relationship between the size of the settlement and how often it is recorded on the chart. Mark these settlements on tracing paper placed on the OS map. Ask children to trace on the paper the shortest route that people could take from their village to each place. Ask other children to describe each journey.

Give all the children a copy of photocopiable page 121 and ask them to complete it. The sheet is based on the idea that larger settlements offer more (and a greater range of) services than smaller settlements; it also involves describing a journey on a map.

Plenary
10 mins Ask a spokesperson from each of the six groups to feedback to the rest of the class. Encourage children from each of the different groups to answer specific questions:
● *What kinds of jobs do people do? Which of the jobs are done in the village? Which are more likely to be done in towns?*
● *How do people in villages travel to work – do most travel by car, bus, train or bicycle? How far do people travel each day?*
● *Whereabouts do people go for different goods and services? Do different places offer different amounts of goods and services? What routes are taken to get to different places?*

Differentiation
More able children could work without direct adult supervision. They should be encouraged to think about how a village is 'linked' to other places: for example, it is part of a network of settlements that form a 'hierarchy' (in terms of size and population). They should also be encouraged to think about the advantages and disadvantages of living in a village in terms of work, travel and services.

Less able children could work in pairs to describe a journey between two places on a map. They should be encouraged to trace their fingers down a road and give directions, including left, right, across and opposite. Ask them to name some of the features they would pass on the way, such as woods and farms.

Assessing learning outcomes
How well can the children collect and interpret information, and relate it to a map? How well can they use maps to find places and trace journeys? How well can they give directions and use a scale?

ICT opportunities
● Use word-processing and desktop publishing to present information in a variety of formats, selecting fonts and layouts.

Follow-up activities
● Consider the lifestyles of people in villages who lack personal transport. Use timetables to investigate the frequency of bus services to a village from a town, and how different people would be affected: someone working from 9am to 5pm, someone shopping for two hours between 10am and 12 noon, and someone wanting to go to the cinema in the evening from 8.30pm until 10.30pm.
● Find out what services are directly available to residents of a village, including shops and mobile services; make a photographic record. (Note that mobile services, such as milk delivery, are still common in villages.)

CHAPTER I
INVESTIGATING OUR LOCAL AREA

Living in a village

How has the village changed?
3 hours

Learning objectives
• Identify and explain changes in the environment.
• Understand that different people have different views about the desirability of environmental changes.

Lesson organisation
Initial teacher-led discussion; fieldwork; group work in the classroom.

Vocabulary
site
environment
impact
environmental change

What you need and preparation
Choose a nearby village for the fieldwork element of this unit (preferably the same one that you have already used). Identify within it sites, buildings or areas that have undergone significant recent change. Make sure that these places can be observed in detail safely and easily. Plan a short 'environmental change' village trail, including areas that have undergone recent extensive change (for example, where a new school has been built on cleared land or a chapel has been converted into a house). Take a selection of photographs of suitable places from ground level and have them enlarged (some photographs from the previous lesson can be reused if appropriate).

Large-scale A4 base maps of the village that cover all of the photographed sites. In rural areas, the largest maps have a scale of 1:2500. These should be marked with the route for the village trail. Copies of at least one large-scale A4 historical map extract of the village; a corresponding modern map extract. Both should be obtainable from local libraries. Large-scale OS maps go back to the end of the nineteenth century, and have been updated at intervals. The historical map extract may have to be enlarged so that the children can compare it more easily with a modern map.

Copies of photocopiable page 122. A selection of old photographs of the village. Books containing old local photographs can often be obtained from nearby bookshops or libraries. Local appeals for photographs can also be worthwhile. Take new photographs from exactly the same viewpoints for comparison.

What to do

Introduction
15 mins
Talk about how and why buildings are altered over the years by their owners – for example, a house might be made larger by adding extensions, or made more comfortable by adding double glazing or central heating. Areas of land also change over time; while the individual changes may be quite small, over the years the environment may be changed significantly.

Explain the fieldwork activity to the children (see below), so that they know what is expected of them. Stress the need for safety. Show the children the village trail route on the map. Show them the site photographs, and discuss what they see and what changes have occurred.

Development
2 hours 30 mins
Walk the village trail together. At each site marked on the map, ask the children to say what change has taken place, why they think this change was required, whether they think the change is an 'improvement', and what they think was there before. They should make brief notes and add a small quick sketch to show what they think was there before.

Back in the classroom, the children should copy up their notes and improve one of their field sketches of a site's previous use, using a modern photograph to provide the background. They should colour and label each site on the large-scale modern village map.

Compare the modern and old maps of the village together. Try to find evidence of what each site's previous use may have been. Ask the children to use these two maps to find out what has been added to the village, what has been removed and what has stayed the same since the historical map was produced. As an alternative, they can complete photocopiable page 122.

As a class, compare the old and new photographs of places in the village. Look for the same changes as above, and also for changes in the types and styles of buildings, the transport and the people. Photographs can be photocopied onto the middle of an A4 sheet of plain paper and annotated.

15 mins Plenary

Look at the enlarged photographs showing areas and places of change around the village. Ask the children to answer the questions asked earlier in front of the class, and to speculate on the original use of each site.

Discuss the changes to the village that the children found when comparing the two maps; ask them to consider whether these changes have been a good or a bad thing. The old and new photographs can be considered in the same way.

Differentiation

More able children could make their own notes during the fieldwork, and write full accounts of particular changes in the village.

Less able children could complete more highly structured work, using charts to be filled in and cloze procedures to help them produce written accounts. They will also need adult support.

Assessing learning outcomes

Can the children use fieldwork techniques and selected primary and secondary source material to gain information? How well do they understand that environments change, and that particular changes can have a major impact on a locality?

Living in a town

The first settlements grew where they did for many different reasons. There may have been fertile soil nearby, fresh water, supplies of timber for building, or extensive views so that the new settlement could be more easily defended. The best sites offered a combination of these advantages, and these settlements grew more quickly than the others.

When people grew more crops or bred more animals than they needed, they would trade, taking their produce along a developing network of paths and tracks to a village that was easy for many people to reach. As a result, some villages developed markets and later grew into market towns, attracting tradesmen who would sell their wares to visiting local people. Some settlements increased in size for other reasons – for example, because they were at a narrow point in a river that could be crossed easily by a bridge or a ford (a shallow crossing-point); or because they occupied a narrow valley, so that people who wanted to travel across the hills had to pass through. Inns, stables, shops and churches were built to meet the needs of residents or visitors. Many of today's towns have names that reflect the reasons for their original growth – for example, 'Bradford' comes from 'broad ford'.

More recently, towns have grown up because they met a need for materials. The towns and cities of West Yorkshire were close to supplies of soft water and hills for grazing sheep; as a result, woollen mills were established and a population of workers grew around them. Other towns and cities owe their origins to cotton or coal, or were ports or harbours. Over the hundred or so years of the Industrial Revolution (1780–1880), many towns grew from populations of a few hundred into sprawling cities of hundreds of thousands. In the 1950s and 1960s, a number of 'new towns' (such as Telford and Milton Keynes) were created to relieve the pressure on cities caused by the expanding population.

The outward growth of a town can be seen in the changing land use, building use and patterns and types of housing. Typically, a journey from the outskirts of a town to its centre will show the following zones:

● Outer suburbs – on the edge of the town or city, made up of large Victorian and Edwardian houses with large gardens and modern (often small) estates of large, 'executive-style' houses.

● Inner suburbs – brick estates of semi-detached houses with small gardens, usually built by local councils in the 1950s and 1960s. There are also some larger terraced houses and occasional blocks of flats.

● Industrial zone – sometimes called the 'twilight zone', this was once a flourishing area typically composed of warehouses, canals, railways, old factory premises and small terraced houses. These are now usually areas of dereliction, though in some towns former industrial premises have been redeveloped into luxury flats. There are also some new, small factory units.

● Town centre – full of shops, offices, hotels, cinemas, theatres, banks and public buildings. In a large town or city, the centre can be sub-divided into a number of different zones, including an education zone, a commercial zone and an administrative zone. Town centres are bustling places during the day, but are often empty at night. Few people live there – in fact, more people live in the centres of smaller towns than in city centres.

A school in the inner or outer suburbs is likely to be close to a wide variety of different land uses that will help children to understand how a town works, as well as to learn a wide variety of geographical skills and concepts. Fieldwork is an important aspect of any local area study, and good safe sites in which to undertake fieldwork within walking distance of the school are essential for this unit of work. Suitable sites for local fieldwork could include: a small parade of shops; a busy road; an area of varied land use; areas that show a variety of building types, styles and usage; and areas that show a high level of environmental change.

A range of secondary source material is also essential, and may include maps of various scales (especially larger scales) that focus on the school and the areas to be used for fieldwork. Old large-scale maps will be needed for comparison when the children are learning to appreciate the nature and extent of environmental change. Oblique aerial photographs will show surface features in three-dimensional form, and vertical photographs of the same areas will aid map work as well as helping the children to understand land use. A good camera will be needed to record different land uses and specific features of the environment. Photographs are useful as evidence; they will also bring the fieldwork experience back into the classroom in a personal way, adding great interest to any display.

The lesson plans that follow are best applied to the study of one town, preferably the town that the school is in or close to. Schools in rural areas will need to undertake more preparation in order to find a suitable town to study and survey. A twinning arrangement with a town in an urban area would be useful.

UNIT 2: Living in a Town

Enquiry questions	Learning objectives	Teaching activities	Learning outcomes	Cross-curricular links
What maps can we use to find our school?	• Investigate different places. • Plan routes and give directions.	Paired work: using the 'best' maps to find places by their addresses; giving directions to different towns using maps; using aerial photographs to give directions to local places; using compass points.	Children: • locate their school and other places on different maps • plan routes to local and more distant places • know the four main points of the compass	ICT: art package, word-processing.
Where would we find different parts of the town?	• Identify the main physical and human features of a town. • Interpret maps and aerial photographs. • Understand why the locality is the way that it is.	Paired or small-group work: describing photographs and locating features shown in them on a map; using aerial photographs to identify features and land uses; locating the school and locality on smaller-scale maps.	• identify nearby physical and human features • know the different land uses close to the school • are increasingly able to interpret local maps and aerial photographs	ICT: word-processing labels, accounts and questions.
What is land use? What is the land around the school used for?	• Collect evidence. • Use fieldwork techniques. • Use secondary sources to obtain information. • Record information using ICT.	Fieldwork in small groups, paired follow-up work in school: land-use mapping around school; completion of base map of the locality in school; ranking local land uses.	• identify different local land uses • record land use information on a map, using a code • present their findings using ICT	Maths: ranking values. ICT: word-processing, scanning, using an art package.
What kinds of jobs do people do and how do they get to work? What kinds of shops are nearby? What kind of traffic uses the nearby roads?	• Construct questionnaires and analyse data. • Use and interpret local maps. • Undertake local surveys.	Paired or small-group work: categorising jobs from completed questionnaires; drawing bar charts to show how far people travel to work and how they travel; mapping advertisements; conducting a shopping survey and a traffic survey.	• collect and analyse data • use local maps • conduct local surveys	Maths: constructing and analysing bar charts. ICT: word-processing, constructing data sheets and graphs.
How has the area around the school changed?	• Use fieldwork techniques. • Use secondary sources to obtain information. • Identify changes and assess their impact locally.	Whole-class fieldwork, paired activity work: identifying local places that have changed; locating sites on a local map; comparing maps and photographs to find examples of environmental change.	• identify changes in the local environment, using fieldwork and secondary sources.	History: using historical maps and photographs. ICT: word-processing, scanning.

Resources
Maps at different scales, road atlases and globes; an A4 base map of the area around the school; photographs of different physical and human features; a completed land use map of the school; clipboards; a camera; photographs of different local land uses; oblique aerial photographs of the locality, with an OHT of one; a simplified base map of a local shopping centre; traffic survey recording sheets; enlarged colour photographs of each shop in the survey; a selection of local newspapers; local maps at 1:50 000 scale; an A4 map of the local area at 1:1250 scale; historical maps of the same area; old and modern photographs of features of the area (for comparison); enlarged photographs of specific sites.

Display
Different maps annotated to show unfolding addresses. Maps, aerial photographs and word-processed directions. Photographs with captions and labels. Children's picture maps. Completed land use maps with codes. Annotated photographs of different land uses. Local maps showing workplaces; charts showing how people travel to work; an advertising map. Shopping and traffic survey graphs, notes and results. Sketches and photographs linked to a local map. Modern and old maps and photographs, annotated.

(1 hour) Where is our school?

What you need and preparation

Copies of a variety of maps at different scales, including a globe and Ordnance Survey maps of the local area at 1:50 000 scale; road atlases; tracing paper; specific maps of the school and its surrounding area – 1:1250 or 1:2500 are the best large-scale maps to use (several of the 1:1250 maps may be needed to cover the catchment area of the school).

A4-sized oblique aerial photographs of the school and the surrounding area (these can usually be obtained locally). Colour photographs are the best to use, but can be quite expensive; black and white are more difficult for children to interpret, but are usually cheaper and photocopy quite well. Check the copyright position. Choose a photograph which relates closely to the OS map to be used.

An OHT of the chosen aerial photograph, and one of the area immediately around the school from the 1:1250 or 1:2500 map.

What to do

(20 mins) Introduction

With the children, look at the base plan of the school; then look at the location of the school through maps of progressively smaller scale, until the globe is reached. (See page 19 for notes on selecting a suitable school.)

Spend a few minutes allowing the children to look at the local 1:50 000 OS map and find places that they know or have heard of. Play a 'point to' game to help the children become familiar with the map; check quickly each time that they can find places quickly and accurately. Gradually concentrate on places that are quite close to the school, in the same settlement. Talk about other settlements and try to categorise them into farms, hamlets, villages, towns and cities.

Together, focus on the location of the school on the 1:50 000 map. Find out which district of the town the school is in, and what the neighbouring districts are called. Introduce the four compass points, and encourage the children to use these when explaining where the other districts are in relation to the school.

Talk to the children about the main symbols used on the map, such as those for churches, bus stations, railway stations and public houses, and why mapmakers use these symbols. Introduce the idea of grid references, and explain how the numbers around the outside of the map are used to find these.

Use the OHT of the aerial photograph to point out the school and specific places nearby; encourage the children to find the same features on their local OS maps.

(30 mins) Development

As a class, trace the area of the town from the 1:50 000 map. Mark in the school, its district and the districts nearby. Using the school's address, find the best maps to show, line by line, where the school is – for example, Ingrow Primary School (the school plan), Broomhill Avenue (local 1:1250 OS map), Ingrow (town map or 1:10 000 OS map), Keighley (road atlas or 1:50 000 OS map), West Yorkshire (atlas showing northern England or 1:250 000 map) and so on. Record which maps were used to find the address. Pairs can try the same exercise with other addresses in the UK.

Ask the children to imagine that they are going to drive a car from your town to other nearby towns. Encourage pairs to write down directions to the towns, using a good road atlas or small-scale OS map. Repeat this several times, making the towns gradually more distant. The children should record the roads they travel on and the significant places they pass.

Learning objectives
• Investigate places in a variety of contexts.
• Plan routes and give directions, using local base maps and commercially produced maps of more distant places.

Lesson organisation
Teacher-led introduction; initially unstructured, then structured map familiarisation work; paired activity work; whole-class plenary session drawing on the experiences of individual children.

Vocabulary
map
aerial photograph
oblique
vertical
routes
directions
landmarks
north etc
settlement
farm
hamlet
village
town
city
symbol

Living in a town

- Use an art package to draw, label and print some map symbols.
- Word-process directions, routes and other written work.

Follow-up activities
- Use place name endings to consider the origins of nearby towns – for example: *...don* – hill; *...bury/borough* – defended place; *...ham* – homestead or farm; *...ley/worth* – clearing. Place names can give information about the characteristics of local settlements in the past, as well as about the surrounding countryside.
- Make a chart showing some of the more common OS symbols and their meanings.
- Draw their journey to school, using OS (or their own) symbols to represent the landmarks they pass.

Ask each pair to use the aerial photographs to give directions to places around the school and record these directions on the local 1:1250 or 1:2500 scale map, identifying and annotating features that they pass on the map. Ask them to use the same map to say whether nearby places (such as the nearest park, bus station or supermarket) are broadly to the north, south, east or west of the school. They should make a picture compass on A4 paper (see illustration) to show the directions in which these places lie.

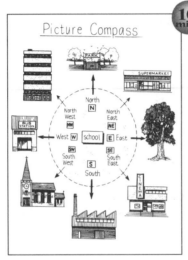

10 mins Plenary
Together, track the school through maps using its address. Ask: *How many maps did we use?* Ask some children to describe another address chase through maps.
- Ask some children to give directions from your town to another by car. Check whether they have described the shortest journey.
- Ask some children to give directions from your school to other local places, using the local map and aerial photographs.

Differentiation
More able children could select their own maps at the scales they think are appropriate, and make a list of directions to places around the school. They could be introduced to the use of eight compass points instead of four.

Less able children should concentrate on the initial task of each activity, and on the language associated with these tasks.

Assessing learning outcomes
Can the children locate their school on maps of various scales? How well can they plan routes around the local area, and to more distant places (using smaller-scale maps)? Are they familiar with the four points of the compass?

1 hour What is a town like?

Learning objectives
- Identify human and physical features of a town.
- Identify local land use.
- Use and interpret maps and aerial photographs.
- Develop an understanding of why the local area is the way it is.

Lesson organisation
Teacher-led introduction; activity work in groups or pairs; whole-class plenary.

Vocabulary
physical features
human features

What you need and preparation
An A4-sized base map at 1:1250 scale of the area around the school, and a corresponding OHT. A selection of enlarged photographs showing different parts of the town or city. A selection of enlarged photographs, taken at ground level, of the main human and physical features of the local area (such as important roads, buildings, shops and parks). Copies (one per child) of an oblique aerial photograph of the area that complements the base map, and an OHT of the same aerial photograph.

What to do
15 mins Introduction
Talk to the children about how towns begin and grow, and how their character changes on a journey from the outskirts or outer suburbs to the city centre. Show them the photographs of different zones or areas in their town; focus on changes in houses and gardens. Ask: *Where would you find factories? Where would you find large shops?*
Give the children copies of the base map. Help the children to become familiar with the map by

asking them a series of quick questions that require them to look at the map closely – for example, *What is opposite the post office?* Use the OHT version to point out features and to run through the answers.

Give out the photographs taken around the school at ground level, and discuss each one in turn. Encourage the children to say (in general terms) what the photograph shows and what the main human and physical features are. In a built environment, most of the features seen will be human ones, since buildings tend to hide physical features.

Give out copies of the aerial photograph. For a few minutes, encourage the children to find places that they know, such as the school, the cinema or their home. Display the OHT version to help them. Ask individual children to trace their journey to school on the OHT, while others follow on their own aerial photographs. Ask questions about the photograph, such as:

- *What is most of the land used for?*
- *Where are the oldest houses?*
- *About how much bigger is the park than the school playground?*

Ask the children to find specific places on the aerial photograph and then find the same places on the map, and vice versa.

Development
30 mins

The children can work in pairs or small groups on these activities.

1. Write a brief description of each photograph showing a feature of the town, then try to match it to the base map and the aerial photograph.

2. Look at the aerial photograph and try to identify the main features and land uses. (Encourage individual children to use the OHT to show others where these features are.) Mark on the outline plan the features and land uses found in the aerial photograph.

3. Try to locate the school and the area around it on a smaller-scale map of the town or city.

- *Where is this area?*
- *What is it like?*
- *Why has it developed as it has?*
- *What are the main land uses in this area?*

Plenary
15 mins

Ask the children to describe what they have found out about the local area. Ask questions such as:

- *Where in the town is the school?*
- *Where are the neighbouring areas? What are they like?*
- *What is most land near the school used for?*
- *Have there been any major changes in the ways that land is used near the school?*

Differentiation

More able children should be encouraged to explore the map and aerial photograph in greater detail, and try to 'zone' the different land uses that they find (such as houses, factories, transport and parkland).

For the less able children, prepare descriptions of the local photographs taken at ground level on separate pieces of paper. Mix the photographs, then encourage the children to match them. Identify the key vocabulary that helps to describe each photograph.

Assessing learning outcomes

Can the children identify the main human and physical features of an area of the town close to the school? How far are they developing an awareness and understanding of land use close to the school? Are they increasingly able to interpret and use large-scale local maps and aerial photographs?

ICT opportunities
- Use word-processing for labels, accounts and questions that can be displayed next to the map and photographs.

Follow-up activities
- Draw a picture map of their normal journey to school, identifying significant features that they pass.
- In four groups, draw and colour houses, gardens, factories and other buildings that would be found on a journey across town (from the outer suburbs to the city centre). These can be combined into a frieze, with an accompanying word-processed account.

3 hours Land uses in the town

Learning objectives
• Collect evidence.
• Use fieldwork techniques to map and record data about land use.
• Use secondary sources.
• Record information using ICT.

Lesson organisation
Whole-class discussion and preparation; fieldwork in groups or pairs; whole-class follow-up and plenary session.

Vocabulary
land use
wasteland
transport
industry
public buildings
survey
colour code

What you need and preparation

A completed 'land use map' of the school, coloured with a suitable key. Base maps (copies of an enlarged and simplified extract from a 1:1250 scale OS map) showing the area around the school. Clipboards; a camera; a selection of photographs taken around the school at ground level, showing a variety of different land uses; an aerial photograph and an OHT version of it. Copies of photocopiable page 123.

Particular care needs to be taken when undertaking fieldwork in an urban area. Ensure that the children are well prepared for the fieldwork, and that they are closely supervised. Choose a survey site that is well away from busy roads.

What to do

40 mins Introduction

Discuss the different ways in which land is used in the school and the school grounds. Make two lists to show the different land uses – for example:

● inside – classrooms, halls, offices, toilets, corridors
● outside – playgrounds, car parks, playing fields, gardens.

Explain that all land is used for something. Look at, describe and explain the completed land use map of the school.

Talk about how the land is used around this locality, and make a class list of land use terms: shops, factories, churches and churchyards, wasteland, transport (roads, footpaths, railway lines, canals) and so on.

Look at the photographs; ask the children to pick out the main land uses shown and make a list of them.

Make a 'land use' colour code key together, showing the main land uses that will be found in the area that you will survey. A related letter code can be used in the fieldwork, to avoid using large amounts of coloured pencils or felt pens; colours can be substituted for the letters on return to the classroom.

Explain clearly what will be expected of the children in the fieldwork: they will survey local land use nearby and record their findings on a base map, using the key. Allow them to spend some time becoming familiar with the land use key and the base map.

2 hours Development

If possible, start the fieldwork by finding a suitable vantage point from which to point out the different land uses of the chosen area. If this is not possible, take the children to the survey area, point out various land uses, encourage the children to identify them, then mark them together on the base map. Mapping land use in an urban area can be difficult, so encourage small groups to work closely with a supervising adult. They should concentrate initially on an area about the size of a football pitch.

Back in the classroom, pairs of children should use the information they have gained in the field to make a coloured map of land use on a new copy of the base map.

Talk to the children about photocopiable page 123, then ask them to complete it. Together, rank the land uses and compare this area with the one they have just surveyed.

20 mins Plenary

Discuss the survey and rank the land uses found, starting with the most important (the biggest area) and ending with the least. Ask the children what kind of area they have surveyed –

ICT opportunities
• Use word-processing for captions, word lists and short accounts.
• Scan the base map and land use key, then colour them in using an art package.

for example, is it a place where people work, live or play? A look at the pattern of land use will provide the answer.

Encourage the children to think about how their results might compare with those of a survey undertaken in another part of the town, or in a village.

Differentiation

More able children could try (as part of their fieldwork) to identify changes in the ways that the land has been used over time, and record any significant changes on the base map. They could complete the land use map in pairs rather than in small groups.

Less able children could produce captions for the photographs, and identify any further land uses that they can see in them. They could develop their understanding of the terms in the class list (see 'Introduction') through a game such as 'I Spy' (for example, 'I spy wasteland' – the children have to find as many examples of it in the photographs as they can).

Assessing learning outcomes

Can the children identify and understand how land is used in different ways? Can they record land usage on a map, using a letter and/or colour code? Can they present their findings using ICT?

**Follow-up
activities**
● Undertake a land use
survey in a different part
of the town that exhibits
different characteristics;
compare the results of
the two surveys.
● Look at land use maps
for other areas (for
example, OS 1:100 000
land use maps),
including ones that
describe agricultural
use.
● Undertake local
surveys to investigate
other aspects of the
school's locality, such as
building use, shops,
transport and wasteland.

③ₕₒᵤᵣₛ Work, commuting and transport

What you need and preparation

A map at 1:1250 scale, showing the local shopping centre in your town. Use this to make a simplified base map for the children to work from – perhaps by removing some boundary walls, going over the outlines of the shops to be surveyed and writing in the door number of each shop (to make them easier to locate). The shopping centre should contain about twenty shops and businesses close to the school, and be a safe environment for the children to work in (with adult supervision).

An enlarged colour photograph of each shop or business. A selection of local newspapers. Maps of the town or city and surrounding area at 1:50 000 scale (OS maps are best). Copies of photocopiable page 124. A large road map of your town or city, showing the street names. Copies of photocopiable page 125, enlarged to A3 size; dice, counters.

What to do

 Introduction
With the children, construct a questionnaire to discover the kinds of jobs that adults do, where they go to do their jobs, how far they need to travel and how they get there. The children can take copies of these home (one for each adult to complete).

Look at the local 1:1250 maps; encourage the children to become familiar with these by finding and identifying particular places and features on them. Look at the photographs; ask the children to name each shop or business, and say what they might sell or what business might take place there.

Tell the children that half of them will conduct a survey of the local shops. Discuss how this will be organised; stress the need for safety. Look at the base map. Construct a colour code for the different kinds of shops in the shopping centre, such as food shops and clothes shops.

Now say that the rest of the children will conduct a survey of local traffic. Explain the traffic survey sheet on photocopiable page 124, and how to conduct the survey. Remind the children about safety near the roadside.

**Learning
objectives**
● Constructing
questionnaires and
analysing data.
● Using and
interpreting local
maps.
● Identifying local
land uses.
● Undertaking local
surveys, using a
base plan and
colour code.

**Lesson
organisation**
Teacher-led
introduction;
small-group
activities; fieldwork
in two large ability
groups; whole-class
follow-up work and
group-led
feedback.

CHAPTER I
INVESTIGATING OUR LOCAL AREA

Living in a town

Vocabulary
primary
secondary
tertiary
manufacturing
service
commuting
commuter
survey
questionnaire

ICT opportunities
● Use word-processing to write up notes and captions, selecting appropriate font types and sizes.
● Use data handling software to construct data sheets and graphs.

Follow-up activities
● Many other surveys can be undertaken to explore and investigate the nature of the urban environment, including surveys of building use, parkland and leisure amenities. Great care must be taken when selecting appropriate sites.

② hours Development

The following preliminary activities are best undertaken in pairs or small groups, each of which can focus on one activity.

● Look at the completed questionnaires; categorise the jobs that people do, how they travel and how far. Categorise the jobs into those done in the town and those done elsewhere. Place coloured stickers on a local 1:50 000 scale map to show where the jobs are located. Now sort the jobs into three broad categories: 'primary' (mining, farming, fishing, forestry, quarrying and so on); 'secondary' or manufacturing (cars, clothes, furniture and so on); 'tertiary' or services (teaching, nursing, police, banking and so on). The terms 'growing and getting', 'making' and 'helping' could be used instead.

● Draw a bar chart to show how far people travel to work: 0–1km, 2–3km, 4–5km, 6–10km, 11–20km or over 20km. Write notes to explain what the chart shows, for example: how far did the greatest number of people travel to work; what was the average distance travelled?

● Construct a bar chart to show how people travel to work: bus, car, walking or train. Write some notes to explain what the chart shows, for example: how did the greatest number of people travel to work? Is there a relationship between the distance travelled to work and the type of transport used?

● Cut out a selection of advertisements from local newspapers. Make sure that each advertisement states clearly what is for sale and which settlement it is in. Make an 'advertisement map' on a large outline base map, showing what can be bought in your town and in other local places.

The fieldwork that follows can be tackled by two large groups.

1. Shopping survey (15 minutes)
In the town, the children should look carefully at each shop in turn to see what it sells or what business it is involved in. They can record this on a copy of the base map, in words or using a letter code (to avoid taking lots of coloured pencils outside), and complete a new base plan on their return to school. This work is best done in pairs.

2. Traffic survey (15 minutes)
This should be tackled in pairs, with one child stating the type of vehicle as it passes a certain point (such as a telegraph pole) on the opposite side of the road and the other child recording. If possible, they should record information they see on lorries – often it is easy to read where the vehicle is from and what it is carrying. They should make a total of all the vehicles seen. On returning to school, they should construct graphs based on the results.

As a classroom follow-up, the game 'Commuter' (photocopiable page 125) can be played by pairs. Talk about the problems of getting to work each day.

③⓪ mins Plenary

Ask each of the large groups to describe their work and say what they have found out. Ask questions as follows.
1. Shopping survey – *What is the most common type of shop? What do they sell? Where in the shopping centre are they?*
2. Traffic survey – *What were the most common types of vehicle seen? Where did some of the lorries come from, and what were they carrying? What could be done to reduce the amount of traffic using the road?* Talk about the problems of 'commuting'. *Who commutes, when and why?*

Differentiation

More able children should carry out the shopping survey, then draw simple bar charts and write descriptions of what they have found.

Less able children should carry out the traffic survey, focusing on collecting and categorising the data.

How has the town changed?

What you need and preparation

Copies of an A4-sized extract of a 1:1250 scale OS map of part of the local area. A4-sized copies of an historical map of similar scale; this can be of any date (large-scale OS maps date from about 1890). A selection of old photographs showing views in the local area, and modern photographs taken from exactly the same positions. Enlarged photographs showing specific sites that have recently undergone radical changes, and with which the children are familiar. Copies of photocopiable page 126.

Undertake a preliminary visit to a local street (possibly Victorian), and take a photograph of each house in a short row of houses.

What to do

Introduction

Talk to the children about recent changes to their homes: perhaps some have been painted, or a dormer window or a satellite dish has been added, or an old garage has been knocked down. Ask about recent changes that have taken place in their street. Help the children to understand that small changes in our environment are taking place all the time; and that if these changes are taken together over a period of time, they may be considerable.

Look at the extract of the modern large-scale map; let the children become familiar with this for a few minutes by finding places that they know. Give them copies of the old map to look at; encourage them to look for things that have changed and things that have remained the same.

Look at each of the enlarged photographs showing a site that has changed. Ask the children to describe what they see, and what they think was there before. Explain the planned fieldwork (see below), and stress the need for safety.

Development

Together, visit a site (or several sites) that has undergone recent, significant change. Ask the children what change has occurred, why they think this change was needed and what they think was there before. They should make small sketches and write notes. If there are several sites to be visited, complete the recording before moving on to the next one.

On return to school, locate these sites on an up-to-date large-scale map of the area. Use the enlarged photographs to help with this. Attach some of the children's small sketches and notes.

Working in four groups, the children should look at modern and historical maps of the area. Each group should work on a different quarter of the map, using a 'window' cut out from a plain sheet of A4 paper to focus their attention. They should note what features have been added, been removed or stayed more or less the same over the years.

The children (in pairs) can go on to look at old and new photographs. They should look for evidence of change, particularly in the buildings and building uses, transport and people's dress. They can stick the

Learning objectives
● Use fieldwork techniques.
● Use other sources to obtain information, including maps and photographs.
● Become increasingly able to identify changes and assess their impact on the local community.

Lesson organisation
Teacher-led introduction (discussion and consideration of work to be tackled); whole-class fieldwork and follow-up; group and paired activities; whole-class plenary session.

Vocabulary
site
environment
urban
impact
change

Living in a town

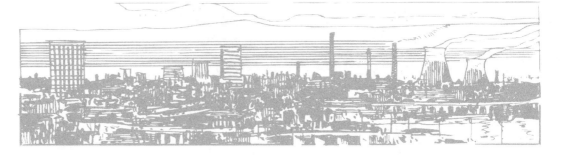

ICT opportunities
• Use word-processing for descriptions and captions.
• Scan photographs and map extracts, then label them on-screen.

Follow-up activities
• Target a wasteland area that is close to the school, safe, and no bigger than half a football pitch. Research the area through historical maps and photographs. Devise questionnaires to discover what local adults would like to see there; record the results using writing and graphs. On an A3-sized base map, draw a plan for the redevelopment of the area.

photographs onto paper or card and annotate them with notes on what has changed.

Explain photocopiable page 126, then let the children work (individually or in pairs) to complete it. There may be local examples of 'infilling' that can be investigated by the children: they can look to see how well the new buildings blend in with the others next to them.

15 mins Plenary

Review the fieldwork: discuss sites nearby that have undergone considerable change, where they are, what used to be there, and what the previous usage said about the original character of the area.

Ask representatives from each of the four groups what changes that they found in their quarter of the local map. *What are the most important changes that have occurred since the older map was produced? How have these changes altered the character of the area?*

Ask the children what changes they found between the old and the new photographs. *Which pair of photographs shows the most change? Which pair shows the least?*

Differentiation

More able children could use the maps to try and find out where the old and new photographs were taken. They could produce detailed descriptions of sites rather than notes.

Less able children should be encouraged to identify changes and use appropriate vocabulary (perhaps from a word list provided) to describe what they see and the changes that have occurred. They should try to pick out only the major changes in the photographs and on the maps.

Assessing learning outcomes

Can the children identify changes to the environment and suggest reasons for them, using fieldwork and other sources such as maps and photographs? Do they understand that environmental change is an inevitable part of the growth of a settlement?

Weather and travel

The **weather** is best thought of as the condition of the atmosphere over a short period of time. It is usually described in terms of pressure, humidity, temperature, rainfall, cloud, wind speed and wind direction. The last five elements can be more easily observed and experienced by children, and so are more interesting for them to investigate.

The weather is rarely the same from one moment to another. Wind speed and direction change and the type and degree of cloud cover vary, altering the amount of sunshine we receive and the temperatures we experience. The saying 'If you don't like the weather here, wait a few minutes' is certainly true in the UK.

Weather should not be confused with **climate**, which is the 'average' of the weather conditions in a particular region through the seasons over a minimum of 30 years.

Measuring weather

Children should be taught to measure temperature in degrees Celsius, although it is often presented to them in degrees Fahrenheit in the press and on television weather forecasts. The chart on the right will be useful for work in this chapter.

Fahrenheit to Celsius conversion	
°C	°F
40	104
35	95
30	86
25	77
20	68
15	59
10	50
5	41
0	32
–5	23

The Beaufort Scale, invented by Admiral Beaufort in 1806 (and adopted for international use in 1874), is commonly used to describe wind strength. It encourages the estimation of wind force from its observable effects on the environment.

			Beaufort Scale	Speed	
Relative force	Description	Results on land		knots	km/h
0	calm	calm, smoke rises vertically		0	0
1	light air	direction of wind shown by smoke drift		1–3	2–5
2	light breeze	wind felt on face, leaves rustle, wind vane moves		4–6	6–11
3	gentle breeze	leaves and twigs in constant motion, a light flag extended		7–10	12–19
4	moderate breeze	light paper lifted, small branches moved		11–16	20–29
5	fresh breeze	small trees in leaf begin to sway		17–21	30–39
6	strong breeze	large branches in motion, whistling heard in telegraph wires		22–27	40–50
7	near gale	whole trees in motion, walking becomes difficult		28–33	51–61
8	gale	twigs broken off trees		34–40	62–74
9	severe gale	slight structural damage, slates blown off roofs		41–47	75–87
10	storm	trees uprooted, much structural damage		48–55	88–101
11	violent storm	widespread damage		56–63	102–117
12	hurricane	catastrophic damage, roofs ripped from houses, cars overturned		64+	118+

Clouds

There are several types of clouds, formed under different conditions in different parts of the atmosphere. They have different effects on the weather.

High clouds, up to 6000 metres above sea level, are usually composed of ice crystals. They include:

● cirrus – white filaments
● cirrocumulus – small rippled clouds
● cirrostratus – transparent sheet.

Medium clouds, between 2000 and 4000 metres above sea level, are usually composed of water droplets. They include:

● altocumulus – layered, rippled clouds, generally white in colour
● altostratus – thin grey layer, breaks up sunlight like ground glass.

Low clouds, below 2000 metres above sea level, are usually composed of water droplets. They include:

● stratocumulus – layered series of rounded rolls, usually white or grey

- cumulus – flat bases, cauliflower-shaped towers, white
- nimbocumulus – flat bases, cauliflower-shaped towers, dark grey, may give rain
- stratus – layered, uniform base, grey in colour
- nimbostratus – thick layer, dark grey bases, cauliflower-shaped towers, may give rain or snow
- fog – at sea level or slightly above, hovers around valleys, uniform grey.

Freak weather conditions

Extreme forms of weather are always fascinating for the children to learn about. They will be able to see the effects of very low or high temperatures, strong winds that dislodge slates or tear branches from trees, intense electrical storms and downpours of rain. Children are also interested in extreme forms of weather that are rarely experienced in the UK, such as hurricanes, tornadoes and drought. When these do occur, they are always well covered by the media because of their rarity and impact on people's lives.

It is unlikely that the children will experience such freak weather as the drought of 1976 or the hurricane of 1987, or even one of the two hundred weak tornadoes that affect the UK each year; but unusual weather does make their work exciting and stimulating. The study of these kinds of weather phenomena can easily lead to looking at catastrophic weather in other parts of the world and how it contrasts with the weather normally experienced here. Television and video are useful for capturing the drama that unfolds when adverse weather is experienced in other parts of the world: they can be used to introduce a theme, tell a story and add an international dimension to work currently being undertaken in the classroom.

In the unit 'Weather around the world', the children find out about differences in climate throughout the world through the imaginary experience of taking a holiday abroad. In role as a family group, they make decisions about where to go, book the holiday with the travel agent, make the journey and send postcards home. The unit encourages them to undertake a considerable amount of research in order to determine their ideal destination. This is a familiar scenario to some children, for whom helping to decide on a holiday destination is an annual event; it will be less real to others, but this gap can be overcome by using colourful resources which the children will find interesting and accessible.

The unit 'My weather' looks at the main weather elements that are observable and measurable by the children. These include temperature, wind speed and direction, rainfall, sunshine and cloud cover. The children are encouraged to experience the weather over the course of the lesson plans, and to play an active part in investigating different kinds of weather phenomena. Recording the weather that they experience, or that they know to be present in different parts of the UK, Europe and the world, is another important aspect of this unit.

(See page 31.)

	J	F	M	A	M	J	Jy	A	S	O	N	D
1. Verkhoyansk (Russia)	−47°C	−40	−20	−1	11	21	24	21	12	−8	−33	−42
	7mm	5	5	4	5	25	33	30	13	11	10	7
2. Archangel (Russia)	−9°C	−8	−2	5	11	18	22	17	13	6	−2	−8
	33mm	28	28	28	39	59	63	57	66	55	44	39
3. Paris (France)	6°C	7	12	16	20	23	25	24	21	16	10	7
	56mm	46	35	42	57	54	59	64	55	50	51	50
5. Lusaka (Zambia)	26°C	26	26	27	25	23	23	26	29	31	29	27
	224mm	173	90	19	3	1	0	1	1	17	85	196
6. In Salah (Algeria)	13°C	18	23	28	34	40	43	43	39	34	28	20
	2mm	3	1	1	1	0	0	2	1	1	3	5
7. Manaus (Brazil)	31°C	31	31	31	31	31	32	33	34	34	33	32
	278mm	278	300	287	193	99	61	41	62	112	165	220

Weather around the world

The climate that a region experiences is governed by a number of different factors, including:
- latitude – its distance north or south of the equator
- altitude – its height above sea level
- its distance from the sea.

Places at or near the equator are much warmer than places nearer the poles, due to the curvature of the Earth and the effects of ocean currents. Temperatures decrease by approximately 1°C for every 100m ascended, so snow falls first and clears last in highland areas. The sea takes longer to heat up and cool down than the land, so it is relatively warm in the winter and cool in the summer. Places near the sea are affected by the prevailing wind from the sea, so they are cooler in the summer and milder in the winter than places further inland.

There is little agreement by the publishers of atlases as to the exact number and nature of the climatic zones that the world should be divided into, but they all broadly agree on the following categories:

1. Polar – very cold, with ice and snow.
2. Cold forest – very cold in the winter, with short warm summers.
3. Temperate – warm summers, cool winters (when most rain falls); includes Mediterranean areas.
4. Mountain – temperature falls with altitude, so extremely cold on the highest peaks (not shown in the statistics below).
5. Tropical grasslands and monsoons – wet season (warm) and dry season (hot).
6. Hot desert – very little or no rainfall, hot in the summer.
7. Rainforest – hot and wet all year round.

The differences between these zones are illustrated by the climate statistics (temperature and rainfall) typical of each zone (see the table at the bottom of page 30).

The climate of the Earth has changed many times. A hundred million years ago, there were no ice caps at the poles, and vegetation extended much further towards them than it does today. For the last one million years, the Earth has been colder than at the present time. Our climate is currently in an 'inter-glacial' phase, between successive ice ages.

People can and do adapt to their climate in a variety of ways: genetically, through changes in their skin pigmentation and body hair; and culturally, through the use of clothing and shelter. The most recent adaptation has come about through the application of technology to provide central heating, double glazing, fans and air-conditioning.

Climatic change has recently been associated with increased fuel consumption and farming, and their effect on the world's weather systems. Most scientists agree that the increasing amounts of 'greenhouse gases' that we produce are raising temperatures around the planet, and that by 2025 the average temperature on the Earth's surface will have increased by approximately 2°C relative to now. 'Greenhouse gases' are largely composed of carbon dioxide (from fossil fuels and vehicle exhausts) and methane (from rice fields and decomposing vegetation).

Some children will have experience of travelling to or living in a country in a different climatic zone from that of the United Kingdom. Children's and their parents' memories are a useful resource for work in this theme: they will provide a direct link to life and work in a different climate. Holidays provide a useful way into the theme of climate. Many children will have travelled abroad, and will have been involved in deciding where to spend the annual family holiday. They will be aware of the information contained within holiday brochures, the location of some popular resorts, the need for a passport, and the things that need to be packed to make the holiday more comfortable.

Some children will have had experiences, good or bad, that are attributable to the weather – for example, being thirsty, having sunburn or gaining a sun-tan. Most of them will have sent or received postcards from different places. A postcard will usually show a view of a place, thus giving some (selective) information about its climate – and the message on the reverse side will usually mention the weather!

UNIT 3: Weather around the world

Enquiry questions	Teaching objectives	Teaching activities	Learning outcomes	Cross-curricular links
Where are the hottest and coldest places in the world? How do people's lifestyles and the foods produced differ between climatic zones?	• Ask and respond to geographical questions. • Recognise patterns in data. • Use geographical data. • Learn about weather conditions around the world.	Whole class or groups: make a booklet about a journey from the North Pole to the Equator, undertaking basic research. Design and make an environment typical of a climatic zone. Arrange labels from foodstuffs around an outline map of the world and show what kinds of foodstuffs originate in the different climatic zones. Carry out a survey in a supermarket to see which foodstuffs are grown in the different climatic regions.	Children: • identify hot and cold places on a map or globe • are aware of the variety of climates in the world and the features of each • understand that climate influences landscape, lifestyles and the flora and fauna of a region	Art: drawing or painting produce from different countries. ICT: word-processing, drawing maps using a graphics package.
Why do people go on holiday? How do they get there and what do they do while they are away?	• Use and interpret globes, atlases and maps. • Ask and respond to geographical questions. • Consider how places are connected by different routes. • Consider climates around the world.	In pairs or groups of three or four: find a holiday destination for different people as shown on the 'profile cards'. Ensure that the holiday selected meets their requirements. Identify routes home and the types of transport that may be used.	• describe the places they have visited and locate them on a map • make decisions about where to send people on holiday • describe the best route between two places and calculate the distance travelled	Maths: calculating journey distances using a scale. ICT: word-processing, using software to locate destinations. D&T: designing 'in-flight' meals, a menu and an airline logo.
How do people choose their holiday destination?	• Use secondary sources to investigate places. • Identify similarities and differences between places. • Know about weather conditions around the world and their effects on human activity.	Group work to include: make a decision about where to go on holiday; select a holiday destination that fulfils the requirements of most 'family' members.	• conduct research and record evidence • understand that weather conditions vary from place to place	English: writing questions for the travel agent about the chosen resort. D&T: making a poster about their resort. ICT: using a CD-ROM to discover the nature of specific holiday destinations; word-processing lists and descriptions.
What do people do on holiday if the weather is poor? How can we find out about the weather in holiday resorts?	• Ask and respond to geographical questions. • Use geographical vocabulary. • Find out about weather conditions around the world.	Paired work: use brochures of UK resorts to discover what different resorts can offer as regards wet/dry weather activities; a similar activity featuring holidays abroad; looking at postcard messages to extract information on the weather, and writing their own.	• are aware of the effects of the weather on human activity • are aware that the weather varies from place to place • use secondary sources to find out about the weather	English: writing postcards home that describe weather and leisure activities. Maths and ICT: using a data handling package to construct a temperature graph; word-processing a description of it. D&T: designing a holiday village for wet/dry weather.
What places have you been to? How can you remember where you have been?	• Use and interpret atlases and maps. • Use secondary sources to investigate places. • Produce a record of work done.	Pairs or groups of children should: make a passport to show some or all of the places they have 'visited' over this unit; make a scrapbook in which to record their visits; contact agencies to obtain further information about some of the countries visited.	• show a developing awareness of different places around the world, with their different climates and weather patterns.	English: writing a letter to obtain information; writing details in a passport. ICT: using e-mail or the Internet; using graphics software to design a passport cover; word-processing.

Resources
A globe, a map of the world, photographs in different climatic zones; travel books, brochures and multimedia resources; materials to make climatic zone models; examples of foodstuffs from different climates; atlases, a large outline world map, a road atlas of Europe, an A4 outline map of Europe and the world; coloured stickers; profile cards; holiday brochures and photographs for different holiday destinations; a number of old suitcases or holdalls; a selection of items that would be packed for a hot country; materials to create a small 'travel agent's office', including posters, maps, box files and a telephone; brochures featuring holiday camps/villages in the UK and family holidays abroad; a selection of guides to attractions near a particular UK resort; road atlases, OS maps; access to Teletext, a broadsheet newspaper and weather reports; a real passport and an A5 facsimile; a holiday photograph album; A3-size scrapbooks; school notepaper, envelopes.

Display
Leaflets and models of typical environments in different climatic zones; foodstuff labels; maps; all survey work from the local supermarket. Different profile cards added to a climatic zone map. Transport routes home from these places, colour-coded according to the type of transport used. Labels added to maps to show the preferred holiday destinations of different families. Commercially-produced and children's own postcards; children's designs for wet/dry weather holiday villages. Children's passports and scrapbooks; replies to children's letters from embassies and tourist offices, and pictorial information that they supply.

CHAPTER 2
WEATHER
AND TRAVEL

Weather
around the
world

Hot and cold places

2 hours 30 mins

What you need and preparation

A globe, map of the world. Copies of photocopiable page 127. A selection of pictures or photographs showing typical views in the different climatic zones, including people, plants and animals. Travel books and brochures; related multimedia resources. A selection of props and materials that can be used to make models of scenes in different climatic zones. Low-cut cardboard trays (as used for fruit in supermarkets) or large school trays. An A2-sized outline map of the world, showing the main climatic zones. Examples of foodstuffs from different countries, such as rice, dates and bananas; tins and packets can also be used (alternatively, provide labels that clearly show the foodstuff and its country of origin).

As an alternative to bringing in foodstuffs, arrange a visit to the fruit and vegetables section of the local supermarket. Obtain permission in advance, and check that this section is easily accessible and the produce is clearly marked. Ask whether an assistant may be available to talk to the children about how the different fruits and vegetables are grown and what climatic conditions they need. A video could be made of the visit.

What to do

Introduction

15 mins

Using a globe, talk to the children about how the climate changes around the Earth and how people's lifestyles, the food that can be produced and the plants and animals that live there change as a result. Show the children the photographs and talk about the differences between them. Look for evidence of what the climate is like in each of them.

Give out copies of photocopiable page 127, which shows the different climatic zones of the world. Talk to the children about where these are and what each zone is called. (Atlases can also be used – but they tend to vary in their statements of where each zone is, how many zones there are, their precise names and the kind of climate that they experience.) Again, use the photographs to make the work more realistic. Explain how to complete the photocopiable sheet, which they will do later (see below).

Explain to the children that much of the food we buy cannot be grown in this country, because our climate is generally too cold. Look at the collection of foodstuffs, and talk about the climate needed to produce them. Alternatively, ask the children whether they have been to the supermarket which you plan to visit. *How often do you go there? What kinds of things do you buy?* Explain the purpose of the visit (see below) and the work planned.

Development

2 hours

Select from the range of activities listed below. They could be tackled by the whole class, or different groups could tackle each one.

1. Make a booklet about a journey from the North Pole to the equator. On the way, stop at a place that is in each climatic zone. On each page, draw and label a map showing the stage of the journey you are at, with a small map of the country you are in. Use photographs and information from CD-ROMs or the Internet, as well as descriptions from travel books and brochures, to talk about the character of the zone that you are in.

2. Use an atlas to complete photocopiable page 127.

3. Use different materials to model a 'typical' environment in a climatic zone (small groups of children could each make a different zone). Design the environment before making it, and list the materials you will need. The models may be constructed in large low-cut cardboard boxes or trays, and should feature aspects of the landscape, human activity (if there is any) and plant and animal

Learning objectives
● Ask and respond to geographical questions.
● Recognise patterns in data.
● Use geographical vocabulary.
● Learn about weather conditions around the world.

Lesson organisation
Teacher-led introduction; whole-class or mixed-ability group work focusing on all or one of the activities described; plenary either teacher-led or with groups feeding back to class.

Vocabulary
climate
zone
weather
hot
cold
polar
tropical
desert
rainforest

life. Adult help and support will be needed for this activity.

4. Arrange labels from foodstuffs (see above) around the outside of a large outline map of the world, and link them to the country of production. Make lists to show what kinds of produce come from each of the climatic zones.

5. Conduct a visit to the fruit and vegetables section of your local supermarket. This may have to be undertaken in small groups, given the level of supervision needed. The visit could be recorded on video. The children can complete a record sheet in the supermarket, naming each type of imported produce and its country of origin, and giving a brief description of its size and colour. It is possible that a member of the supermarket's staff may be able to give the children a guided tour. Bring samples of produce back to school as a stimulus for artwork. Use an A2 outline map of the world to show where the different kinds of produce come from.

 Plenary

Show the video of the supermarket visit; freeze the frame at intervals and encourage the children to name the different foodstuffs they can see and the country and climatic zone that each comes from.

Ask each group to describe their climatic zone model, how it was made and what it shows. They should concentrate on the landscape, people, plants and animals, and say how these are affected by the climate.

Ask some of the children to talk about their journey from the North Pole to the equator, using their booklets and the world map.

Show the children the 'food labels' map. Ask the group who made it to say which foodstuffs came from each climatic zone, and to describe the type of climate that each of the foodstuffs needs to grow.

Differentiation

More able children should try to make a booklet describing the journey from the North Pole to the equator, and conduct the research needed to complete it (with some adult support). They should also attempt to create an environment in a specific climatic zone, generating a design and listing materials for their group to acquire and use.

Less able children should focus on the first-hand opportunities provided by the supermarket visit and the 'food labels' map.

Assessing learning outcomes

Can the children identify hot and cold places on a globe and a map? Are they aware of the world's variety of climates and the main characteristics of each climate? Do they understand that climate influences landscape, people's lifestyles, and the flora and fauna that inhabit a region?

ICT opportunities
• Word-process the descriptions in the booklet, and use a graphics package to draw maps.
• Word-process the materials list, and make initial designs using a drawing or graphics package.
• Word-process a description of the supermarket visit and labels for the foodstuffs found there.

Follow-up activities
• Play a 'Guess what?' game based on the foodstuffs from different climatic zones. Players try to guess what the foodstuff is by asking their partner a maximum of five questions.
• Collect and watch videos that describe the different climatic zones. Plot the places featured on a world map.

CHAPTER 2
WEATHER
AND TRAVEL

Weather
around the
world

① Going on holiday

What you need and preparation

Atlases and a globe; a large outline wall-mounted map of the world; a folded road map of Europe. A4 outline maps of the world, showing the climatic zones and each of the contrasting holiday destinations on the cards (see below). A4 outline maps of Europe. Small peel-off coloured stickers. Copies (one per pair) of photocopiable page 128.

Cards (one per pair or group of children) with pictures of fictitious people (perhaps taken from magazines), each with a comment in a speech balloon outlining that person's idea of a perfect holiday (for example: 'I like to go to a hot country and spent most of the day by the beach or the hotel swimming pool; there must be plenty of nightlife'), and a shortlist of four or five contrasting holiday destinations. (See illustration below.) The shortlist should include only one destination that meets these criteria. All of the cards could have the same shortlist.

What to do

⑮ mins Introduction
Discuss with the children why people go on holiday, identifying the weather as an important factor. Ask children to find on the world map places that they have visited recently, and to mark these places on the map using stickers. Then ask them:
- *How did you get to your holiday destination? What kind of transport did you use? How long did it take to get there?*
- *What was the weather like when you were away?*
- *How did you and your family spend the holiday?*
Introduce the children to the 'profile cards'.

PROFILE CARD

☐ I like hot sunshine and staying close to the hotel pool or on the beach.

☐ I don't want to travel far as I'm not keen on flying.

☐ I want to stay in or near town so that I can enjoy the nightlife.

㉟ mins Development
Divide the children into pairs or groups of three or four.
Give each group a different profile card. Talk through the card with each group, identifying the specific holiday requirements of each holidaymaker. Allow them time to decide where to send the holidaymaker. When they have decided, ask them to find the destination on the map and record which climatic zone it is in.

Each group should mark their destination on an A4 base map of Europe or the world, then mark on a possible route home and identify the kinds of transport they could use for their journey. They should use atlases to find out the best routes from their town to the holiday destination, and try to calculate the length of the journey.

Distribute copies of photocopiable page 128. Look together at the different types of aircraft in the company's fleet: how far they can fly and how fast; how many passengers they can carry. Explain how important it is to match the correct aircraft to the correct group of passengers, for reasons of safety, comfort and economics. Let the children work in pairs to complete the sheet.

⑩ mins Plenary
Ask some groups to read out their profile card and say what kind of place the holidaymaker was looking for, then say where they decided to send the holidaymaker (pointing to the spot on the world map) and describe the climatic zone that he or she would be in.

Discuss the kinds of transport that the children have used to return from their holiday destinations. *What was the most popular type of transport? Why did you decide to use that option?*

Learning objectives
- Use and interpret globes, atlases and maps.
- Ask and respond to geographical questions.
- Consider how different places are connected by transport routes.
- Consider climate differences around the world.

Lesson organisation
Teacher-led introduction, including discussion and targeted questions; paired or small-group activities, involving discussion and problem-solving; teacher-led plenary based on questioning and children's feedback.

Vocabulary
holiday
destination
resort
transport
travel
climate
zone

CHAPTER 2
WEATHER
AND TRAVEL

**Weather
around the
world**

Ask some children to describe routes between their home and a chosen resort in the UK or Europe, again using the wall maps to help.

Differentiation
More able children should tackle the most demanding profile cards, and be encouraged to produce alternative routes back home from their holiday destination. They should work out detailed routes (including ferry crossings, if appropriate), and use the scale of the map to calculate approximate distances.

Less able children should be given a more restricted choice of destinations to which to send their holidaymaker, and use a simplified climatic zone map. They should find the best routes to nearby resorts, and measure the journey distance using string.

Assessing learning outcomes
Can the children describe places they have visited and locate them on a map? Can they make and justify decisions about the best locations for holidays based on specific criteria? Can they find and describe the best route between two places, and calculate the distance travelled?

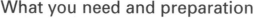

① What will I need to take?
(1 hour)

Learning objectives
● Use secondary sources (including ICT) to investigate places.
● Identify differences and similarities between places.
● Know about weather conditions around the world and their effects on human activity.

Lesson organisation
Teacher-led introduction; group activities in role as 'families'; representatives of each family feedback in a teacher-led plenary.

Vocabulary
holiday
brochure
booking
destination
suitcase
resort
travel agent
temperature
accommodation

What you need and preparation
A selection of holiday brochures and photographs relating to different holiday destinations. Old suitcases, one for each 'family'. A selection of items that would be packed for a holiday in a hot country, such as sunglasses, shorts and sun-tan lotion; a selection of items that would be packed for a holiday in a cold country, such as thick socks and a woolly hat. Copies of photocopiable page 129. A large world map.

With the class, create a small 'travel agent's office' in a corner of the classroom. Include posters, brochures, maps, box files and a telephone.

What to do
⑩ Introduction
Talk to the children about the process of choosing a holiday: agreeing to go on holiday, deciding what kind of holiday to have and where, paying a visit to a local travel agent to gather brochures, deciding on the location and finally making a booking. Show the children a holiday brochure and explain what it contains, how it is designed and what information it gives about particular resorts: location, climate (including temperatures), accommodation, prices and local attractions.

● Ask the children what questions they would ask a travel agent about a resort they had chosen. *What kind of things would you want to know before you decided to book and pay a lot of money for a holiday?* Write some of the most important questions on the board or flip chart.

Display various items (see above). Discuss which things the children would pack if they went on a holiday to a hot country, and compare these with the items they would take with them to a cold country.

⑳ Development
The children should work in groups. Each group should imagine that they are a family, making a decision about where to go on holiday. In role as parents or children, they should argue for what they personally want from a holiday (without having any particular destination in mind). One child should record the most important arguments made by each family member.

CHAPTER 2
WEATHER
AND TRAVEL

Weather
around the
world

Give the 'families' a selection of holiday brochures and ask them to select a place that they would like to go to for a holiday. When they have made their decision, ask them find out as much as possible about the resort. They should compare its climate with that of their home town. Each pair of children should make an A3-sized poster to advertise the resort.

Encourage the 'families' to write down some questions they would like to ask the travel agent about the suitability of their chosen resort. They should use the classroom 'travel agent's office' to visit the travel agent (who could be an adult), ask questions and note the replies. If necessary, they should then rethink their choice of destination.

The 'families' should decide what they will pack for a holiday trip to their chosen destination, then draw the items they have chosen on a sheet of plain A4-sized paper and label them. They should be encouraged to bring in clothing and other items to fill one of the suitcases, then add a sticker to the suitcase stating their destination. Alternatively, they could complete photocopiable page 129.

🔟 Plenary
mins Ask a member of each 'family' to say where they have decided to go for their holidays and to point to their destination on a world map. Ask them:
- *What kind of holiday did each family member want initially?*
- *What did you find out about the likely weather in this resort during the time you intend to go on holiday?*
- *What questions did you decide to ask the travel agent? What were the replies? Did you change your minds as a result?*
- *What things did you decide to pack? Why?*

Assessing learning outcomes
Can the children conduct research and record evidence to answer their own questions and those set by the teacher? Do they understand that weather conditions vary from place to place, and that these conditions affect what people wear and the things they do when they are on holiday?

ICT opportunities
- Use multimedia resources to research the nature of different holiday resorts.
- Word-process all lists and descriptions.

Follow-up activities
- Each family could construct a 'brochure page' to describe the place they intend to go to. They could use information taken from a variety of brochures, as well as material downloaded from the computer. The page should include information on the accommodation available, the weather and climate, the resort and its surrounding area. Combine the pages into a school travel brochure.

① What if it rains?
hour

What you need and preparation
A selection of holiday brochures that feature 'holiday camps' or 'holiday villages' in the UK; a selection of other brochures that feature family holidays abroad. Copies of photocopiable page 130. A selection of 'attraction' guides, leaflets or magazines, featuring things to see and do in and around a particular seaside resort in the UK; road atlases or OS maps at 1:50 000 scale that cover the same area. Blank postcards; postcards with messages from other countries. Access to Teletext, newspaper or Internet information on the weather in different parts of Europe and the world.

Learning objectives
- Ask and respond to geographical questions.
- Use geographical vocabulary.
- Find out about weather conditions around the world.

Lesson organisation
Teacher-led introduction including a short brainstorming session and familiarisation with source materials; paired work from a selection of activities; teacher-led plenary session covering the main aspects of the lesson plan.

What to do
🔟 Introduction
mins Talk to the children about taking holidays in places where the summer weather is unpredictable – such as anywhere in the UK. Find out who has had a summer holiday in the UK recently, and ask them to describe the weather they had. Brainstorm the things the children do on holiday when the weather is poor. Make a list on a flip chart or OHT. Ask the children what they

Vocabulary
holiday
weather
holiday camp/
village
destination
leaflets
entertainment
leisure attraction

CHAPTER 2
WEATHER
AND TRAVEL

Weather
around the
world

can do when the weather is sunny, and make another list.

Talk to the children about holiday camps or villages that cater for children, and holiday destinations abroad that have children's clubs. Show the children the leaflets and 'entertainments' magazines, and talk about the kinds of places people might go to if they had a wet day in a particular UK holiday resort (perhaps one near the school).

Ask the children how they could find out about the weather in different holiday resorts in the UK, Europe or other parts of the world. Show them weather reports in newspapers, and on Teletext or the Internet.

Give out copies of photocopiable page 130 and discuss how to complete it.

40 mins Development

Select from the following activities; the children should work in pairs.

1. Give out brochures that feature holiday camps or villages. Encourage the children to look at what the different holiday companies can offer at various locations. Select one or two different holiday resorts, and for each write down the different activities available if the weather is good or if it is bad. Encourage each pair to share their results with others. Use the class results to make a list, ranking the resorts from the best to the worst.

2. Conduct a similar activity using brochures that feature family holidays abroad. Each pair should select one or two different holiday resorts and make two lists, showing what each holiday can offer if the weather is good or if it is bad. Share the results and rank the resorts from the best to the worst.

3. Allow the children time to look at the postcards with short messages written on. Encourage them to imagine that they are spending a week in one of the resorts they have studied in the activities above. Give them blank postcards and ask them to write a postcard home (or to school), describing the weather that they are having and how they are spending their time. On the front of the postcard, they should sketch and colour a picture of the resort. Display the children's postcards with the commercially produced ones.

4. The children can look at the 'attractions' guides and leaflets that cover the area around a UK resort. They should locate the attractions on a 1:50 000 OS map (or a copy of the appropriate page of a road atlas) and mark them, using different-coloured stickers for wet-weather (indoor) and fair-weather (outdoor) attractions.

5. The children can complete photocopiable page 130.

10 mins Plenary

Ask the children to feed back what made the 'best' and the 'worst' resorts (as far as they are concerned), either in the UK or abroad. Encourage some of the children to read out their postcards to the rest of the class. Ask: *What attractions can be found close to your seaside resort on sunny days? What attractions are there on wet days? Which type are there more of?*

Differentiation

More able children could find out about the weather conditions for particular days at chosen destinations in the UK, Europe or elsewhere in the world. Teletext and

CHAPTER 2
W E A T H E R
A N D   T R A V E L

Weather
around the
world

newspapers give basic information for a number of resorts: the maximum and minimum temperatures, and a brief description of the weather ('sunny', 'cloudy', 'showers' and so on). The children should compare this information with that given by postcards or by temperature graphs in holiday brochures.

Less able children could undertake basic research into a child-centred holiday abroad, where there will be fewer games and activities to record. They should look at real postcards and extract any information they can about the weather and leisure activities, then try to write a brief postcard message. They should focus on completing photocopiable page 130.

Assessing learning outcomes
Do the children show awareness of the effects of the weather on human activity? Are they aware that the weather varies in a given place, and that leisure activities can be provided to take account of this? Can they use secondary sources to gather information about the weather?

ICT opportunities
● Use a data handling package to draw a temperature graph for the resort over the course of a week or two, and word-process a short description of what it shows.
● Use DTP and drawing software to create a postcard from another place, containing a message and a picture of the resort.

Follow-up activities
● Design a holiday village. Provide things for people (especially children) to do when it is sunny and when it is cold and wet. Include places for holidaymakers to stay.

 ## Where have you been?

What you need and preparation
Outline copies of a world map; a selection of atlases. A real passport. Copies of a class passport: an A5-sized facsimile of an adult passport, with spaces for the details of the passport holder, a photograph certified with the school stamp, and a number of blank pages. A photograph album showing holiday photographs, or a child's scrapbook recording a holiday. Blank A3-sized scrapbooks (these can be purchased cheaply or made from sugar paper, with a card cover). Headed school notepaper, stamps and envelopes. Photocopiable page 131. Access to the Internet would be useful.

What to do
Introduction
10 mins Ask the children to remember all of the places they have 'visited' over this unit of work. Make a list on the flip chart or OHP. Locate these places on a map of the world.

Talk about how we record and remember where we have been on holiday. Show the children a real passport and the stamps that have been put inside it on entry to another country (this process is now waived for travel within the EU).

Show the children photograph albums that feature holidays. If possible, show them a scrapbook that gives a child's personal view of a holiday, full of assorted memorabilia. Ask them to consider other ways that they could record information about a country they have visited, or find out about a country they wish to visit.

Development
2 hours 30 mins Encourage individual children to go through their previous work in this unit and record all of the places they have visited. Using an atlas, they should mark and name these places on an outline map of the world. They should add a suitable title to their map, such as 'Around the world with...'

Pairs or groups of children can tackle one of the following activities.
1. Make a passport that shows some or all of the places visited over the course of the unit. Complete photocopiable page 131 and add a small photograph or sketch of the bearer. Each page should contain details of a different country, including: a made-up entry stamp; the country's name; information about the continent and climatic zone the country is in; details of its population, capital city, flag and approximate distance from your town.

Learning objectives
● Use and interpret atlases and maps.
● Use secondary sources to investigate places.
● Produce a record of work done.

Lesson organisation
Teacher-led review of work done and introduction to the lesson; individual, then paired or small-group activity work, including use of secondary sources; plenary with pairs or groups talking about their work.

Vocabulary
passport
scrapbook
photographs
flag
Internet

CHAPTER 2
WEATHER
AND TRAVEL

Weather
around the
world

ICT opportunities
● Use e-mail and the Internet to obtain information about different countries.
● Use a graphics package to design the passport cover and different countries' flags.
● Word-process information for the scrapbook or passport, and letters to send out requesting information.

Follow-up activities
● When receiving replies to e-mails and letters, show them to the rest of the class before using parts of them in scrapbooks, passports or displays.

2. Construct a scrapbook of their visits. It should have an introductory page giving information about the authors and the school, and listing the countries featured. Each following page should contain general and personal information about a different country visited, including the name of the country, the continent and climatic zone that it is in and various memorabilia (such as postcards, postage stamps, maps, decorative sketches, flags, photographs and pictures from brochures).

3. For later display or addition to the passport or scrapbook, send a letter or e-mail to an embassy or tourist office (using the school's address) to request brochures and other publications giving different information from that found in travel agents' offices (the former sources are likely to provide more descriptive material about the country and its culture). Information can also be found in libraries and on CD-ROMs.

20 mins **Plenary**

Ask the pairs or groups to show and talk about their passports and scrapbooks. This can be done as a whole class or in large groups. The children should describe each place they have visited, paying particular attention to the climate that the different countries experience. They should also mention any unusual information they have collected.

Differentiation

More able children should attempt the scrapbook activity, which is not as closely prescribed as the passport activity. They should be encouraged to conduct research to find interesting items to add to the scrapbook. They can write or e-mail to request additional information.

Less able children should try the passport activity, possibly using photocopiable page 131 to help them. They can draw an entry stamp for each country visited and write brief, general information about each one. With support and encouragement, they should write or e-mail to request additional information.

Assessing learning outcomes

Do the children show a developing awareness of different places around the world, with their different climates and weather patterns?

My weather

The four seasons that we experience in the UK have their own characteristic weather patterns, and bring with them changes in the natural world and people's activities. The effects that seasonal changes have on the children need to be explored. They should be given the opportunity to say how the seasons affect them in terms of what clothes they wear, what games they play and what kind of food they eat. Various artefacts associated with each of the seasons can be used to make interesting displays.

The seasons are caused by the tilt of the Earth, which is at an angle of 23.5 degrees to its axis of rotation. As the Earth moves around the Sun, the amount of sunlight that a particular region on the Earth receives per day will vary. When the northern hemisphere leans towards the sun, it is summer in that hemisphere; when it leans away from the sun, it is winter. Spring and autumn represent phases of movement towards the sun and away from it respectively.

In winter, the Sun appears low in the sky and is only seen for a few hours each day. Its heating effect is reduced because of the oblique angle at which its rays hit the land: a given amount of sunlight is spread over a relatively wide area of land. The situation is reversed in summer: the sun appears in the sky for many hours and at a higher angle, so that its rays are more intense and are seen for a longer period.

The temperature and the levels of rainfall, wind and sunshine that we receive in the UK vary throughout the year. The warmest month is July. At this time, the warmest region is the south-east and the coolest is the north-east (especially in Scotland). The temperature gap between these regions is about 6°C The coldest month in the UK is January; at this time, the mildest region is the south-west and the coldest is the north-east. The temperature gap between these regions is about 4°C.

Most rain falls in the west and over the higher land between the months of October and March. These areas are closer to the rain-bearing depressions that come in from the north Atlantic Ocean. Lower and eastern areas are drier; the south-east is the driest region, being away from the depressions and closer to the high-pressure systems that develop over continental Europe at this time. This is also the time of the windiest weather, with western coasts and hills being the most severely affected.

My weather

British Isles climate statistics:

		J	F	M	A	M	J	J	A	S	O	N	D
						average temperature and rainfall							
London	6°C	7	10	13	17	20	22	21	19	14	10	7	
	54mm	40	37	37	46	45	57	59	49	57	64	48	
Oxford	7°C	7	11	14	17	20	22	22	19	14	10	8	
	61mm	44	43	41	55	52	55	60	59	64	69	57	
Plymouth	8°C	8	10	12	15	18	19	19	18	15	11	9	
	99mm	74	69	53	63	53	70	77	78	91	113	110	
Birmingham	5°C	6	9	12	16	19	20	20	17	13	9	6	
	74mm	54	50	53	64	50	69	69	61	69	84	67	
Cardiff	7°C	7	10	13	16	19	20	21	18	14	10	8	
	108mm	72	63	65	76	63	89	97	99	109	116	108	
York	6°C	7	10	13	16	19	21	21	18	14	10	7	
	59mm	46	37	41	50	50	62	68	55	56	65	60	
Ambleside	6°C	7	9	12	16	19	20	19	17	13	9	7	
	214mm	146	112	101	90	111	134	139	184	196	209	215	
Craibstone	5°C	6	8	10	13	16	18	17	15	12	8	6	
	78mm	55	53	51	63	54	95	75	67	92	93	80	
Tiree	7°C	7	9	10	13	15	16	16	15	12	10	8	
	117mm	77	67	64	55	70	91	90	118	129	122	128	
Belfast	6°C	7	9	12	15	18	18	18	16	13	9	7	
	80mm	52	50	48	52	68	94	77	80	83	72	90	

The lesson plans in this unit will help to develop the children's understanding of the weather by focusing on their experiences and observations, and encouraging them to make simple measurements and record their results. They should try to 'sense' the weather as much as possible: to see the clouds and the direction the wind is pushing them in; listen to the wind and the drumming of heavy rain on roads and roofs; feel the heat of the summer sun and the icy blasts of winter. They should be encouraged to write about the weather from personal experience before they begin to take more formal measurements and use more scientific language to describe what they find. How the seasons change, and how they affect the lives of children (in terms of their clothes, activities and food) and of other people, are important aspects of the work in this unit.

Some equipment for measuring the weather will be needed, but most of the lesson plans rely on children's direct observation and recording. Suitable equipment for the children to examine, understand and use may include a rain gauge, an anemometer, a wind vane, some basic classroom thermometers, some large-sized cloud charts and a chart of the Beaufort Scale. There should be some opportunities for the children to make and test their own equipment.

The children should be encouraged to record aspects of the weather that they can observe and measure easily, such as cloud cover and rainfall. This can be done pictorially in the first instance, with single descriptive words being added; older or more able children can be introduced to more accurate recording, using specific measurements.

UNIT 4: My weather

Enquiry questions	Teaching objectives	Teaching activities	Learning outcomes	Cross-curricular links
What is temperature? How and why does it change?	• Use and interpret maps and plans. • Read thermometers. • Make and use a colour code. • Investigate familiar places.	Paired work: make a temperature plan of the school; use it to identify 'hot spots' and 'cold spots', and say why they are hot or cold. Study microclimates in the school grounds; look at how temperature changes with height in a room.	Children: • identify hot and cold places inside and outside the school; understand why some places are hot and others are cold • begin to understand what a microclimate is	Maths: reading scales. ICT: word-processing survey findings; making symbols or signs to represent 'hot spots' and 'cold spots'.
What is wind? How quickly does it blow and where does it come from?	• Use secondary sources. • Record wind speed and direction on a chart and map. • Use correct vocabulary to describe the wind. • Use a compass.	Work in pairs or small groups: make a chart to record wind speed and direction; record wind information from Teletext onto a base map; grade winds according to their visible effects.	• are aware of wind speed and direction and the effect it has on the environment • understand that wind speed and direction change over time • generalise about winds in the UK	English: using key vocabulary to describe the wind. ICT: word-processing; using reference software to research hurricanes and tornadoes.
What is the water cycle and how does it work? How does the weather affect evaporation? What colours keep us warm or cool?	• Investigate aspects of the weather. • Make and test weather equipment. • Appreciate a 'fair test'. • Understand that the colour of clothing alters the effect of sunlight.	Small-group work: investigate evaporation, recording observations; investigate whether different-coloured materials will help keep us warm or cool; investigate rainfall patterns throughout the UK; make and test rain gauges; record amounts of rainfall and sunshine.	• understand the processes of the water cycle • understand that different places receive different amounts of rainfall • know that evaporation is faster if the temperature of the water is higher	Maths: measuring and recording data using scales. Science: testing fabrics and conducting a 'fair test'. ICT: using a spreadsheet to record rainfall and sunshine; making recording charts; word-processing.
What are clouds made of? What different kinds of clouds are there?	• Make geographical observations. • Record data in a variety of ways. • Identify different kinds of clouds.	Small groups make a cloud chart. Pairs of children record cloud cover and cloud types from the playground; photograph different cloud types; make cloud charts using tissue paper and cloud mobiles; design a cloud recording chart.	• are aware of the different types of cloud formation • know why clouds differ and that cloud cover changes constantly	Design and technology: designing and making cloud charts and mobiles. ICT: word-processing captions and titles; using graphic software to draw clouds; designing charts.
How accurate are weather forecasts?	• Know that symbols are used to represent different types of weather. • Use secondary sources. • Know about weather conditions around the world. • Use outline maps, wall maps and atlases.	Paired and small-group activities: record a national and a local weather forecast in symbols on maps of the UK and their home region; make up forecasts and deliver them to the class; record the weather for other towns in the UK and Europe in symbols on appropriate maps.	• describe different places in terms of their weather • find out about the weather locally and abroad • are aware that weather changes constantly and is difficult to predict.	English: preparing weather forecasts to give to the class. ICT: word-processing forecasts for an autocue; drawing symbols using a graphics package.

Resources
Copies of a base plan of the school and its grounds; a number of basic thermometers and beakers of water at different temperatures; access to Teletext; copies of the Beaufort Scale; outline maps and a wall map of the UK; wind speed/direction symbols; a flat area of the playground, water, a recording chart, different-coloured fabrics; sheets of blue paper, cotton wool, black and white powder paints, paintbrushes; clipboards, a camera, photographs and pictures of different cloud types; thin white thread or string, wooden spills, grey/white tissue paper; the weather section of national newspapers, a video of the previous evening's weather forecast, materials for an autocue; A4 maps of the UK and Europe, graph paper.

Display
Annotated temperature plans of the school and its grounds; signs and symbols showing hot and cold spots. Survey findings. Wind charts on graph paper; a wall map showing wind speeds and directions across the UK. All recording sheets, descriptions and records of work done. An annotated picture of the water cycle. Cotton wool and tissue paper cloud charts (showing cloud types and cover) based on playground observations. Cloud recording charts. Maps of the local area, UK and Europe, showing a forecast through symbols; copies of the autocue.

My weather

Temperature around the school

1 hour

Learning objectives
- Use and interpret maps and plans.
- Read thermometers.
- Make and use a colour code on a plan.
- Investigate familiar places.

Lesson organisation
Teacher-led introduction, including a practical investigation; paired practical survey work in and around the school; individual work on photocopiable sheet; teacher-led plenary session reviewing findings.

Vocabulary
rainfall
wind speed
wind direction
temperature
thermometer
degrees Celsius
range
site
aspect
microclimate

What you need and preparation
Copies of a base plan of the school, with areas and classrooms shown and the position of each thermometer marked. Thermometers placed around the school in as many different places as possible, positioned so that they can easily be seen and read. If this is not possible, then locate them in known hot and cold spots.

Copies of a map of the school grounds, with areas shown and the position of each thermometer marked. Thermometers placed in five to ten different parts of the school grounds, in positions that capture different 'microclimates' (for example, the middle of the playground, behind a shady wall, under a tree).

Plastic classroom thermometers (one per pair of children). Sets of five or six different coloured pens (one set per pair). Three thermometers in a line up the classroom wall, from the skirting board to as high as can be read by the children. Three beakers of water, each at a different temperature (not hot). Copies of photocopiable page 132.

What to do

Introduction
15 mins
Talk to the children about the different elements of our weather: rainfall, cloud, wind speed and direction, sunshine.

Talk about temperature: what it is, how it changes over the day and over the year, and how different places have different temperatures. Show the children a thermometer. Explain how it works and how the scale is divided into degrees (Celsius): 0°C indicates the freezing point of water (at sea level) and 100°C the boiling point. Fill beakers with water at different temperatures (be careful not to use hot water) and encourage the children to read the temperature of each, using the scale on the thermometer. Find out what the current temperature of the classroom is.

Introduce the class to the plan of the school, pointing out known areas such as the classroom, hall, headteacher's office and cloakrooms. Explain how the position of each thermometer is shown (by a symbol such as 'T'). Do the same with a plan of the school grounds. Explain the activities to follow.

Development
35 mins
Thermometers need to be placed around the school and grounds at least 30 minutes before the activities begin. Half of the class can do activity 1 while the other half do activity 2, then they can swap over.

1. Give each pair of children a base plan of the school that shows the position of each thermometer. Ask them to find each thermometer and record the temperature it shows by marking it on the plan lightly in pencil. On return to the classroom, ask the children to make a colour code that shows the variation in the temperatures found. Each pair should look at the temperatures recorded and work out five or six intervals to represent with different colours, draw a key and then colour in the plan in the appropriate colours. Ask them to look at the completed plan and identify 'hot spots' and 'cold spots'. Can they suggest why they are hot or cold (for example, near the boiler or near an open window)? What do they think could be done to make certain areas warmer or cooler?

2. Conduct a similar survey in the school grounds. This time, ask each pair to record the temperature and a brief description of the thermometer's location (for example, 'In the middle of the playground' or 'In the garden by the caretaker's house'). Ask the children what they notice about their map. Can they identify 'hot spots' and 'cold spots'? Talk to the children about microclimates: local variations in temperature, rainfall and wind because of differences between particular sites. Ask

the pairs to look at each temperature recorded on the map and the site characteristics of each location. They should try (verbally) to explain the variations in temperature.

Ask all of the children to complete photocopiable page 132, working individually.

Look at the thermometers on the classroom wall and read the temperatures they show. Ask the children to suggest why the readings are not the same. Explain that warm air rises and cool air falls (a draught comes from the bottom of a door, not the top).

10 mins **Plenary**
Remind the children that temperature is not the same everywhere, and that it can vary even over small areas. Ask pairs to describe and explain the temperature variations they found when investigating the inside of the school and the school grounds.

Differentiation
More able children could undertake each investigation with plans and maps that do not have the positions of the thermometers marked on them. They can mark the position of each thermometer when they find it. They should try to say why some areas are warmer than others in the school and outside; they should be encouraged to think about the effects that buildings, surfaces of different colours, shelter from the wind, aspect and shade may have on temperature. ('Aspect' is the direction in which a site faces; a south-facing aspect will be warmer than a north-facing aspect.)

Less able children should concentrate on a few areas of the school, or on completing the photocopiable sheet. Outside, they should collect the different temperatures and rank them, starting with the warmest, then say where each one was located. Encourage them to say why they think there were different temperatures.

Assessing learning outcomes
Can the children identify warmer and colder places inside and outside the school? Can they suggest why there are differences between them? Are they beginning to understand the concept of a microclimate?

ICT opportunities
● Word-process the survey findings.
● Make signs or symbols for 'hot spots' and 'cold spots'. Attach these to a new school plan and grounds map.

Follow-up activities
● Repeat the two surveys at different times of the day. Note the results and compare them with the original surveys.
● Look at the temperature statistics for cities in other countries and compare them with your local town.

2 hours 30 mins Wind speed and direction

What you need and preparation
Access to Ceefax page 402, which will give information on wind speed and direction (NB speeds in mph will need to be converted into km/h) for your region as part of the weather forecast. Information on wind speed and direction for towns and cities across the UK can be found on page 404.

Copies of the Beaufort Scale (photocopiable page 133). Outline maps of the UK with a selection of towns and cities marked (those shown in the Teletext weather reports), including your town. A wall map of the UK; a large blank wind speed and direction symbol (see photocopiable page 133); strips of 5cm² graph paper, 3 squares wide and 11 squares long; a compass. A set of cards giving wind strengths from 0–12; a similar set giving wind descriptions from 'calm' to 'hurricane'; a video on hurricanes or tornadoes.

The school caretaker, a local builder or another adult should be asked to talk to the children about extreme weather.

Learning objectives
● Use secondary sources.
● Record wind speed and direction on a chart and a map.
● Use the correct vocabulary when describing the wind.
● Use a compass.

Lesson organisation
Teacher provides background information; whole-class observation of wind speed and direction in the school grounds; activity work by pairs or small groups; teacher-led plenary session.

Vocabulary
Beaufort Scale
wind speed
wind direction
compass
anemometer
wind vane
breeze
gale
hurricane

What to do

Introduction
15 mins Talk to the children about the wind. Explain that wind is moving air, and that it moves because of differences in atmospheric pressure between places. The wind flows from higher-pressure to lower-pressure areas. Most of our wind comes from the west. Show the children the Beaufort Scale and talk about what is happening in each picture. Ask whether they have experienced windy weather – perhaps a fence near to them has been blown down, or a tree has lost a branch.

Take the children into an exposed part of the school grounds. Ask them what they notice about the wind and the effect that it is having on the surroundings (for example, trees and litter moving). Can they award the wind a force on the Beaufort Scale? Look to see how fast the clouds are moving, and use the compass to find out which direction they are coming from and going to. Even on 'calm' days, clouds will be moving: wind speed generally increases with height.

Look together at the Teletext to explore the information that it gives about wind speed and direction in your town and others in the UK.

Development
2 hours This work is spread over two school weeks.

Ask the children to make a wind chart using the 5cm^2 graph paper. This can be done individually, in pairs, in small groups or as a class. The first column of 3 squares should be used for titles: 'Day and date', 'Wind speed' and 'What the wind is doing'. The remaining 10 squares across, from left to right, cover the two school weeks. When completing the chart, add large wind force numbers (using the Beaufort Scale); along the bottom row, record the observable effect the wind is having on the school's environment and add a direction symbol to show where the wind is blowing from. Talk briefly about the results each day.

Look at Ceefax to discover the wind speed and direction at various towns and cities across the UK. Choose 5–10 towns and cities, including your own. Each day, ask a pair or small group of children to record the information they find on an outline map, using correct wind direction symbols, and add the day and date. They may need help converting mph into km/h. Transfer the information daily onto a wall map of the UK, using enlarged wind direction symbols.

Give out the sets of wind strength number and description cards. Ask the children to cut these out and put them in order, starting with '0 km/h' and 'calm'. They can be made into a mobile and hung next to the class display.

Ask other adults to talk to the children about high winds that they remember and the damage that the wind caused. Show a video about hurricanes or tornadoes.

Plenary
15 mins Ask the children to think about the work they have done on wind speed and direction over the two-week period. Ask:

● *When was the strongest wind and how strong was it?*

● *When was the lightest wind? Were there any calm days?*

● *From which direction did most of the winds come?*

● *Do you notice any patterns in the wind speed and direction?*

Look at the data for your town and others in the UK. Ask the children the same questions.

Differentiation

More able children could use a compass to help them discover the wind direction each day. They could use the information collected to draw graphs showing the wind speed and direction for the school and some other towns in the UK. Using all the information for winds in different towns, they could try to generalise about the variations in wind speed and direction nationally.

Less able children could concentrate on the Beaufort Scale and aspects of the lesson plan relating to it (such as the wind record for the school); they can attempt the Teletext activities with help. They should be able to make the mobile with help or after a demonstration.

Assessing learning outcomes

Are the children aware of wind speed and direction, and the effects of the wind on the environment? Do they understand that wind speed and direction change over time and vary from place to place? Can they generalise about winds in the UK?

ICT opportunities
• Word-process place names and captions to accompany the school wind record sheet.
• Use reference software to find out more about hurricanes and tornadoes; download the information for use in a display.

Follow-up activities
• Design and make your own equipment to measure wind speed and direction. Look at commercially-made anemometers and wind vanes; test them in the school grounds, and compare the results with those gained from school-made equipment.
• Organise a balloon race. Plot the wind directions and distances covered from information received from people finding the balloons and writing to the school.

1 hour Bring me sunshine

What you need and preparation

Copies of photocopiable page 134; chalk; a flat area of playground; a litre of water; copies of a recording chart (see page 47) on A4 paper divided into six squares; five pieces of similar fabric (about 15cm × 15cm) in different colours including black and white; six thermometers; warm sunshine; copies of an atlas showing a basic rainfall map of the UK; some large empty 2l soft drink bottles; a measuring cylinder; cm² graph paper; a commercially produced rain gauge; copies of weather symbols (see photocopiable page 134); an outline of the water cycle on a flip chart or board (see illustration below).

Learning objectives
• Investigate aspects of the weather.
• Make and test their own weather equipment.
• Appreciate what a fair test is and why it is necessary.
• Understand that clothing colour alters the effect on us of sunlight.

Lesson organisation
Teacher-led introduction; small-group activity work to cover all of the activities suggested; whole-class maintenance of recording sheets; teacher-directed plenary with questions answered by the children.

Vocabulary
water cycle
evaporation
condensation
rainfall
mountains
streams
rivers
sea
fair test
rain gauge
funnel

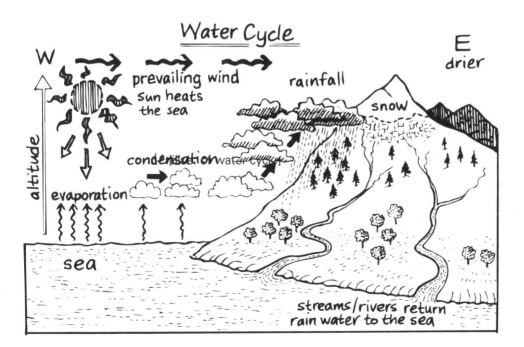

My weather

What to do

Introduction
15 mins Talk to the children about the water cycle, using a diagram on the board or flip chart. Explain its various stages and processes and how they are linked; introduce the relevant terms (see 'Vocabulary').

Talk to the children about the activities to follow. These can be undertaken by small groups, with two groups working on each activity. Ask all the children to complete activity 5.

Development
40 mins 1. *Find out about evaporation.* Find or make a shallow puddle in an area of the school playground that is in full sun. Ask the children to draw around its edge with chalk and note the time on a recording sheet, then draw a quick sketch of it, measure the puddle at its widest and longest point, and record these data. They should check the puddle at intervals of 15 or 30 minutes until it has evaporated.

2. *What colour of clothing keeps us cool?* Ask the group to wrap a different-coloured piece of fabric around each of five classroom thermometers, and place them in full sun in the playground for about half an hour. They should place a sixth on the playground unwrapped to record the temperature. Talk about designing a 'fair test' and how it might apply to this investigation (for example, using fabric samples of the same type and size). After half an hour, the children should quickly unwrap each thermometer and note the temperature it shows on a recording chart. The chart should be a simple grid with a small piece of each fabric, the starting temperatures (which should be the same for all the thermometers), the temperatures after half an hour and the difference between each pair of start and finish temperatures.

3. *Is the rainfall the same all over the UK?* Look at a rainfall map of the UK (this can be found in most atlases), and say in general terms where the wettest and driest parts of the UK are to be found. Look at a map of similar scale that shows the main cities in the UK, and note the amount of rainfall that each is likely to receive.

4. *Make a rain gauge.* Look at a commercially produced rain gauge; talk about how it is made and how it works. Ask the children to make a rain gauge: carefully cut a 2l soft drink bottle in half; invert the top half into the base so that it forms a funnel. They should place it in a secure but open place away from the school building, and use bricks or stones to stop it from being blown over.

5. The children should record the rainfall and the amount of sunshine received each day for two school weeks. They could use the symbols on photocopiable page 134 or make their own. A short description should accompany their record (for example: 'sunny intervals, heavy rain'), along with the day and date. The format could be similar to that used in the previous lesson plan.

Plenary
5 mins Ask each group to feedback on their activity. Encourage each group to describe the activity they undertook, its purpose, the materials they used and the process they followed. Ask questions such as:

● *What did the evaporation activity show? How long did the puddle take to evaporate? Did it evaporate more slowly or more quickly as the weather changed?*

● *Which colour of clothing is best for winter wear? Which is best for summer wear? How did you ensure it was a fair test?*

● *What problems did you have making the rain gauge? How well did it work?*

● *Where are the wettest regions and cities in the UK? Are they distributed evenly, or could you see a pattern from the atlas maps?*

The whole class should be asked which were the wettest, driest and sunniest days over the period of the weather records.

Differentiation

More able children should tackle the clothing activity, and be encouraged to note the steps that should be taken in order to ensure a fair test. They could graph their results using a database. They should look at the rainfall map and describe carefully, using compass points, where the most and least rain falls in the UK, then rank some cities on another UK map from the wettest to the driest. They could produce their own recording charts for the evaporation and clothing activities.

Less able children could tackle the evaporation activity, but may need assistance when drawing the sketches. They should look at the weather conditions in between measuring the puddles to aid their understanding of the process of evaporation. They should be encouraged to produce and use their own rain gauges.

Assessing learning outcomes

Can the children explain simply how the water cycle works? Do they understand that different places receive different amounts of rainfall? Do they understand that evaporation occurs more rapidly if the temperature of the water is higher?

ICT opportunities
● Make and complete a personal recording sheet using a computer spreadsheet.
● Design recording charts for the evaporation and clothing activities.
● Word-process all records, notes and accounts.

Follow-up activity
Complete photocopiable page 134, which looks at belts of rain affecting the UK. Look at the density of the rain and the direction of the prevailing wind, then describe or forecast the kind of rainfall that different towns and cities have had or will receive.

① What are clouds like?
hour

What you need and preparation

A2 or A3 sheets of blue paper; cotton wool; black and white powder paints; a thin paintbrush; glue. Clipboards; photographs and pictures of different cloud types; a camera. Copies of photocopiable page 135; thin white A3 card; thread or string; wooden spills. White or grey tissue paper.

Make and copy an A4 sheet showing a large circle with the four main compass points around the outside; put north at the top of the paper. Add a few small sketches of familiar buildings in the correct positions around the school (this will involve a trip to the playground with a compass). Leave a space on the sheet for children to add the date and an estimate of the proportion of sky covered in cloud.

What to do

15 **Introduction**
mins Remind the children that clouds are formed by evaporation, and that they are pushed by the prevailing wind.

Walk into the playground and look at the clouds. Ask the children to describe the colours and shapes, the direction they are moving in and the amount of cloud. Cloud cover is measured in 'eighths'; some children may be able to estimate values, but for others a descriptive word such as 'most' or 'a little' will be sufficient. Chalk the main compass points on the playground; ask the children which compass direction the clouds are moving from and towards.

Give out copies of photocopiable page 135. Ask the children whether any of the clouds on the chart can be seen in the sky. Talk about the different formations and the Latin cloud vocabulary: *nimbo* – rain-bearing; *stratus* – layered; *cumulus* – heaped; *cirrus* – wispy, at a high level; *alto* – medium level. The cloud names are descriptive combinations of these words.

In the classroom, look at cloud pictures and photographs and ask the children to try to identify some of the clouds. Talk about the activities to follow.

Learning objectives
● Make geographical observations.
● Record data in a variety of ways.
● Identify different kinds of clouds.

Lesson organisation
Initial observation work in the playground; further identification work in the classroom; small-group or paired practical activity and recording work; teacher-led plenary to reinforce work done and consolidate general issues.

Vocabulary
clouds
cloud cover
overcast
cloud names (see page 135)

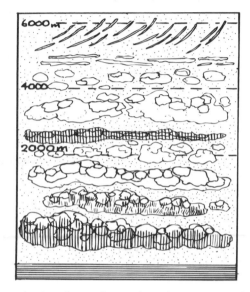

Development

40 mins Ask small groups to make their own cloud chart, using photocopiable page 135 to help them. They need to arrange cotton wool on blue paper, pulling it apart so that it is thin for the higher-altitude, wispy cirrus clouds and using larger, thicker lumps for the lower, towering cumulus clouds; shape the rest of the cotton wool to represent the other clouds; then stick them into position. For the lower rain-bearing clouds, they should mix a small amount of the white and black powder paints to the correct shade of grey and dab some of the dry powder onto the bases of the clouds with a brush.

Pairs of children can go into the playground, stand in the middle of the compass marked earlier and complete the compass sheet (see above). They should ensure that the north point on the sheet matches the one drawn in chalk on the playground, and that the small sketches on the sheet are in the same positions as in real life. They should sketch the clouds that they can see and note the date, the time, the amount of cloud cover and the direction the clouds are moving in. The same pairs can repeat the activity half an hour later and compare the two sheets.

The children can take photographs of different types of clouds and cloud formations seen in the playground over the course of a week, stick these onto sheets of paper and annotate them.

They can make an enlarged (A3) copy of photocopiable page 135 on thin white card and cut out the pictures, then write the name of each cloud formation on the back. They can make a mobile with these cards, using thread or string and wooden spills, and display it near a windows or above a radiator so that the clouds move gently.

Ask the children to design a simple chart on which to record cloud cover and type over ten school days. They should make observations at the same time each day.

Plenary

5 mins Look at some of the cloud charts the children have made. Ask them:
- *What are the differences between high and low clouds?*
- *Which clouds contain raindrops? Which contain ice crystals?*
- *Which clouds are associated with good or bad weather?*
- *From which clouds might thunder and lightning come?*

Explain that lightning is caused when the movement of rain droplets inside a massive cloud causes static electricity to build up: lightning is the sudden discharge of this electricity, and thunder is caused by the sudden air movement as the heat of the lightning makes the air expand.

Look at some of the photographs and see how quickly the children can identify different cloud types.

Later, look at the recording chart and ask the children how many clear and cloudy days there were over that period.

Differentiation

More able children could attempt to estimate cloud cover in eighths, and use eighths on their own recording sheets. They can record cloud cover twice, leaving a half-hour interval, and compare their results in terms of the amount and type of cloud.

Less able children should concentrate on practical activities: making the cloud chart and mobile, and naming the clouds in the photographs.

Assessing learning outcomes

Are the children aware of the different types of cloud formation? Do they understand that clouds differ because of what they contain and their altitude? Do they understand that cloud cover changes constantly?

1 hour How accurate are the weather forecasts?

What you need and preparation

A selection of newspapers that have a weather section with details about the weather in different parts of Europe and the world. Access to Teletext pages detailing the weather for your local area or region. A video of the previous night's main and local TV weather forecasts (to be used the following day). A large wall map of the UK (this could be an A2-sized outline map) with the title 'Today's Weather' and a TV logo incorporating the name of the school. A roll of paper to be used as an autocue; copies of photocopiable page 136; A4-sized outline maps of the UK and Europe; atlases. $2cm^2$ graph paper for the children to make personal recording charts, or a class chart made from $5cm^2$ graph paper.

What to do

15 mins Introduction
Look at copies of photocopiable page 136. Ask children to describe each of the symbols and the weather they represent.

Show the children a video of the previous evening's TV weather forecast. Ask them to identify the elements of the weather that are covered, such as temperature and wind speed. Look at the symbols used, and how the forecaster distributed them over the map of the UK. Point out how the forecaster concentrates on certain parts of the UK (such as the Midlands and Scotland), and on the changing weather over the day. Notice the language used to describe the different weather elements, and make lists of adjectival phrases such as 'sharp showers' and 'chilly breezes'. The video may need to be played several times.

Look at the local forecast part of the video again. Identify the different elements of the weather covered, and make notes recording the details of the forecast.

Learning objectives
● Know symbols used to represent different kinds of weather.
● Use secondary sources.
● Know about weather conditions around the world.
● Use outline maps, wall maps and atlases.

Lesson organisation
Teacher-led introduction and use of a video; a short brainstorming session; paired and small-group activities; work completed by individuals or the whole class; teacher-led plenary session to reinforce the main objectives of the lesson.

Vocabulary
forecast
forecaster
record
elements
symbols

My weather

Development

35 mins Ask a group of children to put symbols on a map of the UK to reflect the previous evening's forecast. Encourage them to make up a forecast for what weather the UK may have during each of the four seasons. They should word-process each forecast and deliver their own 'School TV' weather forecast, complete with symbols, to the rest of the class with the aid of an autocue. They should mark suitable dates on the map to indicate the four seasons. Each of four pairs of children could cover a different season.

Ask another group to add symbols to a map of your own region to show the previous evening's local forecast. They should mark on the map a number of towns, including the one nearest to you. At intervals during the day, they should check to see how accurate the forecast was.

Another group can look at the weather reports for towns in the UK and Europe in newspapers. They can find the towns (or a selection of them that show a variety of weather types) in an atlas, then mark them on an outline map and record their weather by drawing the appropriate symbols (and writing the temperature figures) next to them. They can add a title and date to the outline map. They can do the same for the following day to see how the weather has changed, and make brief notes on these changes for a few of these places (for example: 'Sunshine turning to rain yesterday'). Teletext could be used as an alternative to newspapers.

Ask the children (working individually, in pairs or groups, or as a whole class) to complete a weather recording chart for the school. They should use a variety of weather symbols (see photocopiable page 136), measurements and descriptive words, based on the material in the previous lessons. They should try to measure and record:

● temperature in degrees Celsius, using an outside thermometer and a descriptive word
● rainfall, using a rain gauge symbol and descriptive words such as 'sleet' and 'drizzle'
● wind speed, using a Beaufort Scale force number and a descriptive word
● wind direction, using a compass to determine where the clouds are moving from
● clouds, estimating the amount of cover and naming the main types of cloud.

The children should try to fill in the chart for each day at the same time over ten school days. After lunch at about 2pm will be the warmest time. They should decorate the chart with illustrations, and add a title.

For light relief, you could make a Snap game with the weather symbols on page 136. Photocopy the sheet several times on thin card, and give each pair or small group two sets of cards. You could photocopy brief definitions of the symbols on similar card and add these to the Snap cards.

Plenary

10 mins Put a selection of symbols showing contrasting weather conditions onto a wall map of the UK. Ask different children to describe the weather in a specific part of the UK (such as Wales or East Anglia), or to describe the change of a particular weather element, for example sunshine or wind direction.

Mark about ten cities on a wall map of Europe. Ask individual children to select the correct weather symbol for the weather conditions that you describe for each city – for example, 'sunny intervals' or 'snow showers'.

Ask a group to compare yesterday's local forecast with what actually happened. *How accurate*

My weather

was it? How difficult is it to be a weather forecaster?

Later, look at the class, group or individual weather charts and ask the children to describe the weather in various periods (such as 'the first few days' or 'the middle of the second week') and see how it has changed. Ask them to look for extremes of weather and identify the windiest, wettest, warmest and coldest days.

Differentiation

More able children should be encouraged to look for similarities and differences between the national and regional weather forecast, and to describe in general terms weather trends over the period of the individual, group or class weather records. They could research the weather in places worldwide, using Teletext or the Internet, and compare the weather that these places are receiving with that experienced locally. They could also locate these places on a map of climatic zones.

Less able children should look at the vocabulary associated with the weather and weather forecasts, and make a glossary of terms that they have heard or used. This can be word-processed, and a copy can be given to each child.

Assessing learning outcomes

Can the children describe different places in terms of their weather? Can they research and record information on the weather locally and abroad? Are they aware that weather changes, and that it is often difficult to predict?

ICT opportunities
● Word-process descriptions, comparisons, forecasts for the autocue, place names and captions.
● Use a design package to draw symbols and make collages.

Follow-up activities
● Listen to a taped radio weather forecast. Transcribe the parts that describe the weather for your region, and underline the adjectives.
● Use an outline of the sea areas map (available from the Met. Office) to complete a colour-coded sea areas weather forecast.
● Look at aspects of 'weather lore': sayings meant to forecast the weather. Make and illustrate a collection of them for display.

Improving the environment

Environmental change and environmental protection have been important and topical areas of study in recent years. Environmental change affects both urban and rural areas. It is an inevitable part of the evolution of settlements as they grow and develop to meet the changing needs of their inhabitants and others that use them.

In the countryside, pressure on the land has increased with the expanding population and its demand for faster transport, new houses and increasing supplies of raw materials, food and water. This growing consumption has threatened our supplies of water and the quality of the air we breathe, and caused problems in the disposal of increasing amounts of waste.

There are four main categories of waste:

1. Water. Our water use has almost doubled in the last 30 years. On average, each person uses about 160 litres of water each day – only 3% of which is used for drinking and cooking. Britain discharges treated waste water (sewage) into its major rivers. About 75% of the sewage from coastal towns is passed untreated into the sea. Sewage treatment has four stages:
● screening for such objects as wood and plastic items
● sedimentation – the solid waste or sludge is used as a soil conditioner
● filtration to remove tiny solid particles
● aeration – this allows micro-organisms to feed on the remaining bacteria before the water is returned to the river.

2. Air. There are two main forms of air pollution: particles in the air (grit, ash and dust from chimneys, dust storms and volcanoes) and pollutant gases (usually from vehicle exhausts and industry). Acid rain, the depletion of the ozone layer and the build-up of 'greenhouse gases' (especially carbon dioxide) are also major causes for concern.

Acid rain is formed when water in the atmosphere absorbs sulphur dioxide and oxides of nitrogen (caused mainly by burning fossil fuels); this pollution falls as a weakly acidic rain that causes damage to forests, vegetation and fish in lakes, and buildings. The 'greenhouse effect' is caused by a buildup of carbon dioxide (from fossil fuels and forest fires), methane (from cattle, sheep and rice) and water vapour. These accumulated gases prevent the Sun's energy escaping, resulting in a slow rise in the temperature of the Earth (global warming). The ozone layer is a thin layer in the atmosphere that shields the Earth from harmful ultraviolet rays. This layer has gradually been eroded by the build-up of chlorofluorocarbons (CFCs) used in aerosol cans, refrigerators, air-conditioners and the manufacture of foam packaging.

3. Noise. Our modern world is rarely quiet. Noise is with us constantly, at least in urban areas, from the moment that we wake up (often because of an alarm clock) to the moment that we go to sleep. Most noise is acceptable when the level is not too high, and it is usually considered to be part of the routine of our lives. When it is unwanted or too intrusive, noise can be seen as a form of pollution, since it affects our health and the quality of our lives. Other species are affected too (for example, think of the effect of noise on dogs).

4. Land. In the United Kingdom, about 90% of our waste is disposed of in landfill sites. These are often old quarries, compacted and levelled off with topsoil. Currently, there are 4000 such sites; they accommodate an annual 20 million tonnes of domestic waste, much of it paper and cardboard. Many items that we throw away can be recycled: garden waste, oil, wood, car batteries, plastic bottles, clothes, glass, metal drinks cans and so on.

Environmental improvements are usually supported by everyone who is directly affected by them, since they have a positive influence on people's quality of life. Most of the environmental

improvements that take place are small, and include such activities as tidying up a local park or stretch of canal or turning a forgotten corner of land into a place where people can relax. Some large-scale improvements attract a great deal of publicity and can completely alter the character of part of a town or city – for example, the demolition of blocks of flats to make way for modern housing, or the redevelopment of dockland areas and canal wharves into modern luxury apartments. Other 'improvements' may be more controversial, and be planned in response to a perceived longer-term need – for example, the building of a new road or reservoir.

Improving our school's environment (see pages 56–67)

The school's environment, both inside and immediately outside the building, can be used for extensive fieldwork. The focus for investigations is: *Who creates the problem? Why? What can be done about it?*

The school's very existence makes demands on the environment: it takes up a large amount of space, and consumes resources in order to function. It is useful to produce an 'environmental audit' of the school, looking at (for example) how much noise and litter are produced, how much water and electricity are used and how much of various resources is wasted. Schools with grounds can do much environmental work by looking at the current uses made of them, and how they could be improved.

A case study (see pages 68–76)

This is a real case study, focusing on the village of Gretton in north-east Northamptonshire. Gretton has a population of about 1000 people. Most of the working population commute to the nearby towns of Corby and Kettering. Gretton occupies a position close to old ironstone quarries which, over the years, have been reclaimed due to the closure of the steelworks at Corby. The case study will help to focus the children's attention on the key issues of environmental change by placing these in the context of a real and recognisable situation. The issues they will consider here are similar to those involved in most instances of large-scale environmental change in the UK.

Improving our school's environment

The school and its locality provide a good opportunity to study the issues surrounding environmental improvement on a small scale. The site and circumstances of each school are different; so it will be useful for you to undertake some preliminary work before starting the work in this unit, in order to discover what the school and the locality can offer in the way of opportunities for fieldwork:

● Gather information from the school's budget regarding the amount of money spent on electricity, gas and water, and how much is spent on caretaking, cleaning and maintenance. (This information should be handled carefully. For example, it will obviously not be appropriate to disclose the caretaker's salary. General categories can be used in order to avoid giving away sensitive information.)

● Spend some time surveying and drawing A4-sized base plans of the school and its grounds.

● Look for a local wasteland area to which there is good, safe access no more than 10–15 minutes' walk from the school. Ideally, the wasteland or unused land should be about half the size of a football pitch: large enough to investigate, but not so big as to make the children feel lost within it. Alternatively, if no area of wasteland can be found within easy walking distance, use an area of land with uninterrupted views, such as part of the school's playing fields, some allotments or a park.

● Obtain a large-scale Ordnance Survey map (1:1250 in an urban area or 1:2500 in a rural area) which clearly shows the wasteland area. Make an A4-sized base map from this. Obtain a copy of a large-scale historical map from a local library (OS maps from the late nineteenth century are usually kept there), and use this to make an A4-sized base map of the same area, so that the changing use made of the area can easily be seen. Colour and black-and-white aerial photographs of the wasteland area are useful, particularly if they match the modern OS map. They are available from local newspapers, local commercial and industrial photographers and national aerofilm (aerial survey) companies.

● Talk to a variety of people to see whether they are willing to be interviewed by the children or to talk to the class as a whole. Suitable people might include the headteacher, the Chair of Governors, other school governors, the school caretaker, the local planning officer and local residents. These people can provide valuable information and different perspectives on the local environment.

The caretaker is normally very well informed about the school environment and the changes that have taken place in it over the years. With your support, he or she may be willing to give a guided tour around the school, during which the children can complete a 'school change' trail sheet. Photographs could be taken to supplement the school trail. Alternatively, photographs could be used on their own for an informative and enjoyable 'I Spy' trail, where the children have to find the environmental change shown in each photograph.

The caretaker will also be aware of the particular day-to-day problems, advantages and disadvantages of the school building, as well as whatever plans there may be for its future. The school grounds could feature in an environmental improvement project (in theory, if not in reality). Playground improvement projects, in which the children survey the playground and the play items that it contains, then redesign it according to the class's or year group's wishes, are always interesting – especially if the school agrees to take account of their plans when developing the grounds. Similarly, school garden improvement schemes can be rewarding in themselves, and those that involve active planting can attract sponsorship and voluntary assistance (especially if a wildlife area is planned). Projects of this kind have can a positive impact on the school, as well as on the teaching of geography and science.

The lesson plans in this unit look at issues of environmental concern in the school and the immediate locality. As such, they lead the children to consider environmental issues in a familiar context. The children can observe and measure various changes at first hand, and form a view about which changes are desirable.

UNIT 5: Improving our school's environment

Enquiry questions	Teaching objectives	Teaching activities	Learning outcomes	Cross-curricular links
Where are the noisy parts of the school? Where are the noisiest places locally?	• Ask and respond to geographical questions. • Recognise patterns. • Collect and record data. • Develop fieldwork skills. • Assess environmental impact.	Group work: conduct a school noise survey; carry out fieldwork, looking for noisy and quiet places in the local environment.	Children: • judge noise levels and record that information on maps and plans • understand that there are variations in the flow of children around the school at different times of the day, and that this will affect noise levels	ICT: word-processing; using databases. Maths: using tally charts.
What kinds of things do we throw away from school?	• Collect and record evidence. • Use plans of specific areas. • Suggest ways that we affect the environment we live in.	Individual and group work: collect and weigh rubbish; sort rubbish into different materials; construct graphs; conduct a survey in a recycling centre.	• are aware of the amount and type of rubbish that is thrown away from the classroom • identify waste materials that can be recycled • have a knowledge of the processes involved in recycling	Maths: estimating and measuring weights; constructing graphs. ICT: word-processing; data handling; using an art program; using DTP.
What is litter? Do we need so much packaging?	• Use a plan to locate features. • Understand the difference between reusing and recycling. • Have experience of paper recycling. • Appreciate the cost and wastefulness of packaging.	Paired or small-group work: consider the process of recycling rubbish; investigate litter and rubbish in the school grounds; work out the cost of packaging; use a method of recycling paper.	• are aware of the problems of litter in the environment • understand that most litter is discarded packaging • are aware that packaging is expensive to produce, and that much of it is unnecessary	Maths: calculating the cost of packaging; weighing. ICT: making spreadsheets and graphs; using a graphics package.
What is wasteland? Is there any wasteland nearby? What was the land used for in the past, and what could it be used for in the future?	• Collect and record evidence. • Develop ideas through planning and modelling. • Complete a field sketch. • Compare maps. • Use aerial photographs.	Paired work: consider possible uses for a wasteland; draw a map and write a description to show ideas; visit the wasteland to complete a stimulus sheet, make a field sketch and take photographs; trace the history of the area through maps; develop a questionnaire to canvas opinion about the future of the wasteland; draw graphs and analyse results; plan and model a scheme that fits in with local requirements.	• appreciate the need for environmental improvements in certain areas • are becoming aware that particular groups have responsibility for environmental improvements	English: constructing questionnaires; writing notes and accounts. Maths: drawing and analysing graphs. History: using historical maps to look at changes. Design and technology: designing and making models. ICT: word-processing; using a drawing package.
What do we like and dislike about the area we live in? How could we change parts of it?	• Appreciate the need for environmental improvement in some areas. • Be aware that improvements involve making decisions that will affect people's lives. • Know that improvements are usually a compromise. • Express and justify a view on an environmental change.	Paired work: design a local redevelopment scheme, using a base map and key; write a short account to describe their scheme and the decisions they had to make; redesign a small local area close to school, eg a playground.	• consider the issues involved in redeveloping an area • make decisions and solve problems • create and combine features logically when creating a new environment.	Design and technology: making decisions; designing and making new environments. English: writing accounts and descriptions. ICT: word-processing; using a graphics package to design new environments.

Resources
A base plan of the school; a base map of the school grounds; a 1:1250 or 1:2500 map of the local environment; clipboards, a camera, cassette recorders, stopwatches; weighing scales, dustbin liners, plastic trays and gloves; graph paper; a visit to a recycling centre, a base plan of the recycling centre; a base plan of the school grounds; samples of packaging and cost cards; samples of recycled paper; packaging from a small amount of shopping; a safe area of wasteland, a selection of photographs of it; a large-scale OS map or extract showing the wasteland area; historical maps; oblique or vertical aerial photographs; model-making materials; copies of the local OS map at 1:1250 scale and extracts of it; copies of a simplified A3 base map; scissors, glue, card.

Display
A selection of 'noisy words' in different fonts. Tally charts; noise maps; the local environment noise trail; photographs and descriptions. Rubbish collections and graphs. Examples of rubbish that can be reused or recycled. Fieldwork activity material. Samples of commercially produced and the children's own recycled paper. Litter maps of the school grounds. Samples of packaging with costs. Maps of the children's development scheme and notes. Fieldwork records: maps, stimulus sheets, questionnaires, data analysis, annotated photographs. Completed models with notes. Redevelopment scheme plans, keys and descriptions.

CHAPTER 3
IMPROVING THE
ENVIRONMENT

Improving our
school's
environment

How noisy is our school?

2 hours 30 mins

What you need and preparation

A clear plan of the school and its grounds with key areas, such as car parks, marked on it. A copy of a local large-scale Ordnance Survey map, showing all the places to be visited on the 'noise trail' (see below). A clear base plan (a simple A4 plan, using clear lines) of the inside of the school, with classrooms and areas clearly marked. Clipboards, writing materials. A simple camera for the children to use. Portable cassette recorders. Stopwatches or stopclocks (one per pair of children); alternatively, a central bell could be rung. Copies of photocopiable page 137.

What to do

Introduction
15 mins

Discuss with the children the various environmental problems that your school may have, for example litter, graffiti or broken windows. If they do not suggest it, talk about noise pollution as a possible environmental problem. Find out what different kinds of noise the children hear in different places: in the home, the streets, the supermarket or the local park. Talk about the noises they hear in different parts of the school, and try to identify the noises that cause the greatest amount of irritation or disturbance.

Development
35 mins

Tell the children that they are going to undertake a school noise survey. Tell them that once they are outside the classroom, they will need to listen quietly and write down or record all the sounds they hear over a five-minute period. They should use a stopwatch and tape recorder to help them. Explain carefully how the stopwatch and tape recorder are used. For each noise, they should try to write down a 'noise level' to indicate how loud it is, from 1 for a very quiet noise to 5 for one that is particularly loud. One child in each group will also need to record the number of people (children and staff) who pass by them over the five-minute period. Explain how to construct a tally chart.

The children should be positioned around the school in selected places where different noises can be heard. Suitable places might include: close to a main entrance, in the hall, near the secretary's office, in the dining area, in the car park, in the playground. This investigation can be repeated at different times of the day (for example, at the end of break, at lunchtime and in the middle of a lesson) by the same groups of children to see whether the noises they can hear change during the school day.

Once a group have done their five-minute survey, they should complete photocopiable page 137. Encourage the children to use a wide selection of vocabulary to describe the noises they have heard (see 'Vocabulary'). Once all the groups have finished, a picture plan can be made of the school similiar to that shown on photocopiable page 137. The combined plan will draw on the information gathered from different groups; it should be completed simply, perhaps in cartoon form. Groups can add their pictures while others complete the photocopiable sheet, or after the fieldwork activity.

Fieldwork activity
1 hour 30 mins

As a follow-up activity, a group of children could undertake some fieldwork in the locality to make an environmental 'noise trail' allied to a large-scale local map. They should stop at a number of sites, listen carefully for a few minutes and take notes; alternatively, they could use a cassette recorder with the recording level set to maximum, announcing each time where in the locality they are. On returning, they should play the cassette and note the noises heard. For each location, they

CHAPTER 3
IMPROVING THE
ENVIRONMENT

Improving our
school's
environment

should draw sketches of what they believe made each noise, then attach these to the large-scale local map.

⑤ **Plenary**
mins Talk with the children about their findings.
● *Where are the noisiest places in the school? Are these only noisy at certain times of the day? When are they noisiest?*
● *Where are the busiest places in the school? Do these correspond with the noisiest places?*
● *Do the number of children present or the type of activity going on affect the noise levels that are produced?*
● *Which noises are the most annoying?*
● *Where are the quietest places?*
● *Are there parts of the school where noise is an environmental problem?*

Differentiation
More able children could be encouraged to see a pattern in the location of noisy places, and to see links between pupil movement and noise. The noisiest places will tend to be where children are gathered together. This may be linked to certain times of day, such as between lessons (corridors), the dining room (lunchtime), the hall (PE lessons) and the playground (lunchtime, break).

Less able children could make a collection of 'noisy' words, such as 'slam', 'crash' and 'whisper', and write them out in a pictorial style. They could also be encouraged to make a word bank and use it to sort the words into 'natural' and 'man-made' noises. They could suggest how noisy places might be made quieter.

Assessing learning outcomes
Can the children identify and explain an environmental problem? Can they judge the levels of noise in different places, and record this information on maps and plans? Do they recognise and understand variations in the flow of children around the school? Are they able to relate the number of people to the level of noise?

Follow-up activities
● Carry out an environmental 'noise trail' near the school (see notes at end of main activity).
● Create and display posters aimed at reducing the noise levels in certain parts of the school.
● Find out what 'decibels' are, then look at the decibel levels produced in some everyday situations (for example, whispering is 10–19db, a road drill is 100–109db). Borrow a decibel meter from the local environmental health office to measure the levels of sound produced by different sources.
● A local environmental health officer could talk to the class about noise and health.

---

② hours 30 mins ## Don't throw it all away

What you need and preparation
A set of weighing scales with a pan wide enough to weigh the rubbish collected from the classroom each day; five dustbin or kitchen bin liners; a number of large plastic trays into which rubbish can be sorted; disposable gloves. 1cm squared graph paper (one sheet per child); alternatively, an A1 sheet of 5cm squared graph paper can be used for a pictorial class graph. Copies of photocopiable pages 138 and 139.

This activity can include a field trip to a local household waste recycling centre. Permission needs to be gained well in advance for groups to visit the centre. You will need to undertake a preliminary visit to plan the activity, make a base plan of the centre for the children to complete and take a photograph of each collection point. As the centre will be potentially hazardous, ensure that there is adequate supervision and that the visit follows local government guidelines. The site manager may be willing to visit your school and talk about the work of the centre.

Learning objectives
● Collect and record evidence to answer questions.
● Use plans of specific areas.
● Suggest ways in which people affect the environment they live in.

Lesson organisation
Whole-class discussion; individual and group activities, perhaps including whole-class or group fieldwork; whole-class plenary.

Vocabulary
waste	glass	reuse
recycle	plastic	dispose
paper	metal	bottle
card	oil	bank

CHAPTER 3
IMPROVING THE
ENVIRONMENT

Improving our
school's
environment

What to do

(20 mins) Introduction

With the class, revise the environmental problems within the school that the children have highlighted (see page 58). It is likely that you will have discussed the problems of litter. Now ask the children:

● *What does this litter mostly consist of? Paper? Plastics?*
● *Where should this rubbish be put? What are the advantages of putting it in a dustbin rather than letting it pile up on the ground?*
● *What rubbish is thrown away in our classroom? When? Who throws it away?*
● *What materials is this rubbish is made up of? (Paper, glass, plastics, food scraps.)*

Explain that if rubbish is sorted and thrown away in proper containers, a lot of materials can be recycled. Talk about recycling centres. Ask the children about the local recycling centre: *What is there? Why might adults go there?* Ask the children where they can find a bottle bank, and what kinds of glass items might be deposited there.

If you are going to undertake the fieldwork visit, explain this activity to the children. Emphasise the need for safety. Introduce the children to the site by showing them photographs of the different recycling points and asking them to find these points on the base plan.

(2 hours) Development

The time for this activity should be broken up into five minutes per day for a week. Another 1 hour 30 minutes will be needed for the fieldwork.

Collect the rubbish thrown away from the classroom each day by emptying it into a separate bin liner. Ask the children to estimate, then measure, the mass of the contents each time. Produce a cumulative graph showing the increasing total weight of rubbish thrown away over the week, using a different colour for each day and adding a key.

Arrange for a small group of children to sort each day's rubbish into different categories. These might include paper and card, plastics, metals, glass, cloth, wood. They should weigh the rubbish in each group and use the results to make a daily bar chart based on mass collected. (**NB** the children must take care when handling these materials. Make sure that they wear gloves, and that the trays used for sorting materials are washed daily.)

Discuss with the children what types of rubbish might be recycled or used again, perhaps in a different way (for example, an empty plastic tub could be used as a container for pencil sharpeners). Encourage them to remove some of the items that could be reused and list their possible uses. Keep some of these items and lists for display later.

When the children have completed the litter survey, they can visit their local recycling centre. Many items of household waste are collected for recycling at these centres, including garden waste, plastic bottles, paper, glass, oil and clothes. On the field visit, ask the children to complete the base plan by noting what items are disposed of in which bin or area. Find out how often the bins are emptied, how much is taken away and how the different materials are recycled.

Give out copies of photocopiable pages 138 and 139. Page 138 can be used as an alternative to the fieldwork, or as revision after it. Encourage the children to work out what material each item is made of before drawing a line from it to the correct recycling bin. Alternatively, the items can be cut out and stuck in the correct bins. Before the children work on page 139, talk about how important it is for refuse collectors to find the shortest route to collect the bins in order to save time and resources. The children can practise with string before drawing the best route.

(10 mins) Plenary

Encourage the children to answer the following questions:
● *What kinds of rubbish do we throw away most often?*

ICT opportunities
● Word-process written accounts of the classroom rubbish survey and the visit to the recycling centre.
● Use a data handling package to draw bar charts of types of classroom rubbish collected.
● Use an art program to design a poster encouraging people to throw away less waste and recycle more.
● Use a word processor or DTP package to design a recording sheet for a survey of the rubbish thrown away in the classroom.

CHAPTER 3
IMPROVING THE
ENVIRONMENT

Improving our
school's
environment

● *How can we recycle or reuse some of the rubbish that we throw away?*

● *On which day was the most rubbish thrown away?*

● *What kinds of things are thrown away in recycling centres? What happens to them?*

● *How else can we recycle things?* (Charity shops, car boot sales and so on.)

Differentiation

More able children could attempt to produce their own base plan of the recycling centre and then label it. They could undertake a separate survey to investigate the kinds of rubbish thrown away from their homes, and design their own recording sheet for this.

Less able children could undertake a similar survey using a structured recording sheet from school. For consolidation, they could make a simple chart (on A3 paper) of three large circles, showing which items of classroom rubbish should be 'thrown away', 'reused' or 'recycled'. They should label each circle and then write the name of each item in the appropriate circle.

Assessing learning outcomes

Have the children become aware of the amount and type of waste created in their classroom, and how and why the amount should be reduced? Can they identify kinds of waste that can be recycled? Do they have a knowledge of the processes involved?

Follow-up activities
● Make school collections of items that can be recycled to earn money for school funds, including newspapers and drinks cans. Launch the project in assembly and draw graphs to show how the collections are proceeding.
● Ask the children to think about the rubbish thrown away from their homes. They could carry out a similar survey to the one made in the classroom by looking at what is thrown away at home, when and by whom. They could also find out what materials this rubbish is made up of: paper, glass, plastics, food scraps and so on.

Waste paper and packaging

What you need and preparation

An A4 base plan of the school grounds. A set of weighing scales with a large pan. Dustbin bags or similar, disposable gloves, 'litter grabbers'. Samples of packaging, and two sets of cards giving the approximate cost of manufacture of each item of packaging: large plastic tub 7p, medium tin can 8p, large cereal box 9p, large juice carton 4p, aerosol 12p, plastic bag 1p, large plastic bottle 15p, small glass jar 5p, cellophane cover 1p, polystyrene box or tray 4p, medium plastic bottle 10p, small tin can 6p. Other approximate costs can be worked out from these. Copies of photocopiable page 140, calculators.

Learning objectives
● Use a plan to locate features in the school's environment.
● Understand the difference between reusing and recycling.
● Have experience of paper recycling.
● Appreciate the cost of packaging and the waste involved.

Lesson organisation
Teacher-led introduction; paired or small-group activities; representatives from each group feeding back in the plenary.

Vocabulary
packaging
glass
cardboard
plastic
polystyrene
cellophane
pulp

CHAPTER 3
IMPROVING THE
ENVIRONMENT

Improving our
school's
environment

Samples of recycled paper, such as paper towels, pizza takeaway boxes, some notepads. Equipment for recycling waste paper: plain newsprint paper, rolling pin, liquidiser or washing-up bowl, electric iron, powder paint. Ask each group to bring into school some items of packaging from goods that they would normally buy.

What to do

Introduction
20 mins

This lesson plan deals with two closely related themes: waste packaging and paper recycling.

Talk about litter in the school grounds, where in particular it is and who may have dropped it. Take the children for a walk around the school grounds, pointing out areas of litter and litter bins. Ask the children what most of the litter they can see is made of, and what it was originally used for (packaging).

Back in the classroom, ask the children to think about different kinds of packaging: milk cartons, plastic bottles, aluminium cans, cardboard boxes and so on. Make a class list. Ask the children to think about the things they buy that have no packaging: some fresh fruit and vegetables, fresh bread, petrol and so on. They may find it quite difficult to think of things that don't have any packaging at all!

Refer back to the children's visit to the recycling centre. *Were there areas for recycling paper?* Refer back to the classroom collection of waste. *How much of the waste in school is paper?* Discuss what other packaging materials might be recycled: glass, plastic, metal cans. *Which do you think is the easiest of these materials to recycle?* Point out that paper is probably the easiest, because it can easily be torn up and remade.

Development
45 mins

Show the children some different kinds of recycled paper. Talk about waste bins for paper and the process of recycling. Introduce the children to the equipment to be used for the recycling paper project (see below). Half of the class should work on the following three tasks:

1. Divide the children into small groups and ask each group to investigate litter in an area of the school grounds. Each group should locate its area and mark any litter bins that there might be on a plan of the grounds. They should collect the litter put in the bins each day and weigh it. Make sure that a new bin liner is put into each bin every day, and use the children's findings to mark in the most littered areas on the plan.

2. Produce the two sets of packaging cost cards mentioned in 'Preparation'. Ask groups of children to try to agree on the cost of the packaging items shown in the class list. They should make a note of the costs they have agreed on. Now place the correct cost next to each packaging item, so that the children can see which ones they have guessed correctly. Ask them what they think could be done to package a selection of items more simply (for example, a box of chocolates, a shirt in a box, an Easter egg). These packages can be disassembled in front of the children to demonstrate the quantities of materials used.

CHAPTER 3
IMPROVING THE
ENVIRONMENT

Improving our
school's
environment

3. Put a selection of packaging items into carrier bags (one bag per group). Ask each group to use the packaging cost cards to calculate the total cost of the packaging in their carrier bag.

While half of the class are working on the above activities, the other half should try the following experiment to recycle paper. Tear up a newspaper (or sheets of plain newsprint) into very small pieces and put them in a washing-up bowl. Add enough hot water to cover the paper, then mash it steadily into a pulp. (Alternatively, use an old liquidiser.) Strain the pulp through a mesh, then roll it out into thin layers between paper cloths or towels. Sandwich all of this between two wooden boards. Press them together and leave them overnight. Separate the layers and leave them to dry. Later, trim the sheets of recycled paper and iron each one to produce a smooth finish that will take ink. (To make coloured paper, add a small amount of powder paint to the pulp.)

Ask the children to suggest some possible uses for their recycled paper. They can write their suggestions on their own recycled paper.

5 mins Plenary

Ask two pairs of children from the first group, and a third pair from the paper recycling group, to feed back to the rest of the class.

The first pair should use the plan to show the class where the most littered areas of the school are. They should say who they think drops the litter, how much is dropped every day and what should be done to encourage people to dispose of their litter carefully. The second pair should tell the class how much different items of packaging cost, and how much the packaging in a full carrier bag has cost. Ask the children who pays for the packaging we use. *What kinds of packaging can be recycled?*

Give the children some facts and figures about packaging. For initial dramatic effect, ask the children how much the packaging cost in the carrier bag full of shopping, then throw the same amount of cash into an empty litter bin. (Remember to retrieve it later.) Here are some facts:
● It takes about 1/10 as much energy to recycle an aluminium can or a bottle as it takes to produce a new one.
● We spend about £200m a year cleaning our streets of litter.
● Each of us throws away a tonne of rubbish per year – the same mass as two to three cars.
● 90% of rubbish is paper packaging.

The final pair of children can describe how they recycled paper, and talk about how we use recycled paper in our lives.

Differentiation

More able children could use the packaging cost cards to estimate the costs of other kinds of packaging. They could contact the environmental services department of the local council to discover the location of recycling centres and bottle banks, and mark them on a town map using coloured stickers.

Less able children could find out about rubbish and packaging and construct a series of pictures with captions showing facts and figures about waste, starting with the information given above. They could label recycled paper products brought into the classroom.

Assessing learning outcomes

Are the children aware of the problems caused by litter in their environment? Do they understand that most litter is packaging, that packaging costs money to produce, and that a lot of the things we buy contain unnecessary packaging?

ICT opportunities
● Use the computer to produce spreadsheets and graphs to record data about the litter found in the playground.
● Use a graphics package to design attractive, high-capacity litter bins for the school playground.
● Use a word processor to make captions for recycled paper products, and to describe the recycling paper investigation.

Follow-up activities
● Use photocopiable page 140 to find the cost of the packaging in a shopping list and compare this to the price of the shopping.
● Sort the packaging brought into school according to the material it is made from.
● Collect examples of products that contain 'too much' packaging (such as chocolates, shirts and electrical appliances).

CHAPTER 3
IMPROVING THE
ENVIRONMENT

Improving our
school's
environment

Reclaiming the wasteland

1 hour 30 mins

What you need and preparation
Look for a safe area of wasteland or unused land, such as a cleared factory site or a section of old railway line, about half the size of a football pitch. It should be a few minutes' walk from school and have good access. Undertake a preliminary visit. Take some photographs of specific features of the wasteland and its surroundings, and a series of photographs that can be put together to make a wide-angle panorama of the whole area. Local OS maps at 1:1250 scale that include the wasteland. Copy a section of an OS map in simplified from to make an A4-sized and an A3-sized outline map of the wasteland and its boundaries. A selection of historical maps that show any previous uses of the wasteland and the surrounding area. A selection of small cardboard boxes, such as matchboxes and stock cube boxes, that can be used for small-scale modelling. An oblique or vertical aerial photograph of the wasteland that relates closely to the OS map. A camera. Copies of photocopiable page 141.

What to do
Introduction
15 mins

Talk to the children about the wasteland. Find out what they know about it and what they think of it. Together, find the wasteland on the modern large-scale map and the aerial photograph; locate other nearby places on these. Look at the photographs of features of the wasteland. Talk about each photograph, and ask the children what they see. Collect a list of descriptive words such as *empty, overgrown, abandoned*. Show the children the panoramic set of photographs.

CHAPTER 3
IMPROVING THE
ENVIRONMENT

Improving our
school's
environment

45 mins Development

Working in pairs, the children should decide what they would like the wasteland to be used for. Let them choose for themselves, but encourage them to think about what the local community needs – adults as well as children. Ask them to consider how far it is to various local services such as parks, libraries and cinemas, and think about the services different people might like. Encourage them to consider how their planned facilities would 'fit' into a residential area, and to think about access and the attractiveness of the landscape.

Ask the children to draw or write notes on new uses for the wasteland on the A4-sized outline map. Add labels and a key. They should then prepare a short account of their wasteland redevelopment scheme.

Alternative fieldwork activity

This will take 2–3 hours; two sessions might be needed. The children can work in pairs or small groups. Visit the wasteland with the children and complete the stimulus sheet on photocopiable page 141. Produce a labelled outline field sketch of the wasteland and features around it (this could be prepared beforehand, based on the photographic panorama, for the children to complete in the field).

Back in school, the children can trace the history of the wasteland through large-scale local maps and record the main changes they find.

Together, develop a questionnaire that the children can take home for parents or other relatives to complete, asking them what they would like to see the wasteland being used for. Suggestions might include sports facilities, a library, gardens, shops or an adventure playground. Ask each person to give a rough indication of his or her age, so that there will be something in the scheme for everyone.

From the results, draw a class graph and write a short description of what it shows. Select four or five of the most popular suggestions for redevelopment. Talk to the children about what these might look like. Discuss other things that may be needed in the redevelopment scheme, such as footpaths and car parks.

Working in pairs, the children should plan a redevelopment of the area. They can use an A4 outline map to draw or write notes on how they think the redeveloped wasteland area should look. Ask them to complete two different designs, then produce a final design on an A3 outline map. They should then write an account of what their redevelopment would be like and what it would contain. Each pair should then prepare a two-minute presentation describing their redevelopment scheme.

A much more time-consuming alternative is for the pairs to use an A3 outline map mounted on card and various small boxes to make a model of their scheme. The models will make excellent display material.

30 mins Plenary

Ask a selection of children to present their redevelopment schemes to the class. Ask them to explain:
- what they decided to build and why
- what kinds of people will benefit from the scheme
- what problems they encountered in designing the scheme.

Differentiation

More able children should write full descriptions of the wasteland area and more detailed accounts of how this area has changed over time. They should be encouraged to produce thoughtful presentations to accompany their plan.

Follow-up activities
- Make a display, or do an assembly on this theme, and invite local people to look at the children's finished schemes or listen to their presentations.
- Make 'clean-up' posters for display in the school, focusing attention on the state of the wasteland area and what could be done with it.
- Draw and label sketches to show how the wasteland has changed over the years. This could take the form of a short folded comic strip.

Improving our school's environment

Less able children should complete the stimulus sheet and identify the main changes to the wasteland area over time by comparing two extracts from historical maps. Their presentation may be delivered by an adult or another child.

Assessing learning outcomes

Do the children appreciate the need for environmental improvement in certain places? Are they becoming aware that particular groups of people have some responsibility for improving the environment?

Redevelopment scheme
(1 hour)

Learning objectives
● Appreciate the need for environmental improvement in some areas.
● Be aware that environmental improvements involve making decisions that will affect the lives of other people.
● See that improvements are usually a compromise between what is wanted and what is practical.
● Express a view on an issue and justify it.

Lesson organisation
A brainstorming session followed by brief group discussion and feedback. Paired activity leading to selected children feeding back to the whole class.

Vocabulary
issues
planning
wasteland
redesign
represent
landscaping
draft

What you need and preparation
Copies of photocopiable page 3e, enlarged to A3 size. Copies of a local OS map at 1:1250 scale; an extract from this map enlarged to A3 size, traced to show only the layout of roads and streets (perhaps around the school). A selection of coloured paper shapes of appropriate size to represent the different buildings found in the local environment on the A3 map extract (for example: houses, shops, a library, a church, a park, a playing field). The buildings should closely reflect the school's environment. Scissors, adhesive sticks, card.

What to do

Introduction
(10 mins)
Brainstorm the things that the children like and dislike about the area around the school. For each suggestion made, ask the others whether they agree or disagree. Make two lists on cards to show their likes and dislikes, and display these on the wall next to a local map.

Put the children into small groups, and ask each group to spend a few minutes thinking what things they would like to change in the local environment, what things they would like to keep, and why. Ask each group to say what they like and dislike, giving reasons.

Development
(40 mins)
The children can work in pairs, with several pairs tackling each of the following activities.

1. As a shorter alternative, photocopiable page 142 can be tackled. It should be enlarged to A3 size. The children should colour in the pictures of buildings and areas, then cut them out and position them on the map outline as a plan for redevelopment. They should add a key to the map. They should try to place all of the buildings and areas on the map. Encourage them to think about access, how people get into each building, and the wisdom of placing buildings that have very different functions next to each other. For example, should a retirement

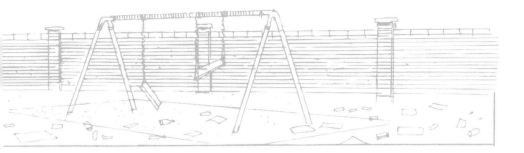

CHAPTER 3
IMPROVING THE
ENVIRONMENT

Improving our
school's
Environment

home be placed next to an adventure playground?

2. A similar activity can be undertaken using an enlarged (A3) extract from a local map. Encourage the children to redevelop a small part of their local environment, using coloured shapes to represent different features. They should produce one or two draft versions which are not stuck onto the base map before sticking down their final versions and adding a key. They should then write a short account of their scheme, describing what they have done and why.

3. Redesigning or redevelopment exercises can be done using a variety of specific small areas such as a playground, garden, park or shopping centre (preferably well-known to the children). Again, a large base plan and various coloured shapes to represent different features will be needed. Try to build in decision-making aspects such as those mentioned in the first activity. Encourage the children to add some form of landscaping (in the form of trees and growing areas) as appropriate.

10 mins **Plenary**

Ask some of the pairs to feed back information to the class about their own redevelopment scheme. They should say what scheme they were undertaking, what problems they had in completing it and how they overcame them.

Differentiation

More able children should redevelop more abstract or unfamiliar areas. They should add landscaping and produce detailed descriptions of what they have done, the problems they faced and the decisions they had to make.

Less able children need to work with smaller, familiar areas or within a tighter framework. They will be able to tackle the photocopiable sheet, or the classroom redesign mentioned in 'Follow-up activities'. Discuss the problems of redesigning with the children as they complete the activity.

Assessing learning outcomes

How well do the children consider the issues involved in redeveloping the area? How well can they make decisions and solve problems? Do they combine features and areas logically when creating a new environment? How well do they present their work to others?

ICT opportunities
- Word-process all accounts, lists, descriptions and decisions made.
- Make attractively printed captions to accompany the plans for the redevelopment schemes.
- Use a graphics package to help redesign or redevelop the wasteland or another area.

Follow-up activities
- Redesigning the classroom is a useful starter activity, and one easily grasped by less able children. Coloured squares and rectangles can be used to represent the different kinds of furniture presently found in the classroom. Children redesigning the room should use all this furniture within the base plan, which should show all the existing walls, windows and doors. A key should accompany the finished design.

A case study: Gretton

Case studies encourage children to look objectively at another place, and to use their knowledge and skills to compare that place with their own locality and understand why it is different. Places used for case studies usually exhibit distinct features: they may be situated in a particular environment, be typical of a certain type of settlement, be the focus for a unique kind of industry or agriculture, or (as in this instance) be undergoing considerable environmental change.

Gretton is a quiet village, set in attractive countryside in north-east Northamptonshire close to the town of Corby. It has a population of about 1000 people. Originally it was a farming community; most of its farmers worked for one of the local landowners. From the mid-1930s, many residents found employment in the steelworks in Corby. The closure of the steelworks, and the redundancy of 10 000 people, in the late 1970s corresponded with a successful large-scale campaign to regenerate the area. Corby is now important as a 'hi-tech' industrial area, with many people being employed in the computer (and software), skilled engineering and service industries.

Around the village are a number of ironstone quarries that have been filled in and returned to agricultural land after the closure of the steelworks. One of these old quarry sites, Deene Quarry, is to be the site of a £50m motor racing circuit that will eventually cater for up to 130 000 spectators. The Rockingham Speedway complex will include a 2.4km (1.5 mile) American-style 'Indycar' oval track, 36 pit garages and over 3km of connecting roads, all enclosed by almost 20km of security fencing. Races will consist of up to 26 cars, competing at speeds of up to 290km/h (180 miles per hour). There may be up to 20 weekend events during each year, and the track will be available at other times for vehicle testing.

Developers believe that the circuit will give a significant boost to the economy of this area of Northamptonshire, which has seen considerable unemployment since the closure of the steelworks. They claim that its construction will create approximately 400 new jobs, with 100 permanent jobs at the track when it is completed and up to 2000 part-time jobs during its main event weekend. It is predicted that visitors will spend up to £30m on accommodation and shopping in the locality during the seven days surrounding each event.

The developers say that they have tried to reduce the effects the track will have on the environment and on the lives of local people. The track will be surrounded by an earth bank 8m high, designed to absorb the sound of the racing cars. The testing of other unsilenced vehicles will take place between 9am and 5pm on only three days a week, between Monday and Friday. It is believed that no household will experience a noise level above 47 decibels.

Some people in Gretton, Rockingham and other local villages have objected to the race track, and have formed a protest group called CARS (Campaign Against Rockingham Speedway). They have called protest meetings, and put pressure on local councillors and MPs. The CARS group say that local people are worried about noise and increased traffic (particularly during race weekends) the effect on wildlife, and the potential health risks from construction work taking place on land that is believed to be contaminated with industrial waste. They say that the protest group has not been consulted about the plans for the race track at any stage.

UNIT 6: A case study: Gretton

Enquiry questions	Teaching objectives	Teaching activities	Learning outcomes	Cross-curricular links
How can we find out where Gretton is? What kind of maps will we need?	● Ask and respond to geographical questions. ● Begin to appreciate the use of scale in maps. ● Give directions and simple references. ● Make generalisations about life in other places, using evidence and reasoning.	Individual or paired work: use maps to locate Gretton; use OS maps to describe the countryside around Gretton; describe journeys to nearby places; look at the village map, giving directions and measuring distances; make a simple land use map of the village, giving basic grid references.	Children: ● are becoming aware of the general characteristics of a village and the surrounding countryside ● appreciate how life in a village compares with life in a town	English: writing descriptions of journeys. Maths: calculating distances. ICT: word-processing; constructing a distance chart, colour code and key using graphic and data handling software.
What is it like to live in Gretton? How will it feel to have a race track nearby?	● Ask questions about a simple map. ● Make decisions that affect the land and the lives of the people nearby. ● Understand more about the impact people can have on the land.	Paired or individual work: assess the impact that the race track would have if sited in different locations; decide where the best site will be and write about their decision.	● appreciate the impact on the environment that the race track will have	English: writing accounts. ICT: word-processing; DTP.
Who will benefit from the race track? Who will be worse off?	● Think about an issue from a particular perspective. ● Understand some of the ways that human activity can affect the environment. ● Understand that environmental changes may benefit some and be detrimental to others.	Large-group work: brainstorm who will gain and lose, ranking 'winners' and 'losers'; suggest reasons why different groups or individuals would benefit or lose.	● are aware of the variety of individuals and groups that would be affected by environmental change ● are aware that these groups have different views ● give their views and empathise with the views of others	English: speaking to the class about who will be affected. ICT: word-processing; using an art package; DTP.
How did the story of the race track begin? How would I feel if it happened here?	● Sequence a list of events. ● Develop a viewpoint about an environmental issue. ● Look at causes and effects. ● Develop reporting skills.	Individual and paired work: order newspaper headlines to tell the story of the race track, adding background information.	● are aware of the sequence of events leading up to the environmental change ● understand that many different people are involved ● appreciate the views of people who are centrally involved	English: writing captions; writing a news story with background information; role-play activities. ICT: word-processing; DTP.
How will the bypass change my life? How will it change the lives of other people?	● Develop an understanding of large-scale maps. ● Understand how people can affect their environment. ● Show empathy with those affected by large-scale environmental change.	Work in pairs: list areas the road will pass through and buildings that will have to be demolished to make way for it; mark areas on the map that will be affected by noise; write letters, as residents, giving views on the proposed new road.	● are aware of the impact that a new road will have on their lives and the lives of others ● express views about it clearly ● describe the kinds of people who will benefit from it ● suggest how the character of the area will change because of it.	English: writing letters to express the views of different people. ICT: word-processing; DTP; scanning.

Resources
A selection of road atlases, maps and globes; OS 1:50 000 maps showing Gretton and its surroundings; an OHP, transparencies and marker pens; scissors, glue, coloured pencils; a school-made race track location chart; name cards; worksheets showing a large speech balloon; school-made activity sheets based on photocopiable sheets; strips of 5cm^2 graph paper; props to help with role-play; a local 1:1250 map of the area around the school with a fictitious road drawn through it, and A3 copies of it; an OHT of the same map; a large envelope with the teacher's name and the address of the school written on it.

Display
Maps of Gretton and its surroundings; maps of the village showing landmarks. Directions from Gretton to other places; distance charts. Maps and descriptions of alternative sites for the race track. Speech balloons under the headings 'winners' and 'losers', next to a sketch of the individual or group who would hold these views. Descriptions of the events behind newspaper headlines. Comic strips and captions. A map showing the proposed route of the road, with areas that will be affected by noise coloured in. Letters to the local newspapers about the bypass.

CHAPTER 3
IMPROVING THE ENVIRONMENT

A case study:
Gretton

(1 hour) Where is Gretton?

Learning objectives
● Ask and respond to geographical questions.
● Begin to understand and appreciate the use of a scale in maps.
● Give directions and simple grid references, using maps of specific places.
● Make generalisations about life in other places, based on evidence and reasoning.

Lesson organisation
Teacher-led introduction, followed by individual or paired activity with a high level of teacher input. Feedback from selected children in the plenary.

Vocabulary
village
countryside
race track
scale
globe

What you need and preparation
A selection of road atlases; a globe map; general school atlases; maps showing Gretton and the area around. A 1:50 000 OS map showing Gretton and the surrounding area; copies of an A4-sized extract of the map showing Gretton, the race track site and the surrounding villages and countryside. An OHP and transparencies. Copies of photocopiable pages 143 and 144; an OHT of page 144. Copies of a sheet showing 10 blank dominoes.

What to do

15 mins **Introduction**
Introduce the children to the different maps and the globe. Explain that these are drawn to different scales, and show different areas and amounts of land. Find your own town (or a nearby one) on each map in turn, starting with the largest-scale map and ending with the globe. Ask the children what happens to the way the town is shown as the scale of the maps gets progressively smaller.

40 mins **Development**
Set the children working, individually or in pairs, on the following activities:
1. The children can use the maps to locate the village of Gretton and the surrounding area, then complete photocopiable page 143.
2. Look at the OS map of the area around Gretton and ask the children to describe the countryside around it (over a radius of roughly 10km). Can they produce written descriptions of the journeys to some of the nearby towns and villages, noting the features they would pass? Some of the children can be encouraged to measure the distances between settlements, using string or a strip of paper, then calculate the real distances.
3. Use an OHT version of photocopiable page 144 to look at a plan of the village. Ask the children to point out various landmarks, such as the church, the school and the post office. Can they give directions from one place to another? Ask them to measure the distances between some of these places, using a copy of photocopiable page 144.
4. The pairs can work together to make a 'land use' plan of the village. They should devise a colour code showing the main land uses, including houses (and gardens), roads and paths, parkland and farmland, then colour in the map using the code. Ask them to rank the main land uses in the village, starting with the most important, and to practise giving simple four-figure grid references for features in the village.

5 mins **Plenary**
Ask the children to arrange the collection of maps in order, starting with the largest-scale map and ending with the smallest. Encourage them to describe the countryside around Gretton (orally) in terms of the features that a visitor would see. Now ask individual children to describe different journeys around the village. Ask the children how this village is different from the area around your school.

Differentiation
More able children should be able to describe in some detail the area around the village and journeys to nearby places. They should be encouraged to measure some of the distances between places on the OS map and the A4 extract. Encourage them to make generalisations about the village (for example, land use or house types seen).

**A case study:
Gretton**

Less able children could list some of the settlements that they can find on the OS map, and order them according to size. Encourage them to pick out some important landscape features close to the village, such as woodland, farmland and rivers.

Assessing learning outcomes

Are the children becoming aware of the general nature and individual characteristics of the village and the surrounding countryside? Do they appreciate how life in a village compares with life in a town?

ICT opportunities
- Use a word processor for all lists and descriptions.
- Construct a distance chart showing how far Gretton is from other settlements nearby.
- Use a graphics package to construct a colour code and key for a chart showing features in the village, with a simple grid.

Follow-up activities
- Work as a group to make an annotated large-scale map of the area around the village. Add sketches of different features or areas.
- List all the features and landmarks in the village, giving a simple grid reference (referring to the OS map) for each.

① Building the race track
hour

Learning objectives
- Ask questions about a simple map.
- Make decisions that would affect an area of land and the lives of the people who live on or near it.
- Understand more about the environmental impact of human activities.

Lesson organisation
Teacher introduction, including revision of previous work and explanation of the activity. Paired or individual activity. Teacher-led plenary, including some paired or individual feedback to the class.

Vocabulary
location
site
impact
planner
decision

What you need and preparation

Copies of photocopiable page 145. Scissors, glue pens. Coloured pencils. An OHP and transparencies. A structured A4-sized chart for each pair (or child) to complete, showing the three possible locations A, B and C and the effects that the race track may have on the lives of people who live there or nearby (as shown on photocopiable page 145).

What to do

⑮ Introduction
mins

Revise the previous lesson by talking to the class about Gretton, the nearby villages and towns and the countryside around them. Ask the children what they think it is like to live there. Make a list of descriptive words using the left-hand side of an OHP transparency. Now remind the children of the planned changes facing the vilage. Ask them what they know about motor racing and race tracks. Talk about race meetings and the crowds and levels of noise that they produce. Make another list of descriptive words on the right-hand side of the transparency. Encourage the children to pick out opposites. Ask them how they think the people of the village will react to the race track.

Find out which of the children would like to live near a race track, and which would not. Encourage them to explain the reasons behind their answers. Ask them to describe how they would feel if a race track, or some other development that would make a great impact on the local environment (such as a quarry or a motorway), were going to be created a short distance from their homes. Talk about the dilemma that planners have when constructing things that we all need when no-one wants them close to where they live. Think about the considerations that might influence a planner's choice of location for something that will have a great impact on the local environment.

㉚ Development
mins

Look together at photocopiable page 145. Talk about the map. What things do the children notice? Talk through the instructions. Explain that they will need to consider, for each location, the impact that the race track will have on the land immediately around it and the people who live or work on or make use of that land.

CHAPTER 3
IMPROVING THE ENVIRONMENT

A case study:
Gretton

ICT opportunities
● Use a word processor for all descriptions and accounts.
● Set up and complete the chart using a word-processing or DTP package.

Follow-up activities
● Look together at a feature that has had a significant impact on the environment near the school, perhaps a new road or a supermarket. Find out what the land was used for before, and what was there – buildings, trees, fields? Ask local people for additional information, and undertake some research using historical maps. Take photographs of the new feature, and use them to help recreate the scene before the new feature.

Encourage the children to complete the A4-sized chart on which they can record the possible effects of the race track on its three possible sites. They can choose what they think is the best site by cutting out the race track insert and placing it on the map. When they are sure which site they consider to be the best of the three, they should stick it in place and write a short account of why they decided to stick the race track in that position.

15 mins **Plenary** [15 mins]
Discuss the following questions with the children:
● *Do you think it was wise for the race track company to build the race track where they have?*
● *What will happen to the value of houses nearby?*
● *What do they think can be done to reduce the amount of noise entering nearby homes?*
Conclude by asking some children to explain where they have placed the race track and why.

Differentiation
More able children could look at four or five possible new sites for the race track and compare the advantages and disadvantages of each. They could be encouraged to consider a variety of other developments (such as a motorway or a reservoir) that might have a major environmental impact.
Less able children could concentrate on the existing site of the race track and one alternative. They should accompany their work with a few sentences to explain their choice of site.

Assessing learning outcomes
Do the children appreciate the impact on the environment of a major change in land use? Do they appreciate the problems involved in locating a feature that will have a significant impact on the environment? Are they becoming aware that all land is used for something, and that a major change in its use will affect the people who live or work nearby or use the nearby land for other purposes? Do they understand that those whose actions seriously affect the environment have a responsibility to reduce the impact of that change on others? Can they assess the likely impact that a significant environmental change might have on Gretton and other nearby villages?

1 hour Winners and losers

Learning objectives
● Think about an issue from a particular perspective.
● Understand some of the ways in which human activity affects the environment.
● Understand that environmental changes may be of benefit to some people and detrimental to others.

Lesson organisation
Teacher-led introduction, including revision of previous lesson and brainstorming activity; large-group activity work; teacher-led plenary.

Vocabulary
issue
debate
spokesperson
presentation
environmental
impact

What you need and preparation
Copies of photocopiable page 146. Name cards for each of the interested parties in the race track debate (see page 146). An OHT and marker for each group and for the teacher; an OHP. A large speech balloon for each child, drawn on A4-sized paper.

15 mins **Introduction**
Recap on the issues raised in the previous lesson. Give the children an idea of the area that the race track complex will cover, and relate this to their own locality. Brainstorm as a class the people who would be affected by the process of its construction, and who would be affected by the noise, crowds and increased traffic that the race track would produce. Remind them to consider both good and bad effects – for example, shopkeepers may welcome the crowds and the increased business they offer.

A case study:
Gretton

35 **Development**
mins Ask: *Who will gain from the race track? Who will lose?* Brainstorm this issue and make a list of winners (those who will benefit from the race track) and a list of losers (those who will have to give up something). Divide the class into six groups: three to look at different winners and three to look at different losers. Give each group a name card (see page 146), an OHT and a pen.

Ask the groups to order their names, from those who would win or lose the most down to those who would only win or lose a little. Each group should elect a spokesperson to read out the group's names in order, together with the reasons for their 'top' and 'bottom' choices. They should do this using the OHT. Some children may wish to ask the spokesperson questions.

Make a note of the main reason for each 'top' and 'bottom' choice. These sentences should be put on an OHT at the end of the presentations. Go through them with the children, to remind them what each group said. Remove this OHT before the final activity.

Go through the instructions on photocopiable page 146. Allow time for children to complete it. When they have finished, show your OHT again so that they can compare it with their own answers.

10 **Plenary**
mins Encourage the children to decide which individual and then which group made the most convincing argument for or against the race track.

Ask the children to vote, perhaps using a secret ballot, to decide whether or not the race track should be built. Discuss whether a compromise could be reached that made concessions to both sides.

Differentiation
The more able children in each group should complete their group's OHT and be the spokesperson for that group.

Less able children do not need to complete the whole photocopiable sheet. They could perhaps just identify each character as a 'winner' or 'loser', or fill in one 'winner' and one 'loser' speech bubble.

Assessing learning outcomes
Are the children becoming aware of the variety of groups of people that may be affected by environmental change? Do they understand that these groups have points of view that they wish to express? Can they begin to express a view on an environmental issue and justify it? Can they empathise with the people most crucially affected by environmental change?

ICT opportunities
• Use a word processor to write up arguments for a particular viewpoint.
• Use an art package to draw a representative from each interest group. Add captions to show who they are and which groups they represent.
• Use a word processor to write a newspaper article with a headline (see 'Follow-up activities').

Follow-up activities
• Each child could take a different role (if possible) from the original brainstormed list. They should think about the kind of comment that this person would make about the race track, then write a comment in an A4-sized speech balloon and draw a sketch of the person to accompany it.
• The children can write a short newspaper article about the race track and quote different people's views, then add a headline and 'photographs'.

CHAPTER 3
IMPROVING THE ENVIRONMENT

A case study:
Gretton

① Track record
(hour)

Learning objectives
● Sequence a list of events.
● Develop a viewpoint about an environmental change.
● Look at causes and effects.
● Develop reporting skills.

Lesson organisation
Teacher introduction to story and explanation of the activities; individual and paired activity work; shared role-play in plenary session.

Vocabulary
sequence
comic strip
headline
protest
site
campaign

ICT opportunities
● Use word processing to produce new headlines, using different fonts at different sizes, and to write the story.
● Use DTP to design new posters campaigning for or against the race track.

Follow-up activities
● Look at other constructions that will have a major environmental impact, such as building a motorway, a quarry or a wind farm. For each, list the kinds of people who would be most affected by it. Sketch each type of environmental change and add a caption.
● Take photographs of sites nearby whose construction had a major effect on the environment. Link the photographs to a local map.

What you need and preparation
This equipment list will cover all of the alternatives.
Copies of photocopiable page 147; a selection of comics. Copies of photocopiable page 148, enlarged to A3 size; A3-sized plain paper. Some activity sheets based on page 147, with a picture mounted on a sheet and questions such as: *What is happening in the picture? What do you think has happened? What might happen next? Who do you think each person in the picture is?* Long strips of 5cm² graph paper paper, measuring approximately 10cm × 35cm. A selection of props to help the children tell the race track story through role-play.

What to do

⑮ Introduction
mins Tell the children the story of Rockingham Speedway. The site was a quarry many years ago, and is now agricultural land with hedgerows and abundant wildlife. Recently, the land was surveyed and permission was given for the development of a car racing track. Concern in local villages about the likely effects of this has led to an organised protest campaign with posters and placards. However, building began and was completed, and the races have now started.
   Talk to the children about the choice of activities for them to tackle.

㉟ Development
mins The children can tackle one or more of these activities, working individually or in pairs.
1. Complete photocopiable page 147. Try to make the pictures amusing, but keep the captions relatively serious.
2. Cut up an A3-sized copy of photocopiable page 148 and arrange the newspaper headlines into the correct order to tell the story of the race track, then stick them down the left-hand side of a sheet of plain A3-sized paper. On the other side of the paper, describe the background to the headlines.
3. Work in small groups on the prepared photocopiable exercises. Each group should tackle one or two different picture sheets, so that all of the picture sheets can be completed.
4. Fold a long strip of 5cm² graph paper along the printed lines to make a 'concertina' shape with seven pages. Use the first page for the title and the remaining six pages for comic pictures, telling the story of the race track. Each picture page should contain a quick sketch to show the 'unfolding' events, with the bottom 2cm left blank for a caption.

⑩ Plenary
mins Put on a short play telling the story of the race track. This could take a variety of forms: children reading from short prepared scripts; a narrator introducing characters who say who they are and then act out the storyline; or a properly scripted play. Make sure that the whole story is covered.

Differentiation
More able children could tackle the more difficult activities, such as the strip cartoon, and should make a significant contribution to the role-play activity.
   Less able children should concentrate on the less demanding activities, including completing photocopiable page 147. They can put the headlines from photocopiable page 148 in sequence without adding an explanation of the background.

Assessing learning outcomes

Are the children becoming aware of the sequence of events leading up to an environmental change? Do they understand that different people are involved, at different times and different levels, within the development of an environmental change? Can they empathise with and appreciate the views of the people most closely involved with the change?

1 hour Building a bypass

What you need and preparation

A local 1:1250 map, with the route of a (fictitious) new dual carriageway road or motorway drawn across it. Make sure that a number of different places, known to the children, are in its path (for example: a park, allotments, some children's homes, perhaps the school). The new road should be about 2cm wide on the map; it should be drawn in outline only.

A3 copies of this map; an OHT for demonstration. Copies of photocopiable page 149. A large brown envelope with the teacher's name and that of the school written on it.

What to do

15 mins Introduction

Tell the children that you have just received a letter from the council, saying that a new dual carriageway road (or motorway) is to be built nearby. Open the envelope and show the children the map. Explain what a dual carriageway is like.

Hand out copies of the map to each pair of children, and ask them to colour in the route (lightly) that the new road will take. Display the map OHT and encourage them to think about the road: *How will it fit in? Which buildings will have to be demolished to make way for it?*

Ask the children what they think about the new road. *How will it change your life? How will it affect the lives of your family and friends?*

35 mins Development

Working in pairs, the children should try to make a list of the buildings that will need to be demolished in order to make way for the new road. They should make another list of the areas that it will pass through, such as churchyards, wasteland and parks.

Ask them to count the number of houses that will have to be knocked down. *If an average of three people live in each house, approximately how many people will have to find somewhere else to live?*

Ask them to mark the area on the map that will be most affected by the noise and pollution that the traffic on the new road will create. Suggest that they do this by drawing two new lines, each 2cm away from one of the lines that mark the edge of the new road. This area could be coloured in a different colour. Ask them to write a short description of what it would be like to live so close to the new road.

Ask them to imagine that they personally will be affected by the construction of, and the

Learning objectives
• Develop understanding of large-scale maps.
• Understand how people can affect their environment.
• Show empathy with those affected by the new road, or by any other large-scale environmental change.

Lesson organisation
Teacher-led introduction, including a few minutes of practical work; activity work in pairs; teacher-led plenary session, including paired response work.

Vocabulary
dual carriageway
motorway
council
demolish
construction

A Case Study: Gretton

ICT opportunities
• Use word processing to write letters to the local press.
• Use DTP to create the front page of a (fictitious) local newspaper, and a letters page with headlines. Scan in photographs of a main road, with children posing as irate residents.

Follow-up activities
• Use a copy of a local map, 1:1250 scale, to plot a different route for the road that minimises the disruption to local people. Describe the new route and explain why it is better. List the kinds of people who will be most affected by it.
• Write a 'front page' story, with headlines and photographs (or sketches), describing the road, its proposed route and its likely environmental impact. Write a second page with letters from local people.

traffic on, the new road. Perhaps they live in one of the houses nearby, send their children to the school, or use the local park regularly. Ask some of the children to write a short letter to the local newspaper, giving their views. Ask others to write letters in role as business people or motorists who want better road links across busy towns. As an alternative, they could complete photocopiable page 149.

10 mins Plenary

Ask some pairs of children to read their letters to the rest of the class. Choose some who are against the building of the new road, and a similar number who are in favour of it. Make sure that they say who they are (for example, a motorist or a resident) and how the new road will affect them.

Ask the children: *What is the main impact of a large-scale environmental change on the lives of the people who live near it?*

Differentiation

More able children should be asked to consider the general effects that the new road will have on the district, as well as its effects on specific places that are on or next to the line of the road. They should be encouraged to tackle the further activities outlined in 'Follow-up activities', particularly the mapping of and accounting for an alternative route for the new road.

Less able children should concentrate on following the line of the road and listing the places that will be affected. They should consider the effects that the new road will have on the lives of the people near to it.

Assessing learning outcomes

Are the children becoming aware of the impact that a new road would have on their lives and the lives of others? Do they have a viewpoint about the road, and can they express it clearly? Do they understand that a new road will have a damaging effect on the lives of people who live near to it?

Settlers

A settlement is a place where people live. It can be as small as a farmhouse or as large as a city. Most people in the United Kingdom and in Western Europe live and work in towns and cities, where manufacturing and service industries are important forms of employment. In developing areas of the world, most people live in villages, with agriculture being the most important form of employment.

There is a long and rich history of settlers coming to live in the UK. The first settlers came in prehistoric times as nomadic people from central Europe. Much later came the Romans, a conquering army whose empire-building crossed these shores. A few centuries later, successive invasions from present-day Germany, Scandinavia and France brought Saxons, Vikings and Normans who carved their identities on the landscape, especially with the names they gave to their settlements.

Most towns and cities (and therefore centres of population) are found in certain areas of the UK: in Scotland around Glasgow, in the north of England around Tyneside, in a broad band between Liverpool and Hull, in South Yorkshire, in the West Midlands, around London, in South Wales and in the east of Northern Ireland around Belfast. The UK has a high density of towns and cities compared with much of Europe. For example, France (our nearest neighbour in Europe) has a similar population to that of the UK (about 56 million), but its land area is approximately twice that of the UK. There are fewer urban areas in France, and more of the population live in villages and small towns.

The **population density** of a country (the average number of people living in each square kilometre) is a useful indicator of the proportion of people who live in an urban area. The highest population densities are in the industrialised countries of Asia.

Large cities are scattered around the world. Many have populations in excess of 5 million, and a number exceed 10 million (see charts on left).

Case studies of cities in other parts of the world, and comparisons with familiar cities in the UK, are both interesting and rewarding. Different parts of a major city may contrast. For example, Rio de Janiero contains the wealthy neighbourhoods of Copacabana and Impanema and the poverty-stricken 'favelas' of Vidigal and Rochina. New York offers contrasts between the wealthy high-rise world of Manhattan and the poorer areas of Harlem, Chinatown and Little Italy. Bombay contains wealthy suburbs and the shanties built by the hundreds of thousands of seasonal workers who migrate to the city for six months of the year.

Population densities (people per km^2)	
Macau	24 850
Hong Kong	5960
Singapore	4667
Gibraltar	3000
UK	300
France	150
USA	40
Australia	7
Mauritania	2
Congo	0.7
Greenland	0.2

Populations of metropolitan areas (in thousands)	
Mexico City	18 748
New York	18 120
Sao Paulo	16 832
Los Angeles	13 770
Shanghai	12 320
Tokyo	11 829
Rio de Janeiro	11 141
London	6378

Village settlers

This unit of work looks at the factors that influenced the siting of settlements hundreds of years ago, and how these early settlements have developed over time. The children look at place-name endings, and use evidence from maps, to find information about the characteristics of the early settlements and the people who lived in them long ago. Maps are used to examine the travel routes between villages, and the symbols on Ordnance Survey maps are used to find out what facilities the villages can offer to their residents. Finally, the children are encouraged to develop an imaginary village by adding physical and human features of their own devising to a base map. Throughout this unit, there is ample opportunity to develop skills in ICT, especially through the use of graphics packages.

How towns grow

The second unit of work looks at how towns and cities have become established and grown, and how their sites and functions have determined what they are like today. The children use maps extensively to find out where towns and cities are and how they influence other towns and villages nearby. The character of a present-day town is explored through maps and other local information, such as estate agents' lists and street maps, to help the children develop a sense of what it is like to live in such a town.

Towns are a focal point for transport: major road networks, railway links and sometimes airports. Links between towns have developed over time, from the wide tracks along which carts and stagecoaches struggled to the motorways along which millions of people and tonnes of goods are carried each day. Like all settlements, towns grow and change in size and character. Sometimes they merge with other towns to form 'conurbations'. The changing size and functions of towns can be observed in many ways, but is perhaps most clear when comparing maps and plans over a period of time.

The characteristics of particular sites determined where early settlers chose to build their houses. Usually a combination of the following site conditions would need to be close by:
● fresh water – for drinking (by people and animals), cooking and washing clothes
● flat fertile land – early settlers were farmers, and expanses of cleared land were needed for growing crops and grazing animals
● supplies of timber – for building houses, fences and animal pens, and as fuel for heating and cooking.
Other common requirements were a hilltop site (a good view, so easier to defend against thieves and bandits) and a dry site (land not marshy or prone to flooding, so that crops could grow). It was also important to consider the climate of the area, as this would affect what crops could be grown.

Place-name endings can provide information on when a place was given its name, and what the location was like when the settlers first arrived. The Romans, Vikings and Saxons all named their settlements in this way. The words they used include:
● *bury/borough* – place defended by a wall
● *den/dene/deene* – pasture for pigs in a wood
● *don* – a hill
● *field* – open fields
● *ford* – river crossing
● *ham* – homestead or farm
● *ing/ingham/ington* – the sons of or home of the people of...
● *ley/worth* – clearing in a wood
● *ton* – hedged or fenced enclosure or village
● *wick* – dairy farm or village
● *by* – a village.

Village settlers

The shapes of the early villages were greatly influenced by the nature of the surrounding countryside. There are three basic kinds of settlement shape:

1. **Dispersed** – farms and buildings are spread out over the countryside. This pattern is found in areas of higher land, as the people who lived there needed to farm a lot of land in order to provide a living.

2. **Nucleated** – buildings are grouped together for protection. This pattern is more common in lower, flatter areas of the UK.

3. **Linear** – where the surrounding hillsides are steep, houses are built in a line along the flat bottom of a valley.

A thousand years ago, the countryside was very different from what it is like today. Isolated farms and villages were dotted around a mostly uninhabited countryside. There were no large settlements. After the Romans, the main group of people to settle in Britain were the Anglo-Saxons (from present-day Denmark and Germany).

Settlers rowed up the rivers in the east, looking for the best places to build their farms and villages. Their houses were rectangular, windowless and built close together for protection. Walls were built from tree trunks split in half; roofs were thatched, with a hole cut into the top to allow the smoke from the fire to escape. These houses were damp, cold and smoky. There was often a small patch of land next to the house for growing vegetables.

The local baron or lord of the manor usually lived in a stone-built house on the edge of the village. His house was large and surrounded by a garden in which there were vegetables, an orchard and perhaps beehives; often a few smaller animals were kept here. The lord of the manor would usually own any surrounding woodland, where he would hunt deer and wild boar. The farming land was divided into strips. Villagers worked a number of strips of land and paid a tax or tithe, usually in the form of crops, to the lord of the manor as rent. There was some common land for grazing animals.

As with all settlements, villages have changed over time: they have developed from the self-sufficient communities of Saxon times to the commuter villages of today. Much of the present-day character of villages can be explored by looking at maps, especially the OS 1:50 000 and 1:25 000 maps (available for all parts of the UK). The symbols used on the map will give information on the services and facilities to be found in the village (such as post offices, churches and public houses) and their links with other settlements nearby (main roads, minor roads, tracks and footpaths). The children should be encouraged to give four-figure grid references, though some preliminary work on this will be needed.

Over time, the shape and function of a settlement, its land use and the number and types of people living there will change. These changes are often more easily seen in a small, well-defined village than in a complex town or one of its districts. Historical maps are a good source of evidence when looking at change. It is possible to obtain copies of maps that date from as early as the sixteenth century; more easily available maps date from the late eighteenth century. Maps from the late nineteenth century correspond more closely to contemporary maps.

UNIT 7: Village settlers

Enquiry questions	Teaching objectives	Teaching activities	Learning outcomes	Cross-curricular links
What was the UK like a thousand years ago? Where did the early settlers choose to settle?	• Investigate the origins of places. • Make simple decisions based on specific information. • Present findings to others.	Small-group work: decide where to locate a farm, ranking locational features.	Children: • talk about early settlers • describe the nature of early settlements • appreciate the importance of site • infer information from place names	ICT: word-processing the characteristics of important locational features.
How can we use maps to find out more about villages? What do place names tell us about the countryside long ago?	• Use maps to obtain evidence. • Know the basic layout and function of a Saxon settlement. • Become aware of how the landscape has changed over time.	Paired work: find settlements with specific place name endings on a local map; look on maps for the site characteristics of local villages; consider how villages may have looked long ago, and what the countryside may have been like.	• use a map to identify reasons for the siting of a village • are aware that villages grow for many different reasons • appreciate what the countryside looked like long ago	History: looking at the Domesday Survey; considering life and the nature of villages in Saxon times. English: linking place name endings with Roman, Viking and Saxon settlers in the UK. ICT: word-processing lists; designing an early village landscape.
How do we find out what villages are like? How do symbols tell us more about villages?	• Learn about the features of a present-day village. • Compare and contrast features of different villages. • Use and interpret OS map symbols.	Paired work: identify OS symbols relating to villages; complete a checklist; describe photographs of villages; link enlarged OS symbols to appropriate features on a map.	• identify a number of OS symbols • understand how and why OS symbols are used • realise that not all villages have the same features	Maths and ICT: producing tally charts; using a drawing package to reproduce OS symbols; word-processing descriptions of villages from photographs.
How are remote farms and houses linked to nearby villages? What kinds of routes are there between them?	• Recognise that most places are connected to other places. • Know that there are different kinds of road or route. • Understand that networks of roads or routes connect settlements.	Paired work: find routeways on local maps, giving grid references; rank photographs showing different routeways; describe a route from a remote farm to a village, and measure the length of the journey.	• give four-figure map references accurately • understand how settlements are connected • understand that there is a hierarchy of routeways	Maths: using a scale to calculate distances; making a distance chart. English: describing journeys accurately. ICT: word-processing all descriptions of journeys and all captions; constructing a distance chart using a data handling package.
How might a village change over time?	• Draw a map of the layout of a settlement, with a key. • Show an awareness of how villages develop over time.	Individual work: draw a map to show how a village might grow and develop, adding specific features; draw a key to explain the symbols used.	• draw a map that shows a logical pattern of settlement • organise various elements of map work into a basic map.	ICT: drawing maps and OS symbols; word-processing descriptions of a village.

Resources
Recording sheets for each 'family'; a settlement name endings sheet; copies of the local (1:50 000) OS map or motorists' atlases; a worksheet showing a limited number of villages; the local 1:50 000 OS map or A3 extracts; enlarged photographs of different villages; a tick list chart; photographs of different routeways; copies of local maps at various scales; coloured pencils; A3 paper for a village map, with a river and some features marked and a blank 'key box'.

Display
Lists of important locational features needed when establishing a farm. Designs for villages generated using ICT. Annotated local OS maps giving the meanings of local place names. A selection of OS symbols commonly used to indicate features in villages; enlarged named photographs of villages with these features annotated. Photographs of different routeways with word-processed captions. The local OS map with journeys marked on and descriptions written alongside. Annotated village maps and descriptions of the village.

① Where did early settlers choose to settle?

What you need and preparation

Copies of photocopiable page 150. Sheets of A4 paper (one per group of three or four), each with a different name of a fictitious Saxon or Viking family written in marker pen on the top – for example: Tosvig, Haldsven (Viking); Fowkes, Berger (Saxon). Copies of a list of word endings associated with early settlements such as *-ley*, *-ton* and *-ham* (see page 78), with descriptions of what each word ending means and spaces for children to write in the names of two examples.

What to do

⑩ Introduction

Talk to the children about what Britain was like over 1000 years ago. It was mostly woodland, and there were potentially dangerous wild animals such as bears, wild boar and wolves. There were fewer people: approximately 1 million, compared with the 56 million of today. Ask the children to imagine that they are living 1000 years ago. Their family are from another land; they have come to settle in Britain, grow crops and keep animals. Encourage the children to consider how they would feel, travelling such a long way across the sea to a distant land with only the sketchiest details of what the new land was like.

Give out copies of the word endings list. Talk about the word endings and what they mean. Ask the children whether they know of any local examples.

⑳ Development

Arrange the children into small groups of three or four. Ask each group, in role as a 'family' of settlers, to think about what kind of land they would consider building their farm on:
- *Ideally, what features should the land have?*
- *What will you need to make a shelter?*
- *What kind of land will help you to keep safe?*
- *What kind of food will you want to eat?*
- *Where will you get water to drink?*

Ask the children to write down these features on the sheet of paper bearing their family name. They should underline the feature that they think is the most important. Encourage the 'families' to share their answers.

In pairs, the children should complete photocopiable page 150. Ask them to write a short explanation of why they have decided to locate the farm where they have.

⑩ Plenary

Find out where the different families would locate their farms. What were the reasons behind their decisions, and what was the most important locating factor? How many children located their farm in the 'best' position? (Position D is the best: it is close to woodland for fuel and building materials, close to a river to provide water for cooking and drinking, and on fertile land for farming.)

Ask the children to describe how they imagine the landscape of the UK was 1000 years ago. How has it changed?

Differentiation

More able children should describe clearly the reasons why they chose the site they did, and why they rejected the others.

Less able children could be given a list of descriptions of different types of land, such as 'The land is flat and easy to build on' and 'The land is close to a river, which sometimes floods'. They

Learning objectives
- Investigate the origins of places.
- Make simple decisions based on specific information.
- Present their findings and explain their decisions to others.

Lesson organisation
Teacher-led introduction; small-group, paired and individual activity work; teacher-led plenary session involving feedback from the children.

Vocabulary
location
site
countryside
landscape
floods
defence

CHAPTER 4
SETTLERS

Village settlers

ICT opportunities
• Use an art package to reproduce in colour the view on photocopiable page 150, as well as the positions of possible sites for the farm.

Follow-up activities
• Find the best location for a farm in each of a number of places sketched by the teacher.
• Relate the 'name endings' sheet to places they know, perhaps places where their relatives live or places that they have visited.
• Find examples of settlements that have a particular name ending. Draw pictures to show the meanings of the name endings. Collect pictures of the settlements to display next to these pictures, showing how the settlements have changed since they were first built.

should tick the statements which describe the best land on which to build their farm. They could use this sheet to help them complete page 150.

Assessing learning outcomes
How well can the children talk about early settlers? How well can they describe the nature of early settlements? Do they appreciate the importance of the 'site' when choosing where to start a dwelling or a farm? Can they use place names to draw conclusions about settlements in Saxon times?

① hour What evidence can we find on maps?

What you need and preparation

Learning objectives
• Use maps to obtain evidence.
• Be aware of the layout and function of a Saxon settlement.
• Become aware of how landscape has changed over time.

Lesson organisation
Teacher-led introduction; individual or paired activity work; individual extension work; individual or paired work in plenary session.

Vocabulary
site
settler
evidence
landscape
countryside

Copies of a local Ordnance Survey map at 1:50 000 scale, or black and white A4 extracts (which are more manageable). As an alternative, you could photocopy a page from a motorist's atlas. Select a rural area on the map showing a number of well-spaced villages; ideally, each should have one of the place name endings mentioned in the previous lesson plan. Use a frame to direct the children's attention to this area.

An OHT of the area to be studied. Copies of photocopiable page 151; a 'name endings' information sheet (as used in the previous lesson plan); and an A4 sheet showing five to eight villages, with appropriate place name endings distributed over the sheet. These places can be taken from a different map, or they can be fictitious.

What to do

⑩ mins Introduction
Give out copies of the map or extract; let the children familiarise themselves with this map for a few minutes. Use the OHT to point out some villages to the children. Look for particular features in the landscape, such as woodlands, hills, streams and rivers. Explain briefly what **contour lines** are (lines joining points of equal height above sea level), and how they can be used to show different physical features.

Look at the place name endings sheet and talk about it. Look at each different name ending and what it means. Discuss how the countryside might have looked 1000 years ago.

㊺ mins Development
Ask the children to use the map or extract to look for examples of local settlements that have the same name endings as those given on the information sheet. They should write some examples of each on the back of the sheet. Ask them to make a collection of name endings not on the sheet, and do some research to find out what these might mean.

Ask the children to choose four or five villages from the map. For each chosen village, they should use the map to discover why it was an attractive site for the first settlers to build their farms – for example, it may be on a hill for defence, on an expanse of flat land for farming, or be close to a river crossing. The children should write down the evidence they can find next to the name of each of the villages they have selected.

Give out copies of a sheet showing real or fictitious villages. Talk about each of the villages'

name endings and what they mean. Encourage the children to draw a small sketch on the sheet to show how these villages may have looked 1000 years ago and colour it in. As most of the countryside would have been woodland, they can fill in the spaces between the villages with trees. Some children could add streams and hills if they wish.

Plenary

5 mins

Concentrate on two or three villages that the children have chosen. For each village, ask who chose it and what evidence they found on the map to suggest why it was sited there. Make a list of the positive features found for each village.

Ask some of the children to describe the landscape that they drew on their sheet. If the sheet was taken straight from a local map, ask the children to describe how the landscape has changed over the last 1000 years.

Differentiation

More able children could make a labelled plan of the village they drew on their sheet. They could also be introduced to the Domesday Survey of 1086, which provides information on most of the villages in England at that time. References for your town or village and others nearby should be available from a local library, and can be used to help draw maps of early villages.

Less able children could try to draw what one or two early villages looked like, and describe the site features of one village.

Assessing learning outcomes

Can the children use a map to identify settlements and reasons for their original siting? Are they aware that a village may develop for a variety of reasons? Do they understand that the landscape 1000 years ago determined where farms were sited, and that it looked considerably different from how it looks today?

ICT opportunities
● Word-process all written work, including lists of local settlements that have particular name endings.
● Use ICT to design an early landscape, with small communities dotted between large areas of woodland.

Follow-up activities
● Complete photocopiable page 151.
● Find out about the Domesday Survey: what it was, who wanted it and why. Collect references for local settlements.
● Model a Saxon settlement. Label it to show the different buildings and areas of land that it contains.
● Collect information about other kinds of early settlements in the UK, such as Roman and Viking settlements.

What are villages like today?

1 hour

What you need and preparation

Copies of the local 1:50 000 Ordnance Survey map. A3-sized OS map extracts which have been produced for examination boards can be purchased much more cheaply than full maps, and are much easier to store. They are identical to the full map, but do not have a key. Check their availability for your area.

Enlarged photographs of different local villages, preferably showing specific physical or human features that can be identified on the local map. A chart showing pictures of a selection of villages (which may include the villages photographed), with a number of OS symbols arranged as a tick list. Copies of photocopiable page 152.

What to do

Introduction

15 mins

The children should already have encountered some basic OS map symbols (see Chapter 1, page 21). Discuss the use of symbols in OS maps: what they are, why they are needed, how confusing the map would be without them. Look at the symbols that the children may find in or near a village when they look at the OS map, such as post office, church (with a tower or spire), chapel, minor road, footpath and bridleway. Discuss how some of the symbols have been constructed – for example, the symbol for a church with a spire is a black circle with a cross on the top: the cross represents the religion and the circle is the plan of the spire.

Learning objectives
● Learn about the features of a present-day village, using maps and photographs.
● Compare and contrast the features of different villages.
● Use and interpret OS map symbols.

Lesson organisation
Teacher introduction; individual or paired activity work; teacher-led plenary session, with children answering directed questions.

Vocabulary
symbols
represent
features
footpath
hostel
viaduct

Village settlers

ICT opportunities
● Produce charts on which to record the number of different symbols found (using tally marks).
● Use a drawing package to reproduce some of the more common symbols; add a caption for each.
● Word-process the descriptions of the villages in the photographs.

Follow-up activities
● Draw pictures or take photographs to accompany the OS symbols in a display.
● Play 'Snap' with cards made from page 152. To make the game more difficult, include the meanings of the symbols as cards and match symbols and meanings.
● Collect more OS symbols, find examples on the map and give simple map references for them.

Allow the children a couple of minutes to look at the OS map and find familiar features.

35 mins Development
Ask each pair to choose a village from the map or extract and identify all the symbols that they can find in or near it.

Give out and discuss the chart (see above). For each village, the children should tick off the symbols for features that they can see in the picture. Ask them to identify the most common symbols. Did they find any symbols that were not on the sheet?

Give out the enlarged photographs of villages. Ask the children to write descriptions of what they see, and to identify particular features – especially any that would be given an OS symbol.

Give out copies of photocopiable page 152. Ask the children to cut out each of the symbols, then write on the back of each one what it represents. The symbols should be attached to the map and linked to appropriate features.

10 mins Plenary
Find out from the children:
● what each of the symbols on photocopiable page 152 represents
● which symbols were most commonly found
● how much local villages vary from one another
● what features were identified in the photographs of the villages.

Differentiation

More able children could try to match some of the enlarged photographs to the actual villages on the map. They could make comparisons between some of the villages portrayed on the chart. They should be introduced to a greater variety of map symbols.

Less able children should describe what they see in the photographs of the villages and make a list of the features found. Having been told the names of these villages, they can try to find them on the map.

Assessing learning outcomes

Can the children identify a number of symbols? Do they know what the symbols represent? Do they understand how and why symbols are used, and how effective symbols closely represent features on the ground? Do they realise that not all villages have the same features?

(1 hour) Remote farms and houses

What you need and preparation
Copies of the local 1:50 000 OS map. Photographs of different routeways, such as motorways, footpaths and cycle lanes, or aerial photographs which will show a variety and combination of routeways. Pieces of string about 15cm long. Copies of photocopiable page 153.

What to do

(15 mins) Introduction
For about two minutes, brainstorm routeways: ask the children to give the names of as many different kinds of routeways as they can. Make a list on the board or flip chart. Talk about each one in turn: *What is it? What is it for?* Look at the photographs of different routeways. Ask the children to identify each type. Discuss how these are shown on maps.

Give out copies of the OS map or extract, and allow the children two minutes to familiarise themselves with it. Encourage them to find their own town or village and others nearby, and to look at the network of links between them. Explain how they can measure the distance between places on a map using string. Go through a few examples with them, using a scale of 2cm for 1km to work out the distances.

(35 mins) Development
Ask the children, working in pairs, to find as many different kinds of routeway as they can on the local 1:50 000 OS map. On finding a type of routeway, they should note what it is and then find three further examples of it, giving a four-figure reference to show the location of each example. They should make a chart to record the routeways and their grid references.

Spread out the photographs of the different routeways used in the Introduction. Ask the children to rank these, from the routeway that would take the most traffic down to ones that wouldn't take any traffic.

Nominate a village on the 1:50 000 map for each pair of children (these could be different villages each time, or a selection could be used in rotation). Ask each pair to choose three or four isolated farms or houses that are some distance from the village. For each of these, the children should describe the exact route they would take to get from there to the village on foot. For example: 'To get from Green House Farm to Westaby, turn left down the track and turn left again over the stream. Follow the edge of the woodland, keeping it close to your right. Pass under the railway line at the end of the woodland. Cross the large field in front of you until you reach the road from Eastley, then follow it to Westaby village.'

The children can then use string to measure the route from each of their isolated places to the village, and so find out which one is closest to the village. They should use the scale of the map to calculate the actual distances. Finally, they can measure the distances between four or five villages and make a small distance chart of the kind that would be found in a motorist's road atlas.

(5 mins) Plenary
Talk to the children about the work they have done. Help them to understand that:
● routeways form a hierarchy (from motorways to footpaths), and all routeways are shown on the 1:50 000 scale maps
● there is a relationship between the size of a routeway and the size of the settlements it connects
● routeways join together to form networks
● different settlements are served by different networks; some people have greater access to networks than others.

Learning objectives
● Recognise that most places are connected to others.
● Know that there are different types of road or route.
● Understand that there is a network of roads or routes that connect settlements together.

Lesson organisation
Initial brainstorm session; teacher-led introduction; paired activity work; teacher-led discussion in plenary session.

Vocabulary
routeway
traffic
grid reference
isolated
connection
network
motorway
main road
minor road
footpath

Village settlers

ICT opportunities
● Word-process all descriptions of routes and captions for different routeways.
● Construct the distance chart using a data handling package.

Follow-up activities
● Find the distances along the routes between a selection of towns and cities, using string and a smaller-scale map of the UK.
● Describe routes between different towns on the local map, or between more distant towns using a smaller-scale map or motorists' atlas. Use accurate directions, and try to give the distances covered.
● Make a routeway map of the area around the school.
● Colour all the routeways on a 1:1250 map, using a colour code (for example: railway lines in orange, roads in red).

Differentiation
More able children could use aerial photographs to identify different kinds of routeways and find out how they link together. They can be encouraged to find examples of routeways combining to form networks. They could find more than three examples of each type of routeway on the OS map; some may attempt to locate these using six-figure grid references. Their descriptions of the journeys from isolated farms to the village should be detailed, identifying many of the features they pass.

Less able children should be helped to find different types of routeway on the map, and give only one example of each. They should be encouraged to rank the photographs, and to describe one journey from an isolated place back into the village. These children, and any who find the small print on the OS maps difficult to read or interpret, should be encouraged to complete photocopiable page 153, which is more simply drawn.

Assessing learning outcomes
Can the children give four-figure grid references accurately? Do they understand how settlements are connected? Do they understand that there is a hierarchy of routeways that have developed over time to link settlements of different sizes?

How do settlements develop?
(1 hour 30 mins)

Learning objectives
● Recognise that settlements have specific features, and are located in ways governed by physical constraints and human choice.
● Draw a map of the layout of a settlement.
● Construct a key to show the symbols used and their meanings.
● Show an awareness of how villages develop over time.

Lesson organisation
Teacher-led introduction, including revision of previous work; individual activity work; small-group feedback in a plenary session, with the teacher discussing some of the children's work.

What you need and preparation
Copies of local OS maps at 1:50 000 and 1:25 000 scale; sets of coloured pencils.

One copy per child of an A3 sketch map of a village. Draw a river (about 1cm wide) on plain paper, and a blank 'key' box to one side. Add the core of a village, including a church and churchyard, a village green, a blacksmith's, an inn and perhaps fifteen houses along a main street.

What to do
Introduction *(15 mins)*
Revise the OS symbols that the children have already encountered. Remind them how important symbols are in our interpretation and use of maps. Give out the OS maps and look at different symbols within a number of villages. Ask which features these symbols represent.

Draw the children's attention to the way in which houses and other buildings are represented on OS maps. Ensure that they are familiar with plan form and how plans are drawn. A plan is a drawing from above, to scale, of a specific place or building. 'Seeing' objects represented in this way is essential to a good understanding of maps, especially detailed large-scale maps. If the children are unfamiliar with plan form, some work will have to be done in advance. Remind them of how high ground is shown on a map by asking them to put their fingers on a high place, a low place and a place where the ground is steep.

Development *(1 hour)*
Give out copies of the A3 village map. Point out the river and other features, and the box for the key. Ask the children to develop the map, using names to identify areas on it and OS map symbols to represent human and physical features. Ask them to include some specific features on their maps, such as an area of high ground, a village pond and a small housing estate (about 15 houses). The area of the map needs to include the village and its immediate surrounding countryside, perhaps including fields and woodland. Encourage them to put in contour lines (representing height) and directions.

Village settlers

Remind the children to complete the key as they are drawing their maps. The key should contain (and explain) all of the symbols they have put on the map. The children should produce a short written description of their completed village.

Plenary

15 mins Ask the children to compare and talk about each others' maps; they can do this in groups of three or four.

Look together at a selection of the children's maps. Point out some of the features they have chosen to include, and how these features are related to each other – for example, minor roads linked to major roads, streets of terraced houses merging with streets of semi-detached houses. Make sure that all the features the children were asked to include appear on each map. Look at how the village in each map has grown, and how the new features added have gradually changed its character.

Differentiation

More able children should draw more closely to scale, add symbols correctly, produce a well-constructed key and add all the features that they were asked to include.

Less able children may need support to undertake this activity. They can be allowed to produce their map in pictorial form (rather than with symbols), but will need help with adding specific features and making them identifiable.

Assessing learning outcomes

Can the children draw a map that shows a logical pattern of settlement, influenced both by physical features and by their own choices? Can they organise the various elements of map work, including plan form, scale, direction, location, height and symbols, into a basic map?

Vocabulary
scale
symbols
plan
height
location
direction
key
village green
blacksmith

ICT opportunities
• Use mapping or graphics software to generate maps and draw OS symbols.
• Word-process the description of the village.

Follow-up activities
• Draw some small sketches of the village, as if looking down and across it from a vantage point. Name the physical and human features that can be seen.
• Look at some larger-scale maps of villages; from their layouts, try to say how they have developed. How are the plans of the oldest buildings different from those of the newest? Colour areas according to their age, to show how the village has grown.

How towns grow

For a town to grow from a village, there must have been a reason: a function or service that this settlement could provide and that others nearby could not. The first towns to have a function were 'market towns'. As most of the people were farmers, these places were very important: they were places where you could sell surplus crops and animals, and buy tools and seed.

Later, around the time of the Industrial Revolution, many towns grew as they became centres of manufacturing. Many of the factories in these towns used the raw materials supplied by local farmers (such as wool) or materials that could easily be imported from other countries (such as cotton). A number of towns grew because of minerals that could be extracted near them – for example, coal, which was either used locally or sold to nearby 'steel towns'. These **industrial towns** included Manchester, Bradford, Huddersfield and Sheffield. Other towns grew as **ports**, becoming important in Tudor times as well as throughout the period of the Industrial Revolution. Through these towns came imported goods that were needed by factories and shops, and manufactured goods exported from Britain to other countries. Towns such as Hull, Liverpool, Bristol, Glasgow and Belfast were important centres for trade and shipping.

Resort towns such as Blackpool, Scarborough and Ayr, and spa towns such as Leamington and Harrogate, grew from Victorian times, when reliable and affordable railways could bring people from nearby industrial towns for a holiday. Consequently, towns such as York, Doncaster, Crewe and Swindon grew as **railway towns**: places where railway lines from different regions converged.

New towns were developed mostly in the 1950s and 1960s, in an effort to reduce the pressure on the major cities (especially London). These towns, which were little more than villages, grew quickly to provide cheap planned housing for people who then commuted to the city nearby. Such towns include Welwyn Garden City near London and Skelmersdale near Liverpool.

Most towns in the UK grew rapidly during the during the time of the Industrial Revolution (roughly 1780–1880). The prospect of regular paid employment drew millions of people from the land and into the expanding towns and cities. Technological advances in agriculture more or less coincided with technological advances in industry and manufacturing, and so the former could supply the latter with a cheap and plentiful labour force. The populations of many established cities rose dramatically at this time; thousands of cheap houses were built quickly; and the boundaries of many towns and cities blurred as they merged to produce many of the urban clusters or **conurbations** that we have today.

Since 1900, the population of many towns and cities has grown much less quickly. The preference for smaller families and the development of the motor car meant that people in the later half of the twentieth century could choose not to live close to where they worked. The populations of surrounding villages and small towns have grown as a consequence: people with no former links with a village could move there, sometimes into purpose-built housing estates, so that they could combine the peacefulness of the village with the amenities of the city just a few minutes away.

Modern towns have a number of functions: they are places for work, leisure and shopping, and the focus of transport links. Over 80% of all paid work is undertaken in towns, and most leisure facilities (including cinemas, theatres, night clubs and restaurants) are found within them.

Patterns of shopping in towns have developed over time. Most corner shops are found in older inner-city areas and in inter-war and post-war housing estates. Streets of shops occur on the approaches to a town centre, or in the suburbs as an exposed front or parade. The idea of shopping malls comes from the USA; they can be found in most town and city centres. They are composed of shop units in a covered area, which is usually embellished with large plants and statues, and there are areas of seating to allow shoppers to linger. Ironically, some malls are designed to look old and interesting – much like the shops that were knocked down to make way for them.

Out-of-town shopping centres are modern developments, built on the outskirts of towns where land is more readily available and cheaper than in the centres. They usually consist of supermarkets and large discount stores, often selling materials or equipment for the home and garden.

The population of Leeds
1781 – 17 121
1801 – 53 162
1821 – 83 797
1841 – 152 054
1861 – 207 149
1881 – 309 119
1901 – 428 968
1921 – 458 232
1931 – 482 869
1951 – 505 219
1971 – 496 009
Today – 676 579

UNIT 8: How towns grow

Enquiry questions	Teaching objectives	Teaching activities	Learning outcomes	Cross-curricular links
Why do some settlements grow into towns and others don't? What are towns like?	• Investigate places. • Use maps to study places and ask questions. • Examine specific places. • Compare different places.	Paired work: find villages on a map, categorise them, make a tally chart; decide how certain towns have grown (their function); look at place name endings.	Children: • show knowledge about the growth of early settlements • understand that different towns grew because they had different functions, and that they have grown at different speeds over different phases of their history	Maths: making a tally chart or drawing a graph. ICT: using ICT to complement the worksheet activity; drawing graphs or tallies using a data handling program.
Where in the UK are most of our towns and cities? How are they different from villages?	• Complete outline maps. • Use atlases to discover the populations of towns and cities. • Plot the locations of cities and calculate their distance from the school.	Individual and paired work: mark important towns or cities on an outline map from memory, then compare with an atlas; mark areas on a map showing the locations of towns or cities; calculate the distance between their town and others.	• understand why some settlements grow and others do not • are aware that the country's main towns and cities are not evenly distributed • use an atlas to locate places	Maths: making tables or drawing graphs; drawing concentric circles. ICT: using ICT to mark in towns or cities and annotate them on a scanned map; drawing graphs; word-processing captions.
How can we find out what towns are like? How can we find places in a town quickly with a map?	• Learn about the features of a modern town. • Use a key to interpret symbols. • Compare the features of nearby towns or cities. • Look for these features on aerial photographs.	Small-group work: find places in a town using four-figure map references. Find features of different towns and complete a check list. Find features on an aerial photograph that could have an OS symbol.	• identify OS map symbols • understand why and how OS symbols are used • understand the importance of grid references in map work	ICT: using a data handling package; using a graphics package to show map symbols and invent others.
How are villages linked to towns and towns to other places?	• Understand that everyone needs routeways to travel around. • Understand that settlements are linked through a network of routeways. • Increase their understanding of maps. • Are aware of the use of timetables, and the importance of public transport for people who live in a village.	Paired or small-group work: use maps to describe routes from a nearby village to a town; use timetables to consider local bus services from a village to a nearby town; use maps to find out about routeways between towns; use timetables to find out about direct links to other cities.	• use four-figure grid references accurately • understand how settlements are connected • are aware that there are communication hierarchies based on the relative size of settlements	Maths: using timetables for work on the 24-hour clock. English: describing routes between villages and towns. ICT: designing flow diagrams to describe routes; plotting towns and cities on a scanned map and calculating the distances between them.
How do towns grow? How can we tell which parts of a town are old and which are new?	• Plot addresses of houses on a town or city map. • Know that street patterns are associated with periods of time. • Identify street patterns.	Paired or small-group work: mark the positions of houses on a town map and colour-code them according to age; look for street patterns that give clues to the age of different parts of a town.	• describe how a town has developed • understand that the character of houses changes with age, and that their location influences their size and style.	History: looking at the layout and style of a Victorian house; understanding the historical basis of housing patterns. ICT: word-processing a list of changing features in the locality; producing estate agents' sheets. for houses close to the school. Design and technology: designing a new neighbourhood.

Resources
A worksheet showing different villages; a flip chart or OHP; glue, scissors; atlases; outline maps of the UK; postcards, photographs and pictures of different towns; a list of place name endings; local and other 1:50 000 OS maps; a school-made worksheet or checklist; photographs of urban features; oblique aerial photographs of your town; paper, pencils; copies of the local 1:50 000 OS map; a selection of timetables from a village to a town; road atlases, world atlases, outline maps of the UK, Europe and the world; A4-sized copies of a large-scale late Victorian map of an area of the town; A3-sized photocopies of a simplified map showing part of a town for children to complete; estate agent's information sheets; street maps of the local town.

Display
Maps drawn using ICT; graphs and tally charts; completed worksheets. Outline maps and computer-generated maps showing and naming larger towns or cities. OS maps and aerial photographs marked with OS symbols. Invented OS symbols. Timetables and descriptions of routeways between places. A colour-coded map of the town, showing the positions of houses of different ages linked to (real) estate agents' sheets. School-produced 'estate agents' sheets' for local houses.

How towns grow

①hour How did these towns begin?

Learning objectives
● To use maps to study places and answer questions about them.
● To examine the characteristics of specific places.
● To compare different places.

Lesson organisation
Teacher-led introduction; paired activity work (or individual work on alternative activity); teacher-directed plenary, with some individual contributions.

Vocabulary
linear
nucleated
dispersed
market town
industrial town
port
new town
prosper
develop
characteristics

What you need and preparation

A sheet with the names of about 15 different villages and hamlets found on the local 1:50 000 OS map spread across it and the terms 'linear', 'nucleated' and 'dispersed' written across the bottom. Copies of photocopiable page 154. Copies of the local 1:50 000 OS map, and of a 1:1250 map of the central area of your own town or one nearby. Copies of a sheet with a set of sentence beginnings (such as 'A market town...') and a set of endings (such as '...is where people travel to buy and sell things') related to the town origins and functions covered in this lesson. Glue, scissors.

What to do

10 mins Introduction

Talk to the children about different kinds of village; explain what the terms **linear**, **nucleated** and **dispersed** mean (see page 79). Discuss why some villages may have developed in these ways, and the effects that the surrounding countryside has had on their development. Write these names on a flip chart or OHT.

Discuss why some villages have grown into towns and others have not. Consider the site, the aspect and closeness to raw materials, good farmland or a coast. Talk about the rapid growth of towns in particular periods of their development: market towns from early times until the Industrial Revolution; industrial towns and ports during the Industrial Revolution; resort towns in the late nineteenth and early twentieth centuries; new towns in the inter-war and post-war periods. Talk about the characteristics of each type of town.

Ask the children some key questions about their own town or one nearby, for them to answer using the 1:1250 map. For example:
● *Are there areas of housing laid out in a 'grid iron' pattern?* (There usually are in inner-city areas, within 2km or so of the city centre, implying a large population increase in Victorian times.)
● *Are there large areas of factories, mills and warehouses close to the city centre?* (Again, there usually are, due to rapid expansion in industry that took place around the old town in Victorian times.)
● *Does the town centre retain a pattern of old, irregular streets and roads?* (Some still do, especially those that grew as market towns: growth was slow, so it followed the lines of medieval tracks and routes.)
● *Are there areas of housing laid out in crescents and cul-de-sacs spread around the town?* (These are usually found in the outer suburbs, implying expansion of the town in the inter-war years.)
● *Are there large areas of terraced housing and warehouses around a harbour?* (These are found around ports such as Hull, implying rapid growth in population with expansion of the port and its facilities during the Industrial Revolution. Warehouses to house imported or exported goods would develop as the port grew.)
● *Are there areas of wide roads and large houses close to the seafront?* (This would occur with the expansion of a resort town, implying a growing importance of the town during late Victorian or Edwardian times. The wide streets would allow coaches or pedestrians to pass by easily.)

40 mins Development

Give each pair of children the local OS maps and the 'villages' sheet. Ask them to find each village or hamlet named on the sheet and put a ring around its name, using a different colour to show whether it is linear, nucleated or dispersed. Try a few examples together initially. Ask the children to make a tally and/or draw a simple bar chart to show how many of each type there are.

Ask the pairs to complete photocopiable page 154. Encourage the children to look for the clues

about each town found in its picture, and to make a note of these before deciding what kind of town it is.

Give out the 'beginnings and endings' sheet. The children need to match each beginning with its correct ending, then cut them out and stick them onto a plain sheet of paper.

10 mins Plenary

Encourage the children to answer the following questions:
- *What are linear, nucleated and dispersed villages like?*
- *Why have they developed as they have? Give some examples from the local map.*
- *Why have some grown into towns and others not?*
- *Why, specifically, did market towns, industrial towns, ports, resort towns and new towns grow?*
- *What features do the types have that make them different?*

Differentiation

More able children could look at more than 15 villages and hamlets, construct a graph to show which is the most common type, and produce a short written account of their findings.

Less able children need not complete the 'villages' sheet, but should find two or three examples of each type of village on the map. They should concentrate on identifying the different types of towns on photocopiable page 154, and on joining the sentences together.

Assessing learning outcomes

Do the children show knowledge about the growth of early settlements, and the effects of their location on their growth? Do they understand that different towns had different original functions that were responsible for their growth? Do they know that towns have grown at different speeds and at different times over the last few hundred years?

ICT opportunities
- Use mapping software to make a map showing the different villages investigated.
- Use a data handling package to draw the graph or tally, and word-process all descriptions.

Follow-up activities
- Look at the Domesday Survey entry for your town. Draw a picture of what the town might have looked like over 1000 years ago.
- Find out more about the origins of your town and how it has developed. Make notes on the highlights of its development. Draw a pictorial timeline, showing the main events in the town's history.

---

1 hour Where are our towns?

What you need and preparation

A selection of atlases. Copies of an outline map of the UK; A4 copies of the same map. Postcards, photographs or pictures of different towns and cities in the UK. A large chart showing various common place-name endings and their original meanings (see Chapter 2, page 78).

What to do

10 mins Introduction

Brainstorm towns and cities: see how many the children can name in two minutes. Record the names on the board, flip chart or OHT. Count them together.

Ask the children to explain what makes these places towns or cities. *How are they different from villages?* Show them some pictures, photographs and postcards of different towns and cities. Find out whether any of the children have been to the places named in the brainstorming session.

Explain that long ago, all of these towns and cities were small villages, and that they grew into what they are today for different reasons. Talk about how place names and word endings such as *-ham* and *-ton* can provide information about what a place was like when it was first settled (see page 78).

Learning objectives
- Complete outline maps.
- Use an atlas to determine the sizes of towns and cities.
- Plot the locations of cities and calculate their approximate distances from a reference point (the school).

Lesson organisation
Initial whole-class brainstorming and teacher-led introductory work; individual or paired activity work; teacher-led plenary session.

Vocabulary
town
city
atlas
suffix
concentric

How towns grow

Development

45 mins Give each child or pair a blank outline map, and ask them to mark on some of the main cities in the UK (such as London, Belfast and Glasgow). They should do this without using their atlases. Most children will have difficulty in completing this activity. When they have finished, ask them how they would find out where these places are. Give out the atlases and ask the children to find the 'best map' of the important towns and cities in the UK. They should compare their own map with this one, to see how close they were in placing each city.

Ask the children to mark on new outline maps where the most important towns and cities actually are. Encourage them to mark and name about 15 major towns and cities from those originally brainstormed. The key on the map in the atlas may give information about the relative sizes of the different towns and cities marked. Direct the children's attention to this.

Ask the children to look at the towns and cities they have marked and compare their name endings to the list provided. They should write down the name of each city and the meaning of its name ending on the back of their outline map.

Now ask them to work out how many of the large towns and cities are within 50, 100, 150, 200 and so on kilometres of your school by drawing concentric circles on a copy of the outline map. They should record the results in a table, then in a graph. *Which city is the closest, and which is the furthest away?* Ask them to find other large cities in Europe and the rest of the world.

Plenary

5 mins Ask the children what they have noticed about the distribution of the largest towns and cities in the UK. *Whereabouts are they?* Talk to the children about where most of the cities are found. Explain why this pattern has emerged. The cities are grouped in regions where there was major industrial growth during the Industrial Revolution: shipbuilding and steel in Strathclyde; the port at Liverpool; cotton in the Manchester region; wool industry in West Yorkshire; shipbuilding, coal and engineering in Tyneside; coal and steel in South Yorkshire; ceramics and other light industry in the Midlands; commerce in London.

Ask the children how far most of the major towns and cities are from the school. Ask them to say how far away specific cities are, such as London, Edinburgh, Cardiff and Belfast.

Differentiation

More able children should be able to complete the activities individually. They should be able to locate the best map quickly, and to plot more than 15 towns and cities. They should be encouraged to draw around the areas of the UK that have the most cities, and describe (using compass points) where these regions are in the UK. They should be able to draw a graph showing how many cities there are within particular distances from the school.

Less able children may need to be told which map to use, and may need to be given a list of the towns and cities that they should plot on their outline map. They may need help to do this. They should be given an outline map with concentric circles drawn on it to help with the final activity.

Assessing learning outcomes

Do the children understand why some settlements grow and others do not? Do they understand why major towns and cities are not evenly distributed, but tend to be found in certain areas? Can they use atlases to locate places?

ICT opportunities
• Mark towns and cities on an outline map using *Claris Works* or clip art.
• Find out the distances between the school's town and others.
• Use a data handling package to draw graphs showing how many towns are found within different distances of the school.
• Word-process the names of the most important towns and cities in large fonts for display.

Follow-up activity
Rank the towns and cities plotted on the outline map in order of distance from the school. Write their names in order, starting with the closest and ending with the most distant city. Undertake a similar exercise with major cities in Europe and the world.

1 hour What are towns like today?

What you need and preparation

Local OS maps or extracts at 1:50 000 scale; a selection of other OS maps at the same scale. A sheet with different OS symbols and their meanings (using urban examples, such as bus stations and motorways) down the left-hand side, and the right-hand side drawn into a grid with spaces at the top for the names of towns, so that the children can tick off the symbols found. Photographs of urban features that can be given as an OS symbol; copies of oblique aerial photographs of your nearby town, or a selection of aerial photographs showing areas of other towns. Plain paper and coloured pencils or felt pens; cotton or wool thread.

What to do

10 mins Introduction

Give out the maps or extracts. Ask the children to look at the map and think about what information it provides about a particular nearby town or city. After two minutes, they must report back to the rest of the class, saying what facilities they have found.

Talk to the children about how important symbols are when we want to use and interpret a detailed map: without them, understanding and using maps would be much more difficult and time-consuming.

Ask the children to locate places on the map, using simple four-figure grid references. For example: *Where is the hospital? What grid reference does the park have?*

Lead the children through a few examples of finding grid references. Be careful to explain that **eastings** (E–W) are given first and **northings** (N–S) second. Ask them why it is useful to know and understand grid references when you are using maps (they enable you to locate a feature quickly and precisely in a large area).

40 mins Development

Give out the OS symbols sheet; talk about its format and how to complete the tick list. In pairs, the children should look at different towns and cities (perhaps using different OS maps, to increase the number of settlements being investigated). The name of each town or city considered should be written at the top of the sheet. They should try to choose places that are discrete (have clear boundaries), rather than conurbations where towns merge and their boundaries become unclear. Where possible, they should record grid references (either four-figure or, preferably, six-figure) for the OS symbols found.

Give out the aerial photographs to each pair of children, with another copy of the OS symbols sheet. Ask the children to look carefully at the photographs to see whether they can find any features that would be marked with a symbol on an OS map. They should mark the ones they find on the sheet. Finally, they should draw each symbol found on a small piece of plain paper, colour and label it, then link it to the correct place on the aerial photograph using cotton or wool thread.

10 mins Plenary

Compare the children's results from the map work activity. Find out who has found the most OS symbols, and who has found the most in specific categories (such as churches or bus and coach stations). Find out how different towns and cities compared: *Did larger cities have more symbols or not? Do all the towns have the same facilities? Do they all have the same amount of facilities?*

How towns grow

Ask the children what they found when they looked at the aerial photographs: *What features were found that would have an OS symbol? What features were found most often?*

Differentiation

More able children could study the larger, more complex towns and cities and the most detailed aerial photographs. They should try to invent their own symbols to represent important features of urban environments.

Less able children could study smaller, more discrete settlements where there are fewer OS symbols to record and less possibility of becoming confused by the quantity of symbols that they can see. Similarly, their aerial photographs should be of a smaller area containing only a few important buildings or structures.

Assessing learning outcomes

Can the children identify a variety of symbols, knowing their meaning? Do they understand how and why map symbols are used? Do they understand the importance of grid references in the accurate use of maps?

① Can't get there from here
(1 hour)

What you need and preparation

Copies of the local 1:50 000 OS map. Bus timetables from a selected village to a local town; bus, coach, rail and air timetables from a local town to other places. Road atlases; a selection of world atlases. Outline maps of the UK (and, if possible, of Europe and the world).

What to do

⑩ (10 mins) Introduction

Ask the children to say what kind of routeways there are between villages and towns (such as roads, railways and so on). *What kinds of traffic would use these routeways?* Ask them to describe the transport links within a large town or city and between cities; talk about such transport links as local buses, national coaches, trains and perhaps air traffic. Find out which of the children has used each form of transport. Where did they go to and why?

Discuss the best ways of getting from a village to a town, from a town to another nearby town, to a city in the UK, and to a city abroad. Why would the children choose those particular forms of transport?

⑩ (40 mins) Development

Choose a village that is quite close to your nearest town. Ask the children to find the village on the OS map and then to write a description of the routes from it to the nearest town. Give each pair or small group of children another village that is more distant, and again ask them to write a description of the routes into the same town. They should include road numbers and particular features passed.

Ask the children to look at the timetable for local buses from the village to a nearby town. *How often do the buses run? At what times? Are the buses likely to be convenient for the people in the village to use?* If appropriate, they could look at train times too. Ask: *What might the cost of a taxi be?* (Suggest that they calculate it, based on a standard fare of £1 per km.)

They can look at the OS map of a local town, find the routeways into the town from another

nearby town, and make a list of these. They should give four-figure map references for some of these (at their closest point to the local town centre).

They can use the road atlases to discover which other towns and cities it is possible to get to easily by using main roads, motorways or railways from your local town. They should list the connections available through each kind of transport, showing which towns can be reached most easily.

They can look at a selection of timetables that give information on the different forms of transport available from the local town to other towns. Encourage each group to look at the timetables relating to one form of transport, and make a list of the places that they can get to easily using that form of transport. Bring the class together to share the results, in the form of a map showing the towns that can be reached by various means. Maps of Europe and the world may be needed if there is an airport nearby.

10 mins Plenary

Ask the children to describe the range of routeways that link villages to towns. Find out which type of routeway (or mode of transport) they would choose to visit a farm, travel to another small village, or go into the town. Repeat the exercise, looking at routeways and modes of transport in, around and between towns and cities. Find out which routeways and modes of transport the children would use to visit:

● another local town
● a town at the other end of the country
● a town in a completely different country.

Compare the answers. *For which journey is there the most choice?*

Ask the children where people can get to from the local town or city by coach, rail or air. Ask who they think is 'better off' for access to routeways: people who live in a village or people who live in a town.

Differentiation

More able children should look at villages that are further away, and describe the routes to the town in detail. They should look at bus timetables (or extracts from them) and decide whether the buses are convenient for local people. They could also use timetables to find out which other towns can be reached, and map them on a blank outline map.

Less able children need to look at a small village close to the town, where the connecting routeways are clear and easy to follow. They should look at the variety of routeways within a town, and the more obvious links between towns. With support, they can find various places that it is possible to get to from the local town.

Assessing learning outcomes

Can the children give four-figure grid references accurately? Do they understand how settlements are connected? Are they aware that there are communications hierarchies based on the relative sizes of settlements?

ICT opportunities
● Design flow diagrams to describe routes from a village to a local town, and from the town to more distant towns.
● Plot towns and cities on outline maps, and use mapping software to find out the distances between various towns and cities in the UK, in Europe and around the world.

Follow-up activities
● Play a team game for two pairs, using an extract from a local 1:50 000 scale OS map. One pair describe a route from a village to a nearby town. The second pair have to find the route and name the town they will arrive in. The second pair describe a route from that town to another village, and so on.

How towns grow

① In the neighbourhood

1 hour

Learning objectives
• Plot the addresses of houses on a town or city map.
• Identify and describe street patterns.
• Know that different street patterns are associated with different periods of time.

Lesson organisation
Teacher-led introduction; activity work in pairs or small groups; children feed back to class in plenary session.

Vocabulary
plan form
detached
semi-detached
terraced
flats
estate agent
street plan
index

What you need and preparation
Copies of an A4 extract of a local, large-scale, late Victorian map of a local town. A selection of 1:1250 OS maps covering the same area as the historical map. Copies of photocopiable pages 4c and 155. Copies of a street atlas of the local town; a map of the town, showing its boundaries, districts and streets. A3-sized photocopies of a simplified map of a fictitious or real town, with 6–10 roads (including a main road) and a blank key at the side; sets of coloured pencils. A selection of estate agents' house sale information sheets that show a photograph of the house for sale, its address, its age (estate agents will supply this verbally) and its price.

What to do

⑩ Introduction
10 mins   Show the children the extracts of the large-scale local historical map and ask them what they notice about it. Compare it with the corresponding extract of a modern 1:1250 map. Ask what has changed since it was produced, what has gone and what has remained the same. Concentrate on the area around a main road. Ask what it might have been like to live here at that time.

Talk about the plan form of the houses found on the modern 1:1250 map. Use the board, flip chart or OHT to draw plans of detached, semi-detached and terraced houses. Ask the children what the plan of a modern block of flats might look like. Look at the street patterns and explain how these are associated with different times in the development of a town or city:
• Medieval – narrow, irregular streets running at different angles.
• Victorian – 'grid iron' inner-city terraced housing with yards to the rear (no gardens); large, detached suburban houses with gardens.
• Edwardian – similar large, detached suburban houses.
• Inter-war – curves, crescents and cul de sacs; semi-detached houses, often with garages, bay windows and gardens to the front and rear.
• Post-war – irregular roads (some cul de sacs), often with a mix of housing styles, all with gardens and garages; a lot of conversion development in old mills, dockyards and barns; large, detached or semi-detached houses in the suburbs with large gardens and sometimes double garages; blocks of flats separated by public areas.

Give out the estate agents' sheets. Encourage the children to look at the house details. Together, use a street atlas of the town to find these places.

⑷⓪ Development
40 mins   The class can all work on one of these activities, or be divided into three groups to cover them all.
1. Give outline city maps and street atlases to each pair or group. Ask the children to look at each house on the estate agents' sheets and give it a colour code to show how old it is (for example: yellow for eighteenth-century houses, red for early nineteenth, green for late nineteenth, blue for up to 1918, orange for up to 1939, purple for up to to 1960, black for up to the present time). They should use the outline map to find the streets that these houses are on, and mark their positions with correctly coloured dots. The group can combine their results onto a single outline map.

2. Ask the children to look out for street patterns that give a clue to the age of different parts of the town (see above). The date of the house given by the estate agent should help to confirm the date of its street. The children can use the estate agent's sheets (with the outline street maps) to look for specific features of houses from different periods, such as: large ornate chimneys and stained glass in Victorian houses; smaller bay-windowed houses from the 1930s.

3. Give out copies of photocopiable page 155. Remind the children of what different street patterns can tell us about the age of houses and the development of a town. Encourage them to look carefully at the map on page 155 and decide how old different areas are, then colour them in according to a colour code. They can do this individually or in pairs.

10 mins **Plenary**
Ask the children the following questions:
● *How do street patterns change with the distance from the city centre?*
● *What kinds of different patterns are there? What periods do they come from? Does the evidence of estate agents' sheets support this?*
● *What differences in style and architecture do houses from different periods show?*
● *Where are the oldest and the newest houses? Where are the biggest and the smallest houses?*

Differentiation
More able children should be encouraged to relate their findings to the changing nature and character of the town in each of the activities. The first two activities are more appropriate to the more able children.

Less able children should concentrate on the more obvious and immediate examples of change in a town. The third activity is more appropriate to the ability level of this group.

Assessing learning outcomes
Can the children describe how a town has developed? Do they understand that the characteristics of houses vary according to when they were built? Do they understand that the location of a house influences its likely size and style?

ICT opportunities
● Word-process the list of changing features in the local area.
● Use scanned photographs and a DTP package to produce estate agents' sheets for houses of different styles, sizes and periods that are close to the school.
● Design a new neighbourhood using a graphics package.

Follow-up activities
● Follow an 'I Spy' trail in the local environment, using photographs of specific features and a base map (provided by the teacher).
● Compare the historical and modern maps; identify and list changes that would be visible to someone walking along the main road. Consider how these may have affected the character of the area.
● Use the A3-sized outline map to design a new neighbourhood. Use OS symbols, and include features such as old terraces and an inter-war housing estate. Name the roads and complete the key.

Village case studies

Much of children's work in geography involves learning about developing countries and peoples. In Key Stage 2, this includes looking for similarities and differences between two cultures. The lesson plans in this chapter will help children to develop ideas about an economically developing country. They focus on two villages: Chembakolli in southern India and Clapham in North Yorkshire. The children will consider where these villages are, their functions, their climate, how they have developed, and the work patterns and lifestyles of their inhabitants.

The lessons on Chembakolli involve using information and photographs from the ActionAid website www.chembakolli.com (see resources list on page 101 for details of these and other resources on southern India published by ActionAid). The lessons on Clapham draw on a pack entitled 'Clapham in the Yorkshire Dales' that was published by Ingleborough Hall Outdoor Education Centre in Clapham, but is no longer available. This chapter is about using secondary sources and background knowledge; neither of the two case studies requires the children to visit the place being studied.

Case studies can give pupils the opportunity to study a locality in some depth without requiring them to travel there. They allow pupils to empathise with others on a personal level. The children should be encouraged to see and appreciate the challenges that people in other places face each day in doing things that are taken for granted elsewhere. Time should be taken to help the children identify the similarities between cultures, and to recognise that societies separated by huge geographical distances can nevertheless have much in common in terms of how they live and work.

The children should understand that a case study is a snapshot of life within one community in one locality in a particular country; as such, it is not representative of life in that country as a whole. As in the UK, there are great contrasts in the form and function of different Indian villages and the lifestyles of the people who live in them. To overcome the limitations of a case study, it is useful to study other localities within the same country – not only to avoid stereotyping, but to highlight the existence of contrasts within one society.

When studying a settlement in a locality far away, it is important that the same approaches are used and the same questions asked as would be the case if a similar study were undertaken close to the school. Finding out what gives a place its character involves asking serious geographical questions that require considered answers based on real evidence – not just on looking for the 'unique' aspects of life in that place. At culturally diverse schools, it may be possible to invite speakers into the school who can talk about their own experience of life in or near the case study village. Such visitors add a sense of immediacy and realism to the work being done, and can provide an insight into the form and functions of villages and the lifestyles of the people who live there.

India

India is bordered by Pakistan to the west, Bangladesh and Myanmar (Burma) to the east, and China, Tibet, Bhutan and Nepal to the north. Covering an area of 3.3 million square kilometres, it is home to over 1 billion people. India is broadly triangular in shape; it is about 3200km from north to south and 2900km from east to west at its widest point. The coast of India meets the Arabian Sea to the west, the Bay of Bengal to the east and the Indian Ocean (in which lies Sri Lanka) to the south.

India is the seventh largest country in the world, but it is second only to China in size of population. 73% of India's population live in the countryside, giving a density of 329 per km^2, compared with 243 for the UK. The annual population growth in India is 1.8%, compared with 0.3% in the UK.

India's landscape is varied. The high Himalayan mountains (reaching 8848m above sea level) in the north descend into forest-covered hills. To the south is the North Indian Plain, which extends from the Bay of Bengal in the east to the Arabian Sea in the west and is where most of the great

cities of India are located. South of this plain are the Vindhya mountains and the high, arid Deccan Plateau (one of India's major regions). The average height of the Deccan is about 600m above sea level. To the east and west of the Deccan are the 'ghats' or 'high places' that separate it from the sea. Between the ghats and the sea are broad coastal plains where bananas, coconuts and spices are cultivated.

India's most important rivers flow across the Northern Plain. They are the Ganges and its tributaries: the Jumna, Gogra and Brahmaputra. The Indus, another important river, flows through Pakistan and the disputed Kashmir region in the north-west. Some of its tributaries flow through India, and are important in irrigating the dry North Indian Plain.

The climate of India is also varied. The northern mountains and hills are cold in the winter and temperate in the summer, with temperatures similar to those of Europe. In the Northern Plain, the summers are hot and the winters are mild; rain occurs in the summer, though there are sometimes dust storms. The Deccan is dry, but catches the monsoon between June and September. Towards the coast, especially in the west, the rainfall is very heavy. The Deccan is hot in the summer, when temperatures reach 40°C; the coastal areas are more temperate. In the north-west, around the southern border between India and Pakistan, desert conditions prevail: the land is always dry, there is little rainfall and summer temperatures are very high. Areas in the south-east and north-east that catch the monsoon are extremely wet, often receiving 10m of (mainly monsoonal) rain each year.

Bangalore – climate statistics

	Jan	Feb	Mar	Apr	May	Jun	Jul	Aug	Sep	Oct	Nov	Dec
Temperature (°C)	24	25	27	28	30	29	28	27	27	28	27	25
Rainfall (mm)	0	1	0	0	20	647	945	660	309	117	7	1

North Yorkshire

North Yorkshire is a county in northern England. It has an area of 8321 km², making it the largest county in England. It consists mainly of two upland areas: the Pennines to the west and the Cleveland Hills and North York Moors to the east; in between these is the Vale of York. The Pennines in North Yorkshire reach a height of over 670m above sea level; they are broken up by deep river valleys known as the Yorkshire Dales. The Dales cover an area of 1761 km², and extend into Cumbria. The North York Moors are an area of moorland and woodland, covering an area of 1432km² and extending into Redcar and Cleveland. The population of North Yorkshire is approximately 723 000. Towns tend to be located in the Vale of York and around the North Sea coast; Harrogate and Scarborough are the most important towns.

The climate of North Yorkshire is variable. Winters are often long, with appreciable snowfalls on the higher land. Rainfall is moderately high compared with other areas in the UK. Temperatures are cold in the winter and mild in the summer.

Clapham – climate statistics

	Jan	Feb	Mar	Apr	May	Jun	Jul	Aug	Sep	Oct	Nov	Dec
Temperature (°C)	4	7	8	10	15	18	18	17	14	9	8	4
Rainfall (mm)	9	8	16	12	9	8	6	14	12	9	14	15

Chembakolli: village life in India

The state of Tamil Nadu, once called Madras State, occupies the extreme south of the Indian peninsula. To the north are the Nilgiri Hills, that reach to a height of more than 2600m above sea level; to the west are the Western Ghats. The main river is the Cauvery, an important source of irrigation and power generation; other, smaller rivers dry out in the hot, dry weather from March to June. The climate in Tamil Nadu is tropical. In the south-west monsoon, from June to December, there is torrential rainfall and cyclones sweep in from the Arabian Sea, sometimes causing considerable damage.

Tamil Nadu has a population of 56 million, about the same as the UK. Over 5 million people live in the state capital, Madras (India's fourth largest city). Groups of tribal people called the 'Adivasi' (a Hindu word meaning 'original inhabitants') live in the Nilgiri Hills. These tribal Indians are scattered throughout India, but most of them live in the countryside (especially in the highland areas). They are poor, and this affects their health and opportunities for education. Less than half of the children go to school, even though it is free, as many parents cannot afford to pay for the books and materials that their children will need. Many children help their parents on the farms, or look after the youngest children.

The farming year in the Nilgiri Hills is closely linked to the cycle of the monsoon, before which fields are cleared and seeds planted. The rains keep the crops well watered until they are harvested in December or January. Most families typically farm a small area of land, in which they grow small-scale cash crops and vegetables for their own consumption. Wealthier farmers, usually non-tribal people who live outside Chembakolli, grow cash crops, often on irrigated land, such as rice, cotton, bananas, potatoes, tea, spices and groundnuts; these are sold in the local markets or to large commercial organisations. They often employ the Adivasis to work for them as labourers.

Adivasi village groups or 'sangams' meet regularly to discuss how they can improve their lives. These groups will lend money to individuals (the banks will not), and are a forum for community discussions and decision making. Many nursery schools, using the Adivasi languages rather than Tamil, have been established to bring education to the youngest children of poorer families. Junior and secondary education are taken up by a minority of children; those that do attend have to travel long distances, and some stay at the school during the week (which adds to the families' expenditure). Many health problems are caused by the lack of safe water: few of the people have piped water, and most of the water used is collected from springs and streams that may be used by animals. New boreholes have been sunk, and health centres have been set up to provide basic health care. Teams of health workers travel the region to immunise children and advise local people on health care.

There are about 125 houses in the village of Chembakolli. Families tend to be 'extended', with many family members living under the same roof or close by. Everyone is involved in agriculture, and almost all of the vegetables that are produced in the family's plot go to feed the family. Crops grown in Chembakolli include bananas, potatoes, millet, okra, onions, tomatoes, herbs and spices. Villagers grow some tea, coffee and pepper as small-scale cash crops. A few animals are kept: a family will typically have chickens and a cow. Around the village, non-tribal landowners grow cash crops such as tea and coffee in plantations. Many women are employed in picking tea leaves, for which they are paid about 50 rupees (equivalent to 70p) a day, plus bonuses.

UNIT 9: Chembakolli – village life in India

Enquiry questions	Teaching objectives	Teaching activities	Learning outcomes	Cross-curricular links
How can we find out where these places are? What are they like?	● Investigate places. ● Respond to geographical questions. ● Use and interpret globes, atlases and maps. ● Use secondary sources. ● Use ICT to access information. ● Identify the physical and human features of places.	Work in small groups: locate the positions of Europe, the UK, Asia and India; find out the names of countries that border India and information about the climate of India; add physical and human features to outline maps; make large outline maps, using the information collected.	Children: ● locate Europe, the UK, Asia and India on maps ● draw maps to show locational information ● are aware of the main physical and human features of India ● appreciate the diversity of the landscape of India	English: writing letters or sending e-mails for information on India. Maths: drawing climate graphs. ICT: using CD-ROM, Internet and e-mail facilities; word-processing.
How would we get to India? Which places would we pass?	● Find out how different places are connected. ● Use and interpret maps and globes. ● Use secondary sources.	Work in pairs: plan routes from the UK to Chembakolli; list the countries and capital cities flown over, and the distances between them.	● complete a map showing a route from the UK to India ● ask questions about what distant places are like	Maths: calculating distances between places; drawing graphs. ICT: word-processing questions about India and Chembakolli.
What is the land around Chembakolli like?	● Make maps from pictures. ● Give simple grid references. ● Learn how to use scale and calculate distances from a map. ● Describe a route. ● Make a land use map.	Work in pairs: draw a map of Chembakolli, labelling physical and human features; give four-figure grid references; use the map to give directions and to estimate distances; make a land use map or plan a tour around Chembakolli.	● make a map to show the main features of a village ● use a map to give directions and calculate distances ● recognise and describe the main features of a village	Maths: estimating and calculating distances; using a scale. ICT: word-processing captions and descriptions.
What are the buildings in Chembakolli like?	● Use secondary sources. ● Know about the similarities and differences between places.	Work in small groups or pairs: look at the similarities and differences between Chembakolli and local villages; annotate a picture of a house in Chembakolli; make a model of a house or classroom in Chembakolli.	● are aware of, and able to discuss, the similarities and differences between houses and schools in Chembakolli and locally	Design and technology: designing and making a house or a classroom in Chembakolli. English: writing letters. ICT: word-processing descriptions and annotations.
What kind of jobs do women do in Chembakolli? What kind of jobs do men do?	● Use secondary sources. ● Consider the similarities and differences between places. ● Annotate pictures of features in the village.	Work in pairs: make lists of and describe the jobs that men and women do in Chembakolli; look for similarities and differences between shops and markets in the UK and in India.	● understand the different kinds of jobs people do in Chembakolli ● identify similarities and differences between shops and markets in India and in the UK.	English: writing brief descriptions of jobs. ICT: word-processing captions and descriptions; using a CD-ROM to access information on climate and tea and coffee production.

Resources
Globes, world maps and atlases; aerial photographs of India; copies of an A4 outline map of India, and one A2 outline map, showing its borders with other countries; Indian posters, photographs and artefacts; wall maps showing the UK and India; outline maps showing the countries and positions of capital cities between the UK and India; access to Teletext; a list of countries and capital cities flown over on the way to India; airline routes to India; access to the ActionAid website *www.chembakolli.com*; labelled photographs and copies of the base map of Chembakolli from the website; copies of a large-scale OS map of a local village; photographs of a selection of local houses; a school-made worksheet about houses and schools locally and in Chembakolli; a selection of materials to make a model house or a classroom; A3 paper; pictures of markets and shops in the UK and in India; 5cm^2 graph paper; a selection of produce typically grown in and around Chembakolli.
  Further resources available from ActionAid Education (Chataway House, Leach Road, Chard, Somerset TA20 1FR; tel. 01460 238000) include: a photopack, *Chembakolli: a village in India*; a CD-ROM, *Take me to Chembakolli*; a video, *Working Together: the people of Kanjikolly* (exploring life in a neighbouring village to Chembakolli); a series of printed and CD-ROM resources, *Village Life in India*; a big book, *Footprints in the forest: a Chembakolli story* (with a reader and a CD of clipart and songs); and two A1 wallcharts produced in association with PCET Publishing, *India and her neighbours* and *Chembakolli journeys*.

Display
An A2 map of India, or a picture map using a collection of paintings or sketches as a collage. Children's maps showing their routes to Chembakolli, linked to published maps. Leaflets describing a tour around Chembakolli, linked to the pictorial chart (see above). Children's maps of Chembakolli. Annotated pictures and models of a house or classroom in Chembakolli. Pictures and photographs, with captions, of shops and markets in the UK and in India.

CHAPTER 5
VILLAGE CASE STUDIES

Chembakolli:
village life in
India

① Where are Asia, India and Chembakolli?

① hour

What you need and preparation
Globes, world maps and atlases. CD-ROMs and access to the Internet and e-mail facilities would be useful. Aerial photographs of India. An A4 outline map of India, showing its borders with other countries. Other resources, including posters, photographs and artefacts that show various lifestyles and landscapes and the cultural diversity of India. An A2 outline map of India and its neighbouring countries.

What to do

⑩ mins Introduction
Start with a short brainstorming session to assess the extent of the children's knowledge about India. Write down their ideas on the board, flip chart or OHT. Explore some of these ideas with the children to emphasise key points such as aspects of India's location, climate, landscape, agriculture, people and culture. Correct any misconceptions the children may have.

Talk to the children about Chembakolli.

⑩ mins Development
Give small groups of children a selection of maps, atlases, aerial photographs and globes, as well as access to CD-ROMs, the Internet and e-mail facilities (if possible). Ask them to locate the positions of the UK, Europe, Asia, India and Chembakolli. You will not find Chembakolli on a map, as the Forest Department say it is an illegal settlement; but you will find the local town of Gudalur. Land rights are very important in this and other parts of India, and tribal people have been pushed off their land.

Now ask them to find out the names of the different countries, seas and oceans that share a border with India, and the main centres of human activity within the country. Encourage them to find out as much as they can about the climate of India. The climatic maps found in atlases and CD-ROMs will be useful here. The children should use the information collected from their research to add the main physical features, including seas, rivers, mountains and some of the main cities, to the blank outline map of India.

The groups should then collect their information together to make a larger-group or whole-class map of India for display. This could take the form of a large picture map, using sketches and paintings to show India's changing landscape and human activities; or a collage of photographs and pictures, some of which may be downloaded from a CD-ROM; or an outline map with photographs placed on it and annotated. Some children could write letters or e-mails to embassies and tourist information offices, asking for general information about India.

⑩ mins Plenary
Complete an unlabelled A2 map of India and the surrounding countries with the children. Ask some of the children to point to India and the surrounding countries on this map and label them, then do the same for the surrounding seas and oceans. (An **ocean** covers a very large area of water; a **sea** covers a smaller area, and may be a geographically distinct part of an ocean or an inland mass of water.) Ask them to say what shape India has. Now ask some children to mark on and label some of the important cities and natural features. Ask a child to try to locate Gudalur and the Nilgiri Hills, the region that Chembakolli is in.

Ask individuals or pairs of children to give pieces of information about India from the research that they have done (for example, the names of cities or rivers). Add additional information to the map if possible.

Differentiation

More able children should be encouraged to find out about and describe the climate of India. Climatic maps and graphs in atlases and CD-ROMs can be used for this. They should try to draw a climatic map of India on one of the blank outlines, and add a key and colour code.

Less able children should be given clearer, more elementary material to use for their research, and can help to put the key physical and human features onto the outline map.

Assessing learning outcomes

Can the children locate the UK and India in various types of reference material? Can they draw maps to show locational information? Are they becoming aware of the main physical and human features of India? Do they appreciate the diversity of India's landscape, climate and culture?

Follow-up activities
Find out about the state of Tamil Nadu in southern India. Construct a factfile about the state, using the headings *Landscape, Climate, People, Agriculture, Industry, Beliefs and customs, History, Education* and *Transport*. Print some facts about Tamil Nadu in a large font for display next to a class map of India with the state highlighted on it.

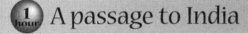

A passage to India

What you need and preparation

Atlases, maps and globes; wall maps showing the UK and India. Access to Teletext. Outline maps showing the countries between the UK and India. A list of countries and capitals flown over on the way to India, cut up and mixed up. A battery clock to display Chembakolli time and a sheet of six clock faces.

Information on airline routes between the UK and India, including distances travelled and countries crossed. Travel agents or airlines may be able to supply this information; they will need to be contacted well in advance. In-flight magazines may also be useful for information; often they show an airline's flight network around the world.

A visitor from India would be useful for the plenary session, but is not essential.

What to do

Introduction
Talk to the children about how they would travel to India. *What are the advantages of travelling by air instead of by sea?* Show the material obtained from travel agents or airlines about routes and flight times.

Scroll through the pages of Teletext that relate to flights from regional and national airports on any particular day. Note any flights from the UK to India during that day. Use a wall map to locate airports in the UK and India.

Discuss with the children what they think India and Chembakolli are like. Brainstorm some questions they would like to ask in order to find out more about these places.

Development
Ask each pair of children to plan a route to Gudalur, a town near Chembakolli in India, using maps, atlases and other information sources. They should plot their route to India on the outline map, using the airline route or one of their own devising; list the countries they will be flying over and their capital cities; and work out the approximate distance of their flight. (The flight should not have intermediate stops.) They should also try to plan their journey to the airport in the UK, and from the airport in India to Chembakolli. Ask them to think about how they will reach Chembakolli from their flight destination.

Plenary
(This will take 30 minutes if a visitor can be arranged.) Ask a selection of pairs to describe

Learning objectives
● Find out how places are connected.
● Make maps and draw routes.
● Use and interpret maps and globes.
● Use secondary sources.

Lesson organisation
Teacher-led introduction, including use of Teletext; paired or small-group activity work; results shared with the class or large groups in the plenary session, when a visitor from India may be present.

Vocabulary
route
distance
kilometre
airport
airline

CHAPTER 5
VILLAGE CASE STUDIES

Chembakolli: village life in India

ICT opportunities
● Word-process questions about India and Chembakolli.
● Draw a line graph to show the distances between capital cities and the time it would take to travel between them.

Follow-up activities
● Find out the actual flight path of aircraft from the UK to India. Photocopy an outline map onto acetate and draw on the flight path; place this on top of the children's maps for comparison.
● Look at time zones. Use two clock faces to work out what time it is in Chembakolli. Put a clock on the wall, giving Chembakolli time, while this unit of work is being covered.

their route to India, using a wall map or globe, to the rest of the class or a large group. Ask them to give the names of the countries they will fly over, and the total distance of the flight.

Ask the children to read out their questions (from the initial brainstorming session) that they would ask to find out more about India and Chembakolli. Discuss the sources of information that could be used to find out the answer to each question. (If possible, ask the visitor these questions and note the answers.)

Differentiation

More able children can be encouraged to calculate the approximate flight time to India, if they travel at 800km/h using their own route, and compare it to the flight times advertised. They can measure the distances between capital cities on the way to India.

Less able children should be given the countries and capitals list; using an atlas, they should put the countries in the order in which they will be flown over, starting with the UK and ending with India. Next to each, they should place its capital city.

Assessing learning outcomes

Can the children complete and follow a simple map showing a route to India? Can they ask questions about what places are like?

1 hour The landscape of Chembakolli

Learning objectives
● Make maps based on pictures.
● Give simple grid references.
● Learn how to use a scale and calculate distances from a map.
● Describe a route.
● Make a land use map.

Lesson organisation
Teacher-led discussion and questioning using photocards; individual activity work (including an alternative for more able children); teacher-led plenary session to assess the children's knowledge and understanding.

Vocabulary
landscape
market
community centre
well
temple
tank
clinic
agriculture
crops
irrigation
valley

What you need and preparation

Photocards 1–2 from the Chembakolli website www.chembakolli.com; a series of labels for them, including *forests, Nilgiri Hills, farmland, valley bottom, cleared hillsides, crops*; a main title, *The Landscape Around Chembakolli*. Copies of photocopiable pages 156 (copied onto cm² graph paper) and 157; plain A4 paper. Copies of the base map of Chembakolli from www.chembakolli.com. A copy of an OS map of a local village.

What to do

10 mns **Introduction**
Look at photographs 1–2 from the website and discuss what the landscape is like in each of them; look in turn at the shape of the land, the amount and kind of vegetation, and the agriculture – especially hillside clearances, irrigation and the shape and size of the fields.

Look at the map in the pack, and ask the children how Chembakolli would compare with a village in the UK. Look for awareness of differences in styles of buildings, village layout and land use, as well as common features such as roads, bus stop and post office.

Identify and talk about specific buildings in the village, and how the land around it is used. Look to see how the map of Chembakolli compares with an OS map of a local village.

40 mns **Development**
Ask the children (working individually) to use the map from www.chembakolli.com to draw a small map of the village. They should label the human and physical features shown in the map. Ask them to compare their map with the map on page 156 to see how accurate they have been.

Help the children to put grid numbers on the map photocopied from page 156 onto graph paper. They should use two-figure references up the side of the map (northings) and different two-figure references from left to right (eastings). Remind them to mark the references on the lines of the graph paper, not in the spaces between them. Ask them to list the physical and human features of the village, with a four-figure grid reference (eastings followed by northings) next to each.

Ask the children to give directions from places in the village to other places – for example, from the 'balwadi' (nursery school) to the well or from the coffee nursery to Bospara. They should use the scale to estimate the distance they would need to walk, and use the compass points to give the approximate direction. Encourage them to describe the features of each route.

As an alternative activity, the children should use photocopiable page 157 to plan a tour guide to Chembakolli. After filling in the sheet, they should fold a sheet of A4 plain paper into three equal parts and use it in a similar way to draw and describe features in and around the village, as if they were showing a stranger around.

Plenary
10 mins
Ask the children to describe the landscape of Chembakolli and the features of the village. Discuss how it compares with a local village.

Ask a selection of children to describe a journey around Chembakolli, concentrating on the landscape and land uses. Other children can follow the journey being described on their maps.

If the alternative activity is undertaken, ask some children to act as tour guides to Chembakolli, using their leaflets for reference. Other children can use their maps to 'follow' the tour guide.

Differentiation

Throughout the activities, more able children should be encouraged to use and interpret the map of the village rather than the picture maps. They should look at the similarities and differences, in terms of form and function, between Chembakolli and a local village. They should undertake the tour guide activity.

Less able children may respond more positively to the picture maps, and should not draw a map to compare with the map on photocopiable page 156. They should be encouraged to complete all the activities except making the tour guide.

Assessing learning outcomes

Can the children make a map to show the main features of a village? Can they use a map to find directions and distances? How well can they recognise and describe the main physical and human features of a village?

ICT opportunities
● Access information on the Chembakolli website www.chembakolli.com.
● Word-process captions, descriptions of features, directions around the village and the tourist guide (if tackled).

Follow-up activities
● Working in groups, make a model of the village and label the key facilities.
● Word-process a description of the village; draw or paint pictures of it.

The buildings in Chembakolli
1 hour

What you need and preparation
Photographs 7 and 16 from the ActionAid website www.chembakolli.com; copies of photographs 17 and 29. Photographs of a selection of local houses. Copies of two worksheets, each divided into two columns: the first entitled 'Houses in Chembakolli' and 'Houses close to school', the second 'The school in Chembakolli' and 'Our school'. A selection of materials the children can use to make models of houses in Chembakolli, including smaller cardboard boxes and straw or hay. Plain A3 paper.

What to do

Introduction
10 mins
Encourage the children to look at the photographs of the houses in Chembakolli. Ask them to describe what they can see, and how the traditional houses in the village compare with their own. Use the board or flip chart to note their responses.

Describe the inside of a traditional house: one room which is a sleeping area, and a kitchen with a hole in the thatched roof to allow smoke from the fire to escape. Ask the children to

Learning objectives
● Use secondary sources.
● Consider the similarities and differences between places.
● Annotate pictures of features in a village.

Lesson organisation
Teacher-led initial discussion; small-group and paired activity work (larger groups if models are made); plenary session with children feeding back to larger groups or the class.

Chembakolli: village life in India

compare the insides of these houses with their own.

Look at the photo of the 'balwadi' (nursery school) in Chembakolli. Again, ask the children to describe what they can see and how the school compares with their own.

40 mins Development

(This will take two hours if the model is made.) Divide the class into groups of three or four. Half the class should look at the similarities and differences between houses in Chembakolli and in their local area, while the other half look at similarities and differences between the schools. In pairs, they should complete the appropriate worksheet, using local photographs to help them.

Give out copies of photographs 17 and 29 (the school and a house in Chembakolli). Ask pairs of children to glue their copy into the middle of a plain A3 sheet. Around the margin, they should note differences and similarities between the school and their own, or between the house and a local house, linking each annotation to the appropriate place on the picture. They should add a title.

Alternatively, small groups of children can use secondary sources to model a house or classroom that they would find in Chembakolli. Houses could be based on a shoe-box, with a roof made of card overlaid with straw. Encourage the children to design the house so that the roof can be taken off to reveal its internal layout of the house. The classroom could be larger, with the inside revealed via a cut-away side.

10 mins Plenary

Ask pairs of children to feed back to the opposite groups, so that children looking at houses feed back to those looking at schools and so on.

Use the board or flip chart to list and rank the five most significant differences between houses in Chembakolli and locally, then the five most significant differences between the schools.

Differentiation

More able children should be encouraged to write a short paragraph to describe houses or schools in Chembakolli.

Less able children can complete a structured chart to identify similarities and differences between houses and schools in Chembakolli and locally. This will identify specific characteristics for the children to comment on, such as (for houses) roofs, windows, doors, walls, overall size, inside layout and gardens.

Assessing learning outcomes

Are the children aware of, and able to discuss, the main similarities and differences between homes and schools in Chembakolli and in their own local area?

① How do people earn a living in Chembakolli?

What you need and preparation

Photographs from the Chembakolli website www.chembakolli.com: 5–7 (work), 21–23 (farming) and 25 (market). Pictures of other markets and shops in India and the UK. Strips of 5cm² graph paper, 13 squares long and 2 squares wide. A selection of produce (from a local market or shops) of the kinds typically grown in and around Chembakolli: onions, tomatoes, potatoes, okra, garlic, bananas, peppers, tea and coffee beans.

What to do

⑳ Introduction

Show the children photographs 5–7 from the website, and ask them to say what jobs are being done by the women. Explain the importance of the jobs that women do in the running of their homes in Chembakolli, and how difficult they are – for example, carrying six litres of water for 300m up to four times a day. Talk to the children about the jobs that the men do in the fields of the big estates: clearing the land, hoeing and planting crops. Explain how difficult these jobs are without the modern conveniences that we take for granted.

Look at photographs 21–23. Ask the children to say what is happening in each picture; cover the titles on the cards and ask the children to put them in order. Talk about how difficult picking tea leaves is, and how poorly the women tea pickers get paid compared with people in the UK: approximately 50 rupees per day. The cost of living is, though, much lower in India than in the UK.

Look at photograph 25 (a market stall) and ask the children to identify the produce for sale. Look at other photographs of markets and shops in India and the UK.

㉚ Development

Ask the children, working in pairs or small groups, to make a list of jobs done by women and another of jobs done by men. They should write a brief description of what each job involves.

Ask them to use what they know to plan a typical day for a woman in Chembakolli. They should incorporate some of the forms of unpaid, but necessary, work that are done to maintain a household.

Ask them to compare the pictures of markets and shops in India and the UK. They should look for similarities and differences in size and layout, and in the types of produce sold.

⑩ Plenary

Ask some pairs of children to talk about the differences between the jobs done by women and by men in Chembakolli. Ask which jobs they would find the most demanding, and why. Ask which of all the modern facilities that we have in the UK would be the most useful in Chembakolli, and why.

Ask the children how they think they would manage if they and their partner together earned about £2.00 a day. *What kinds of things would you need to buy? How would you save up, in case you were ill and could not work?* Your children should understand that the relative costs of everyday items are much lower in India, but that basic rights are denied to tribal people.

Ask the children to describe the main similarities and differences between shops and markets in India and in the UK.

Differentiation

More able children could undertake some work on the three main seasons of southern India (see 'Follow-up activities'), collecting statistics for temperature and rainfall. Encourage them to consider what it would be like to work outside in this type of climate. They can compare their findings with

Learning objectives
• Use secondary sources.
• Know about similarities and differences between places.
• Understand that the farmer's year is dictated by the weather.

Lesson organisation
Teacher-led introduction, using secondary source material; paired activity work; opportunity for an adult to prepare food; teacher-led plenary session with children answering questions.

Vocabulary
market
shops
trade
cash crops
occupation
estates

Chembakolli: village life in India

ICT opportunities
- Access information on the Chembakolli website www.chembakolli.com.
- Word-process captions and descriptions.
- Use a CD-ROM to access information on India's climate, and on tea and coffee production.

local climate information in the UK.

Less able children could produce captions for the jobs done by men and women instead of writing descriptions. They will need help in showing a farmer's year (see 'Follow-up activities'), and in identifying similarities and differences between the markets and shops of India and the UK. They should use a minimum number of photographs.

Assessing learning outcomes

How well are the children aware of the different economic activities practised in Chembakolli? Can they use secondary sources to identify similarities and differences between the ways of selling and trading goods in Chembakolli and in a village in the UK?

A farmer's year

Cool season: Nov–Mar. Hot season: Apr–May. Monsoon: June–Oct.
Harvest: Dec–Feb. Planting: June–July. Weeding: Sept–Nov. Farmers work on tea and coffee estates throughout the year, as well as on preparing their own land.

Follow-up activities
- Help the children make an Indian meal, using foodstuffs typically produced around Chembakolli. Talk about what it is called, what the ingredients are and what it tastes like.
- Use the strips of 5cm² graph paper to show a Chembakolli farmer's year. Use the first pair of squares for the title, the 12 upper squares to sketch different farming activities, and the 12 bottom squares to name the activities and the season (see above). Similar activities can be merged.
- Find out about tea production in India: planting, picking, drying, processing and retailing. Ask UK companies for information on the tea industry.

Clapham – a village in the Yorkshire Dales

The Yorkshire Dales National Park comprises 1769 square kilometres of limestone countryside in the Central Pennine uplands. It is home to about 19 000 people. It is the third largest National Park in the country. Most of the land in the Dales is privately owned farmland.

The Dales began as a series of river valleys, worn and shaped by glaciers from three successive ice ages that gradually scoured and flooded the area. The base rocks of the Dales are over 280 million years old. These sedimentary rocks were formed under the sea and consist of limestone, shale, slate, gritstone and sandstone. Erosion and weathering have exposed many of the area's characteristic limestone formations, such as scars, caves, gorges and dry valleys, which are seen each year by millions of visitors.

The Yorkshire Dales has about half of the **limestone pavement** in the UK. This is a formation in which the natural cracks in the limestone have been weathered and widened to produce a distinctive scenery of grooved and ridged limestone. There are three major peaks in the Dales: Whernside (736m), Ingleborough (723m) and Pen-y-ghent (694m). The Gaping Gill cave system is approximately 110m deep, and is an impressive part of an 8km complex of underground passages and caves.

The Dales are, on average, 300m above sea level, and so the climate is predominantly cool and wet. Rainfall is high: the west of the Dales receives approximately 1800mm of rain a year, the east 1000mm. There are many days of frost, and often significant amounts of snow.

The whole of the Dales is criss-crossed by miles of dry stone walls that separate hay meadows and fields for grazing sheep. Beef cattle are raised on the lower, better-quality farmland on the valley floors. Quarrying is an important source of income for local people: limestone quarry products are used in the construction, road-building and soil-conditioning industries. Tourism is the newest and fastest-growing industry in the Dales, with almost 10 million visitor days being spent in the National Park annually. Visitors come for the walking, climbing and cycling opportunities. Money from tourists helps to support the economy of the area. However, increasing numbers of tourists can create problems for the countryside they come to enjoy: traffic congestion, worn footpaths, broken-down walls and cottages sold as holiday homes are some of the problems that increased popularity and accessibility have brought to the area.

Clapham is an estate village. It owes much of its present-day character to its owners, the Farrer family, who lived in Ingleborough Hall in the village and owned some 35 000 acres of land. Today, the estate has shrunk to about 10 000, acres most of which is moorland. Of the original sixteen farms, nine remain. Over 40 of the 100 homes in the village are still owned by the Farrer family. About 250 people live in the village.

Ingleborough Hall, a late Georgian building, is reached from the village by a short drive and a tunnel. In Victorian times, a public right of way that ran close to the Hall meant that people walking or riding along it could see inside. The tunnel was built to keep road users out of sight of the Hall; the Farrers kept the original road (above the tunnel) as a private road to the woods nearby. In 1946, staff employed at the Hall comprised two labourers, two joiners, two plumbers, two masons, one storeman, one slater, four woodsmen and at least two gardeners, as well as some domestic staff.

The reservoir was constructed in 1833 to supply the village with water by damming Clapham Beck, which flows through the centre of the village. In 1897, a small generator turned by water flowing from the reservoir was used to provide one light for each house in the village and street lighting – this was the first community in the country to have electric streetlamps.

Clapham – a village in the Yorkshire Dales

Information needed for this unit of work

The farmer's year
Jan. muck-spreading, feed sheep, pre-lambing vaccinations.
Feb. scan sheep in lamb, test cows for pregnancy, feed sheep, muck-spreading.
Mar. vaccinate cows, calving starts, feed sheep, muck-spreading.
Apr. calving, lambing, put cows to pasture (if weather is good enough).
May dehorn calves, send last year's calves to market, spread fertiliser on land; test, worm and mark all lambs.
June dip sheep, make silage and hay into bales.
July make hay, fertilise fields after cutting, take last year's fatter calves to market.
Aug. cut second silage, dip all lambs, buy in straw.
Sept. dip female lambs, clip their undersides and send them to market.
Oct. send hogs to Cheshire for the winter.
Nov. bring in cows for the winter.
Dec. send more lambs to auction, give hay to sheep (bring some in in bad weather). Other jobs done: mending fences and walls, digging drains, cleaning buildings, maintaining water supplies in fields, unloading fodder and fertiliser, buying equipment and materials, doing business administration.

Jobs people do in Clapham (full-time and part-time)			
Market gardening	11	Post office	1
Garage	19	School	8
Publishing	6	Estate	4
Outdoor Education Centre	19	Show cave	3
Building contractors	12	Contract transport	19
Joiner	1	Fitted furniture	2
Cabinet maker	1	Farm	9
Guest house	4	Gamekeeping	2
Café	4	Electrician	1
Hotel	13	Artist/lecturer	2
Gift shop	8	National Park Info. Centre	2
General store	3	Hairdresser	1

Where do the people of Clapham work?	
Place	**Workers**
Clapham	48
Austwick	2
Ingleton	3
Horton	1
Bentham	2
Settle	6
Lancaster	5
Kendal	3
Burnley	1

Visitors have come to Clapham from:			
Powell River, Canada	Exeter	Ottawa, Canada	Stoke
High Wycombe	Rawmarsh (S. Yorks.)	Sheffield	Northampton
Keswick	Sherbourne	Southport	Edinburgh
Rugby	Halifax	Chester	Brussells, Belgium
Crewe	Clitheroe	Leicester	Lund, Sweden
Bradford	Sunderland	Baden-Baden, Germany	York
Warrington	Leeds	Oakham	Hultsfred, Sweden
Chatham	Grantham	Hull	Derby
Ipswich	Basingstoke	Potter's Bar	Accrington
St Helen's	Mansfield	Aldershot	Sandbach
London	Skipton	Rotherham	Stafford

UNIT 10: Clapham – a village in the Yorkshire Dales

Enquiry questions	Teaching objectives	Teaching activities	Learning outcomes	Cross-curricular links
Where are North Yorkshire and Clapham? How can we find out about these places?	• Investigate places. • Use globes, atlases and maps. • Use secondary sources to access information. • Identify physical and human features.	Work as individuals or in pairs: locate North Yorkshire and Clapham using maps of different scales; mark physical and human features of North Yorkshire on an outline map; find out about the climate; make a poster using secondary source material.	Children: • locate North Yorkshire and Clapham • complete an outline map showing the main physical and human features • access information about climate	Maths: drawing and interpreting graphs. ICT: using a CD-ROM to access information; word-processing text.
How is Clapham connected to other places? How easy is it to get to and from Clapham?	• Understand how places are connected. • Use atlases and maps. • Use timetables.	Paired or individual work: describe routes between Clapham and local places; work out and describe routes from Clapham to more distant places in the UK; complete a worksheet using bus timetables.	• find a route and prepare a map for a journey to Clapham • describe what Clapham might be like • understand how limiting public transport can be for commuters	English: describing routeways. ICT: word-processing descriptions of routes; using software to locate places and calculate distances on a scanned map.
What is the area around Clapham like?	• Complete a field sketch. • Draw a route and label parts of it. • Use a scale and calculate distances. • Identify important OS symbols.	Paired work: construct a walk around Clapham using maps; complete a generalised relief map and field sketch; make a colour code.	• make a walker's map • complete a relief map and colour code • complete a field sketch • compare villages using an OS map	Maths: calculating distances on a map using a scale; calculating journey times. ICT: drawing a walk using a graphics package; word-processing labels for the walk.
What are buildings like in Clapham, what are they made of? What is the land used for?	• Use secondary sources. • Talk about the differences and similarities between places. • Interpret a large-scale map. • Make a land use map and key.	Work in pairs: make a land use map and colour code; use large-scale maps to describe a short walk; describe building types and other features.	• are aware of the differences between different types of buildings • identify different kinds of land use • describe a walk using large-scale maps	ICT: word-processing; using a graphics package to design a land use key.
What kinds of jobs do people do in the village? Where do people who live in the village go to work?	• Appreciate the importance of tourism. • Consider differences in lifestyle and patterns of work between people who live in Clapham and in Chembakolli. • Construct a chart from geographical data. • Estimate and calculate distances using maps.	Paired and some individual work: draw a diagram to show a farmer's year in Clapham and compare it to Chembakolli; look at ways of earning a living from tourism in Clapham, and other jobs (and journeys to work) for local people; plot where visitors to Clapham have come from.	• use secondary sources • understand how different places are connected • discuss the similarities and differences in farming between Clapham and Chembakolli.	Maths: constructing pie and bar charts; using a scale to calculate distances. ICT: word-processing lists and descriptions.

Resources
Globes, atlases, road atlases, OS maps of North Yorkshire; A4 outline maps of North Yorkshire; CD-ROM facilities; holiday brochures and leaflets featuring North Yorkshire; climatic maps of the UK; A4 and A3 plain paper; road atlases; maps of Clapham and the surrounding area at 1:25 000 scale; an A4 outline map of the UK; a school-made worksheet on bus timetables; copies or A4 extracts of a 1:25 000 OS map of Clapham; A4 tracing paper; a land use key; samples of building materials; graph paper; OS maps at 1:25 000 and 1:50 000 or road atlases; 'farmer's year' background information; an A4 map showing the different regions of the UK; worksheets listing various people's jobs and where they come from to visit Clapham.

Display
Children's maps of North Yorkshire. Maps at different scales showing the position of North Yorkshire and Clapham. Posters of North Yorkshire. Routes Cland descriptions of journeys to Clapham. Relief maps and field sketches showing walks in the area around Clapham. Completed land use maps and descriptions. Diagrams of the farmer's year. Graphs and charts relating to employment and tourism in and around Clapham.

CHAPTER 5
VILLAGE CASE STUDIES

Clapham - a village in the Yorkshire Dales

① Where are North Yorkshire and Clapham?

Learning objectives
• Investigate places.
• Use globes, atlases and maps of different scales to find places.
• Use secondary sources, including ICT, to access information.
• Identify physical and human features of places.

Lesson organisation
Teacher-led introduction, including brainstorming session; paired or small-group activities involving small-scale research; some children feeding back in plenary session.

Vocabulary
county
settlement
town
city
river
climate
landscape
human features
physical features

What you need and preparation
Globes, atlases, road atlases. A selection of OS maps of North Yorkshire; a wall map of the UK; an A4-sized outline map of North Yorkshire. CD-ROM facilities; holiday brochures; leaflets that feature North Yorkshire. Climatic maps of the UK (found in atlases). Plain A4 paper; A3 poster paper.

What to do
🔟 Introduction
Divide the class into small groups, and give each a sheet of A4 paper to brainstorm what they know about North Yorkshire and Clapham. On the back of the sheet, they should write down questions they would ask to find out more about the two places. They may have many more questions than facts! After about five minutes, ask each group to read out what they have. List the information on the board or flip chart, talking briefly about each item as it is added. On another board or flip chart sheet, list the questions they would ask to find out more about North Yorkshire and Clapham. Keep these lists on display.

🔟 Development
Give each small group of children a selection of globes and maps; ask them to locate North Yorkshire and Clapham unaided, using the method of working down from smaller-scale to larger-scale maps (see page 21). After a few minutes, ask them to point to North Yorkshire on one of the maps that they have, and to Clapham if possible.

Ask the children to use the atlases to mark important physical features on outline maps of North Yorkshire, such as the North Sea and the Pennine Hills. They should mark some human features also, including towns such as Harrogate and Scarborough, and mark on the position of Clapham.

Look at the climate maps of the UK in the atlases, especially those showing patterns of rainfall and summer and winter temperatures. Ask the children to locate North Yorkshire and Clapham on these maps and describe the climate they experience. Compare their findings with the climatic information given in this book (see page 99).

Groups of three or four children should use a CD-ROM and other secondary source material to find out about North Yorkshire, then make an A3 poster to advertise the county. They should focus on contrasts within the county (for example, the Dales and the beaches on the east coast), as well as on the area around Clapham.

🔟 Plenary
Encourage the children to feed back on each activity:
• *Locate North Yorkshire and Clapham on maps of different scales. Label them on the wall map.*
• *Describe some of the main physical and human features in the county, and show where they are.*
• *Talk about the climate of North Yorkshire. How it is different from our climate? Why?* (See 'Differentiation' below.)
• *Talk about the posters you have made to advertise North Yorkshire.*
Ask the class: *Can you now answer any of the questions about North Yorkshire and Clapham that you thought of at the start?*

Differentiation
More able children should be encouraged to produce a detailed map of North Yorkshire, putting on

CHAPTER 5
VILLAGE CASE STUDIES

Clapham – a
village in the
Yorkshire
Dales

neighbouring counties and adding compass points. They could compare the climate statistics for Clapham with those for their home town and write about the differences.

Less able children should be given clearer resource material that will allow them to find North Yorkshire and Clapham more easily. They could be given a map of North Yorkshire (closely based on a specific atlas map) and add to it some physical features and towns as directed by the teacher. They could describe the climate of North Yorkshire using climatic maps, but not make comparisons.

Assessing learning outcomes

Can the children locate North Yorkshire and Clapham, using maps to 'narrow down' the search? Can they complete an outline map to show locational knowledge of the main physical and human features of the region? Are they able to access data on climate and compare it with similar data about other places?

ICT opportunities
• Use a CD-ROM to access information for the poster.
• Word-process text for the poster and comparisons of weather data between places.

Follow-up activities
• Construct a factfile about North Yorkshire, dealing with landscape, climate, agriculture, population and settlements.
• Compare the climate data for Clapham and for Chembakolli. Look at rainfall, temperature and seasonal variations.

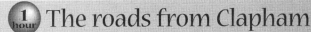

① The roads from Clapham
hour

What you need and preparation

Road atlases or maps of the Clapham area at 1:250 000 scale; OS maps (or extracts) of Clapham at 1:25 000 or 1:50 000 scale. A4-sized outline maps of North Yorkshire and of the UK; plain A4 paper.

Prepare a worksheet about the bus services from Clapham, including the bus timetable information given below. Add some fictitious questions from local people, perhaps in speech bubbles – for example: *I have a dental appointment in Settle at 10.30. What time must I catch a bus to get there?*

Populations	
Settle (with Giggleswick)	4770
Ingleton	1990

Clapham to Ingleton

Mon–Fri
 0847 1026 1106 1258 1748 1919
Sat. (no Sunday service)
 1055 1255 1515 1745
Journey time: **10 mins.**

Clapham to Settle

Mon–Fri
 0817 0909 1139 1409 1705 1845
Sat (no Sunday service)
 0817 0909 1139 1409 1704
Journey time: **13 mins.**

Learning objectives
• Understand how places are connected.
• Use atlases and maps.
• Use timetables.

Lesson organisation
Teacher-led introduction; paired or individual activity work; children feed back in plenary session, with the main teaching points being covered.

Vocabulary
route
distance
road
motorway
lane
track
bridleway

What you need

⑩ **Introduction**
mins Look at Clapham on the 1:25 000 or 1:50 000 map. Talk about the routeways that connect the village to other villages and towns. Look at the road atlas or 1:250 000 map; find Clapham and other nearby towns and villages.

Clapham – a village in the Yorkshire Dales

Look at the bus timetable for Clapham. Ask: *How often do the buses run?* Consider how useful they would be for local people who needed to get to work, the shops or a doctor's appointment at a particular time.

Ask the children what they think Clapham is like as a place to live.

Development
40 mins

Look at the local OS maps or extracts. Ask the children to describe the routeways between Clapham and some local farms, some other villages and a nearby town (verbally). They should write descriptions of one or two of these routeways, based on the map information.

Use the road atlases or 1:250 000 maps to see how Clapham is connected to more distant places. Ask the children to work out the most direct route from two or three places in the UK to Clapham. They should record the routes they would take on the outline map of North Yorkshire (if the place is close by) or the outline map of the UK (for more distant places), marking on important towns that they would go through or past.

Ask the children to complete a teacher-made worksheet (see above) about the bus services from Clapham to neighbouring settlements. For the 'doctor's appointment' example, they could consider how convenient the buses are by looking at the waiting time between arriving in Settle and the appointment.

Plenary
10 mins

Ask individuals or pairs to describe how Clapham is connected to nearby villages and towns. Encourage the other children to follow these routes on their own OS maps, and to contribute to the discussion if they feel they can add accuracy and clarity. Ask other children to describe journeys to Clapham from more distant places. Again, other children can follow these routes and say whether or not they could make the journey shorter.

Ask the children to comment on how useful the local bus service to Clapham is. *How would you like to live in Clapham if buses were your only form of transport?*

Differentiation

More able children should be asked to describe the longer and more difficult journeys, and should provide more detail about the landscape they pass through. They should calculate the waiting times between events and subsequent buses on the worksheet.

Less able children should concentrate on the shorter journeys, and use the OS maps rather than the road atlases. They should be encouraged to find the 'best bus' for each event on the worksheet, but not to calculate the subsequent waiting times.

Assessing learning outcomes

How well can the children find a route and prepare a map of a journey from Clapham? Can they describe what they think Clapham might be like? How well do they understand how limiting the public transport currently available can be?

ICT opportunities
- Word-process descriptions of routes to Clapham from nearby and more distant places.
- Use mapping software to locate various places in the UK and calculate the distances between them.

Follow-up activities
- Encourage the children to give accurate (but brief) descriptions of routes from places in the UK to Clapham. They can draw simplified 'topological maps' (places joined to others using straight lines, with circles for destinations, as in the London Underground map) to help them.
- Find routes and calculate the approximate total distances between chosen towns and cities in the UK.

1 hour The landscape of Clapham

What you need and preparation

Copies or extracts of the 1:25 000 OS map of Clapham and the surrounding area (*Outdoor Leisure 2 – Yorkshire Dales, southern and western areas*). A4 extracts should be in portrait format, with Clapham in the middle towards the south and Ingleborough in the far north. Colour photocopies of this area are cheaper, longer-lasting and much quieter than large folded A1 maps in the context of classroom work.

Copies of photocopiable page 158. A4 tracing paper and plain paper. A generalised A4 relief map showing the landscape around Clapham: the lower land (the area divided into fields), the reservoir, the areas of scars and the higher land (including Ingleborough and the main road).

What you need

10 mins Introduction

Ask groups of children to look at the OS map and find various villages on it, such as Clapham, Newby, Ingleton and the various hamlets in between. They should also find: the A65T main road from Skipton to the Lake District, Clapham Beck, the cave system between Clapham and Ingleborough, Ingleborough itself, areas of woodland, and 'scar' areas of exposed and eroded limestone (which are typical of this part of the Yorkshire Dales). They should also look further, into the surrounding Dales areas.

Look at the village of Clapham and ask the children to describe its facilities and character, based on the OS map. Compare Clapham with other villages nearby, such as Newby and Ingleton.

Give out the generalised relief map and describe it to the children. Ask them to identify different areas and to describe how the land rises from the south to the north.

Give out copies of photocopiable page 158. Talk to the children about **field sketches**: simplified sketches that focus on the main physical and human features of a landscape.

40 mins Development

The children should work in pairs on these activities.

Use the map extracts and tracing paper to construct a walk around Clapham and the surrounding countryside. The walk should start and finish in the village, and visit places that give this part of the Dales its unique character (such as the scars, caves and peaks). Trace this route on tracing paper, and label interesting features and stopping points on the way. Work out how long the walk is, where the easy and difficult parts of the walk are, and approximately how much time the walk might take. (3km/h is a good average walking speed in this environment.)

Complete the generalised relief map to show the different types of land around Clapham; use the OS map extract for reference. Make a colour code to show the different types of land (see above), and colour the map in the appropriate colours. Name specific places and areas, and add spot heights. Together, talk about the general landscape of the area, saying where the main highland areas, scars and fields are, and describing the position of Clapham. (It is in a small wooded valley.)

Look at photocopiable page 158 and discuss what each feature is. Use the list to label them.

10 mins Plenary

Find out from the children what the landscape around Clapham is like.

Ask a selection of children to describe their walk while other children follow it on their map extract. Ask each pair to say why they decided to visit the places they mentioned.

Ask other children to describe the landscape around Clapham in general terms, using the relief map. *Where is the highest land and where is the lowest? What is the difference in height?*

Learning objectives
- Complete a field sketch.
- Draw a route and label parts of it.
- Use a scale to calculate distances.
- Identify OS symbols.

Lesson organisation
Teacher-led introduction; paired activity work; teacher-led plenary session, pulling together ideas from the lesson.

Vocabulary
landscape
peaks
scars
valley
woodland
erosion
weathering
limestone
caves
scale

Clapham – a
village in the
Yorkshire Dales

Follow-up activities
● Make a leaflet describing a walk around
Clapham. Use an A4 sheet folded into three.
Include a large map with stopping points,
information about each stopping point,
approximate distances between them, the total
length of the walk and the approximate time it
will take to complete it. Give the leaflet a name
such as 'The Caves Walk' or 'The Scars Near
Clapham'. Some of the leaflets can be enlarged,
labelled and displayed.

Differentiation

More able children could work out the distances between the stopping
points on their walk around Clapham. They could make written comparisons
between Clapham's features and facilities and those of nearby villages.

Less able children will need assistance in constructing their walk around
Clapham and in copying it onto tracing paper. They should concentrate on
completing the photocopiable sheet.

Assessing learning outcomes

Can the children make a walker's map that shows a selection of the main
physical features of the village and the surrounding countryside? Can they
complete a generalised relief map, make a code and use it to show features
of the landscape? Can they use an OS map to identify features of the
village and compare it to other villages?

① hour The buildings in Clapham

**Learning
objectives**
● Use secondary
sources.
● Talk about the
similarities and
differences
between places.
● Interpret a large-
scale map.
● Make a land use
map with a key.

**Lesson
organisation**
Teacher-led
introduction
including map
work; paired
activity work;
teacher-led plenary
session.

Vocabulary
distance
land use
detached
semi-detached
terraced
limestone
slate
rendered
tiles

What you need and preparation

Copies of photocopiable page 159; an enlargement of the map on it. Copies of a land use key (see
below). Tourist information on North Yorkshire from previous lessons. Samples of limestone, slate
and tiles (if possible). Various materials (such as small boxes and cardboard) that the children can
use to model a Dales house.

Land use key
H   houses and gardens
T   transport: roads, paths and car parks
I   industrial: mills, factories and warehouses
S   shops: post office, grocer's and so on
E   entertainment and catering: restaurants, cafés, hotels, tennis courts
P   public services: schools, churches, tourist information offices
W   woodland and parkland
R   rivers and reservoirs
F   fields

What you need

⏱ 10 mins Introduction

Talk about the village of Clapham. Show the children the kinds of materials that houses and
other buildings in the village are made of. The houses are typically built of local limestone and
slate. There are a few variations: some walls are rendered (covered with a thin layer of cement),
and occasionally roofs are made from stone slabs or tiles. Encourage the children to hold samples
of these materials and to comment on their colour, texture and weight. Show the children some
pictures of houses in the Dales from tourist information.

Look at the map of the centre of Clapham on the enlarged extract of photocopiable page 159;
allow the children two or three minutes to explore it. Spend another two or three minutes
encouraging them to find specific places and familiarise themselves with the map. Talk about
detached, semi-detached and terraced houses, and what the differences are.

40 **Development**
mins Give each pair of children a copy of photocopiable page 159 and the land use key. Ask them to use these sources to make a land use map of the village. Some letter codes have been added to the map to help. Remind them that all of the map inside the frame should be coloured in. Ask them to rank the land uses in terms of how much land area they take up, from the largest (estimated) area to the smallest.

Ask the children to use page 159 to devise and write a description of a walk from 'Gildersbank' house to the school. They should write about the function, layout and size of each different type of building passed. They should also mention other nearby features, such as the Beck and the bridges.

Give the children an enlarged copy of the map on page 159. Ask them to use different colours to colour in detached, semi-detached and terraced houses and buildings. Ask them: *Which type of building is the most common in Clapham? Where can each type be found? Where is the oldest part of the village? Is there a pattern to the distribution of the different types of building in the village?* These questions could be written on the board or flip chart to prompt the children while they are completing this activity.

10 **Plenary**
mins Ask the children to describe the land uses in the village. How do they think the pattern of land uses would be different in a town?

Ask a selection of children to describe their walk through Clapham and the buildings that they pass.

Ask other children where they think the centre of the village is, and where most of the detached, semi-detached and terraced buildings are. *Why are there so few detached and semi-detached buildings in the centre of the village?* Ask them for their answers to the questions displayed in the last activity.

Differentiation
More able children could rank the land uses by calculating the areas, using a cm² squared grid copied onto acetate or tracing paper. They could calculate whole and part squares taken up by different land uses.

Less able children could concentrate on the vocabulary used in each activity, and try to complete the building type and basic land use surveys.

Assessing learning outcomes
Are the children aware of differences between types of building? Are they able to identify different types of land use? Can they devise and describe a short walk through a village?

ICT opportunities
• Word-process the description of the walk through Clapham and answers to questions about patterns of housing in the village.
• Use a graphics package to design a land use code and key.

Follow-up activities
• Link the pictures down the right-hand edge of page 159 to the map of Clapham.
• Use materials brought into school to model a Dales house. Different children could model different buildings found in Clapham.

1 **Making a living in Clapham**
hour

What you need and preparation
Copies of photocopiable page 160. Strips of 5cm² graph paper, 13 squares by 2. OS maps of the local area at 1:25 000 or 1:50 000, or road atlases. 'Farmer's year' data (see background information on page 110). A regional map of the UK, including Scotland, Northern Ireland, Wales, East Anglia, the West Midlands, the East Midlands, Yorkshire and the south-west, south-east, north-west and north of England.

A worksheet on where people work, listing the jobs that

Learning objectives
• Appreciate the importance of tourism to a community.
• Consider similarities and differences between life in Clapham and in Chembakolli.
• Construct a chart from geographical data.
• Estimate/calculate distances with maps of different scales.
• Describe routes and journeys.

Lesson organisation
Teacher-led introduction; individual and paired activity work; teacher-led plenary session.

Clapham – a
village in the
Yorkshire Dales

Vocabulary
job
employment
tourist
tourism
farmer
pastoral
route

ICT opportunities
• Word-process all lists and descriptions of routes from Clapham to other settlements.

Follow-up activities
• Imagine you are a tourist visiting Clapham from another part of the UK or Europe. Write a postcard home, telling friends or relatives what Clapham and the landscape around it are like.
• Using the background information, calculate the number of tourists coming from each region of the UK; mark this on a regional map.
• Draw some pictures of (fictitious) tourists and local people on a sheet of paper. Give each person a speech balloon. Write down what the tourists might think about Clapham and surroundings, and what the local people might think about the tourists.

people do in Clapham and where people from the village go to work. (See page 110.) There should be spaces for the children to write in the distances people travel to work, and the best routes for them to take to get there.

A worksheet on where people come from to visit Clapham, giving each home town or country and leaving a space for the distance travelled. (See page 110.) Small maps of the UK and Europe should be drawn on the back of the sheet.

What you need

🕐15 mins Introduction
Using the background information to this unit (see pages 109–110), talk about the farmer's year and the different jobs that need to be done on a pastoral farm in North Yorkshire. (A **pastoral** farm is one that rears livestock, such as sheep and cattle; an **arable** farm is one that grows crops; a mixed farm combines the two.)

Give out the school worksheet about jobs that people do in Clapham. Read through the list of jobs done in the village and decide which ones have to do with tourism. Look at the list of places that other people in the village go to in order to work. Ask: *Which ones do you think are the furthest away?* Explain how to complete the sheet.

Give out the school worksheet on visitors to Clapham. Ask the children to estimate which people have travelled furthest to get to Clapham, and which have come from most nearby. Ask: *Who do you think has come for the day, and who might be staying in or near the village?*

🕐40 mins Development
Ask individuals or pairs to complete photocopiable page 160 by drawing a diagram of the farmer's year. As an alternative, they can construct a farmer's year in strip cartoon form, using a strip of graph paper with one square for each month and another square for the title. Sketches can be drawn on the top row of squares, with the name of the month, the main jobs done and the season written underneath. In discussion, the children should compare the Clapham farmer's year with the farmer's year in Chembakolli (see page 108).

Working in pairs, the children should list the jobs to do with tourism in the village and calculate the number of people employed in these jobs, compared with the number doing other jobs in the village. They should construct a simple pie chart to show the results. Ask them to find the places that people from Clapham travel to in order to work, using a road atlas or OS map. They should use the scale to calculate how far the people travel each day; then choose one place and describe the best route to it.

Ask the children to use atlases and the relevant worksheet to estimate how far some of the visitors have travelled to Clapham, and then to calculate how far all of the visitors have travelled. They should compare the calculation with the estimate and write down the difference in km; then plot where the visitors live on the back of the sheet. Note visitors living outside Europe (for example, in Canada) in the margin of the map (or use a wall map).

Plenary

5 mins Ask the children: *When is the busiest time of the year for farmers in Clapham?* Find out which of the farmer's tasks they think is the most important, and why. Ask:

- *How many of you would like to be a farmer in North Yorkshire?*
- *How does a farmer's year there compare with a farmer's year in Chembakolli?*

Ask how important tourism is to the village, and how far people come especially to visit Clapham or to visit it as part of a holiday in the UK. *What kinds of things do people do when they come to Clapham?* Look at the photocopiable map of Clapham, and find out what places in the village are there for the tourist trade.

Ask where people from Clapham travel to get to work. *Why do you think they travel instead of working in the village? How do you think they get to where they work?*

Differentiation

More able children could think of other ways to show the farmer's year, and look for similarities and differences between farm work here and in Chembakolli. They could construct a pie chart to show the origins of tourists, and describe the 'best routes' between Clapham and local people's workplaces.

Less able children could look for similarities and differences between specific aspects of the farmer's year, such as the jobs done each month. They could be helped to construct a bar chart to show the origins of tourists, and could use an atlas to relate the origins of tourists to the map of the UK.

Assessing learning outcomes

Can the children use secondary sources to explore the nature of farming and the extent of tourism in the area around Clapham? Do they understand how different places are connected? Can they see and discuss the similarities and differences between farming in Clapham and in Chembakolli?

Village land use map

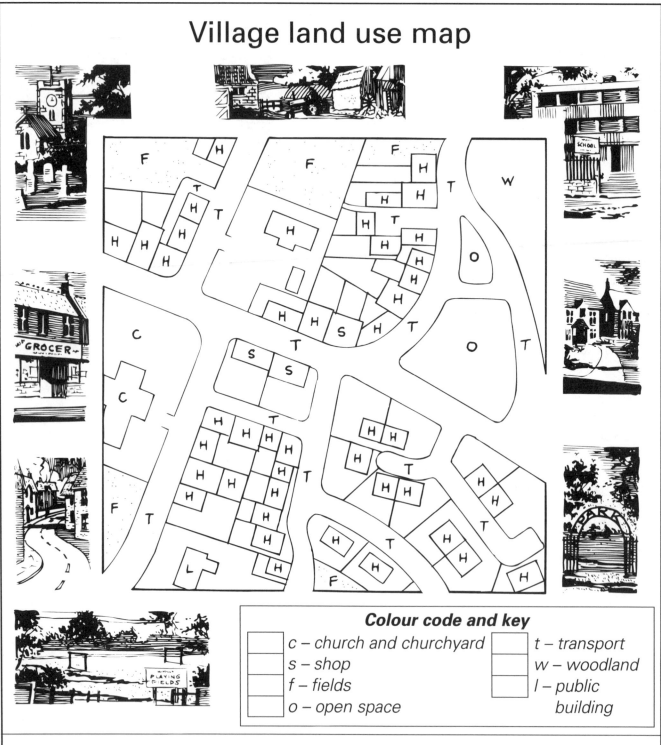

Colour code and key

c – church and churchyard | t – transport
s – shop | w – woodland
f – fields | l – public
o – open space | building

● Colour in the colour code and use it to make a land use map of the village.

● Join each land use shown around the outside to a correct part of the map.

● Rank the land uses, starting with the most important.

● What is most land used for? What is least land used for?

INVESTIGATING OUR LOCAL AREA: **Living in a village**
Work, commuting and services. Page 14

PHOTOCOPIABLE

At your service

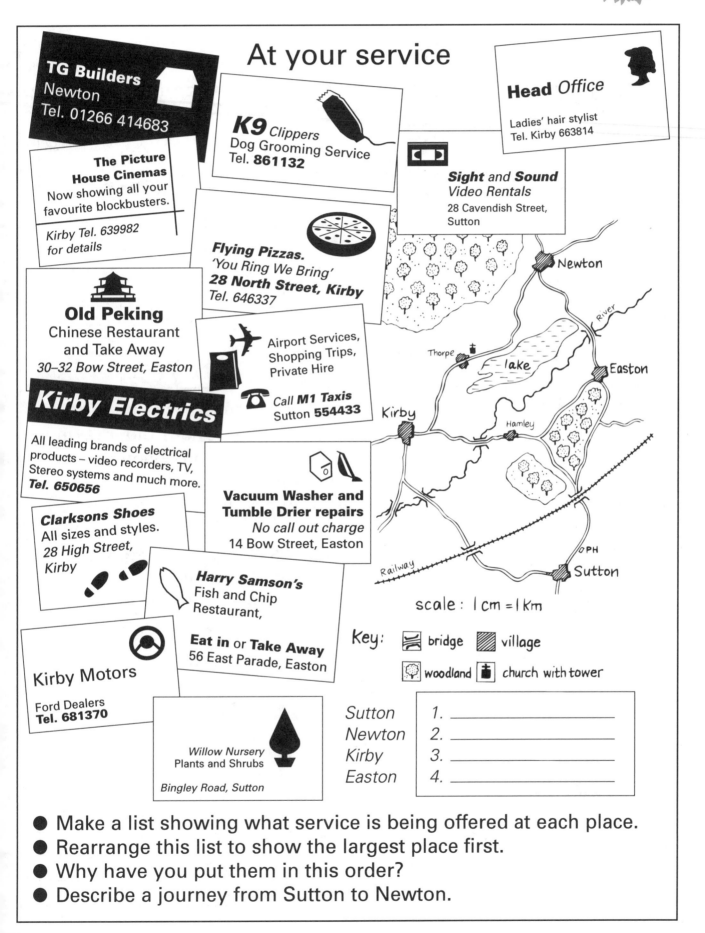

TG Builders
Newton
Tel. 01266 414683

The Picture House Cinemas
Now showing all your favourite blockbusters.

Kirby Tel. 639982 for details

K9 Clippers
Dog Grooming Service
Tel. **861132**

Head Office
Ladies' hair stylist
Tel. Kirby 663814

Sight and **Sound**
Video Rentals
28 Cavendish Street, Sutton

Flying Pizzas.
'You Ring We Bring'
28 North Street, Kirby
Tel. 646337

Old Peking
Chinese Restaurant and Take Away
30–32 Bow Street, Easton

Airport Services, Shopping Trips, Private Hire
Call **M1 Taxis**
Sutton **554433**

Kirby Electrics

All leading brands of electrical products – video recorders, TV, Stereo systems and much more.
Tel. **650656**

Vacuum Washer and Tumble Drier repairs
No call out charge
14 Bow Street, Easton

Clarksons Shoes
All sizes and styles.
28 High Street, Kirby

Harry Samson's
Fish and Chip Restaurant,
Eat in or **Take Away**
56 East Parade, Easton

Kirby Motors
Ford Dealers
Tel. **681370**

Willow Nursery
Plants and Shrubs
Bingley Road, Sutton

scale : 1 cm = 1 km

Key: bridge   village
 woodland   church with tower

Sutton
Newton
Kirby
Easton

1. _____
2. _____
3. _____
4. _____

- Make a list showing what service is being offered at each place.
- Rearrange this list to show the largest place first.
- Why have you put them in this order?
- Describe a journey from Sutton to Newton.

Then and now

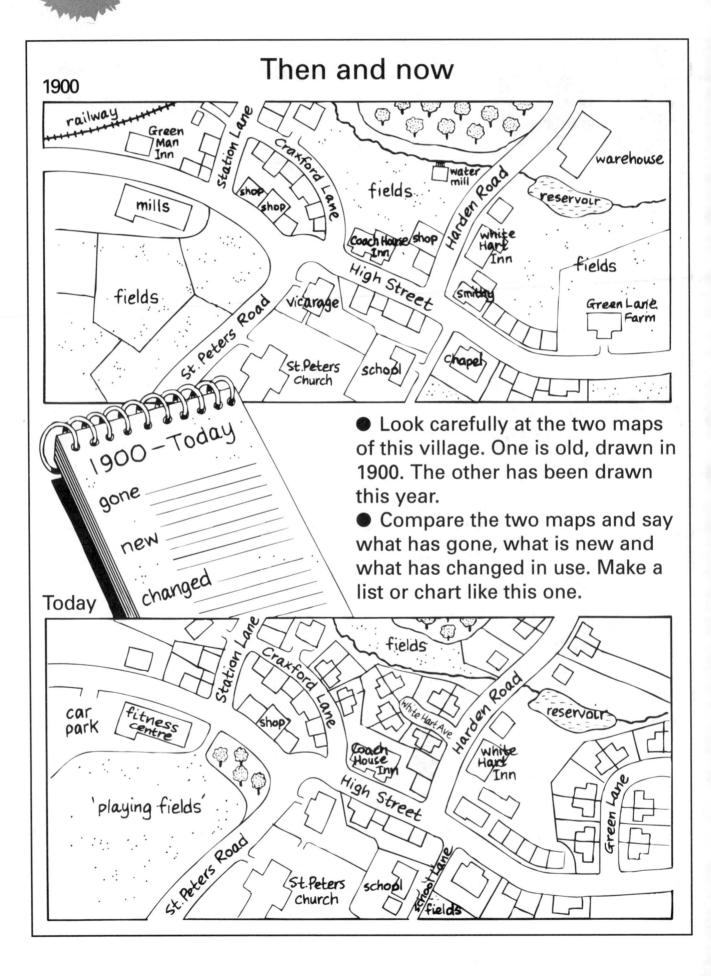

1900

● Look carefully at the two maps of this village. One is old, drawn in 1900. The other has been drawn this year.

● Compare the two maps and say what has gone, what is new and what has changed in use. Make a list or chart like this one.

1900–Today

gone _____

new _____

changed _____

INVESTIGATING OUR LOCAL AREA: **Living in a town**
Land uses in the town. Page 24

PHOTOCOPIABLE

Urban land use map

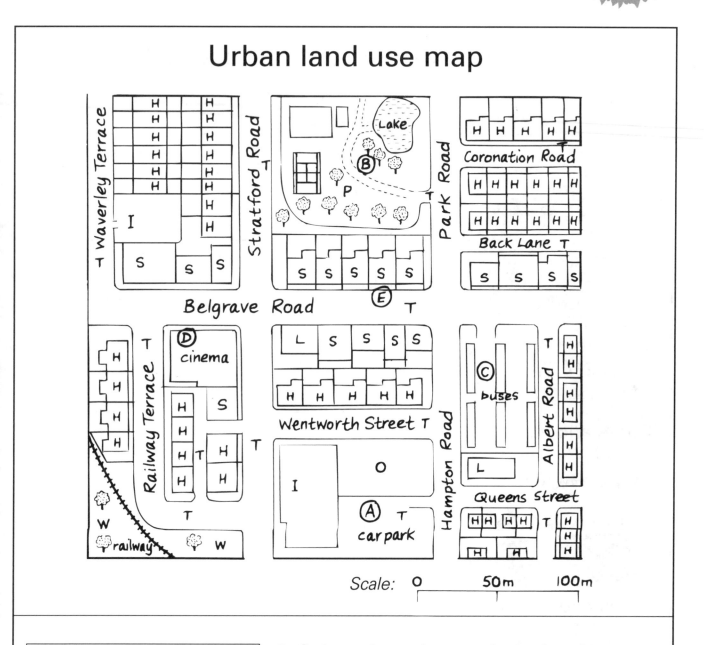

Scale: 0 ___ 50m ___ 100m

Colour code and key

T – transport	
H – house/garden	
S – shop/yard	
I – industry	
W – wasteland	
O – open land	
L – public building	

● Colour the colour code and make a land use map.

● What is most land used for? What is least land used for? Rank the land uses, starting with the most important.

● How do your results compare with those from the 'Village land use map'?

● On the back of the sheet, draw sketches of what you think you would see at each of the places marked with a circled letter from A to E.

PHOTOCOPIABLE

INVESTIGATING OUR LOCAL AREA: **Living in a town**
Work, commuting and transport. Page 25

Traffic survey recording sheet

Name: _____   Road: _____

Date: _____   Time: _____

		Total
Bicycles		
Motorcycles		
Cars and taxis		
Trucks and vans		
Lorries		
Buses and coaches		
Others – list		
	Total of all traffic:	

● Work out the total of all traffic and draw a bar graph.

● What kind of traffic is the most common?

● Do you think the survey results would be different at other times of the day – for example, at 8am, 1pm or 3am?

Commuter – a game for two office workers

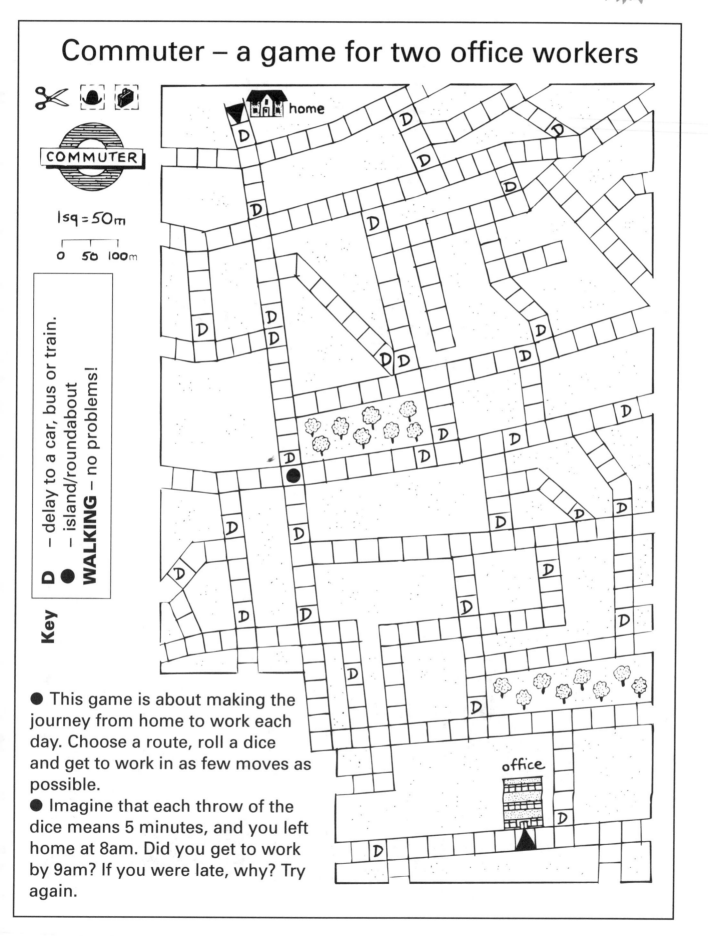

Key

D – delay to a car, bus or train.
● – island/roundabout
WALKING – no problems!

1sq = 50m

0 50 100m

● This game is about making the journey from home to work each day. Choose a route, roll a dice and get to work in as few moves as possible.

● Imagine that each throw of the dice means 5 minutes, and you left home at 8am. Did you get to work by 9am? If you were late, why? Try again.

Filling the gap

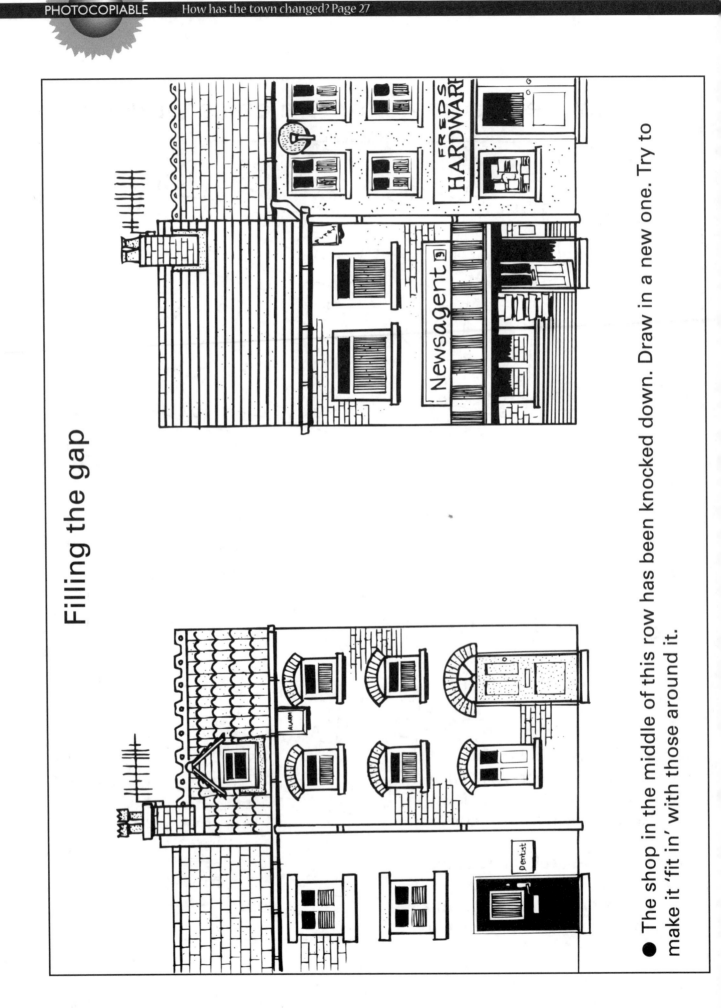

● The shop in the middle of this row has been knocked down. Draw in a new one. Try to make it 'fit in' with those around it.

WEATHER AND TRAVEL: **Weather around the world**
Hot and cold places. Page 33

PHOTOCOPIABLE

Climates of the world

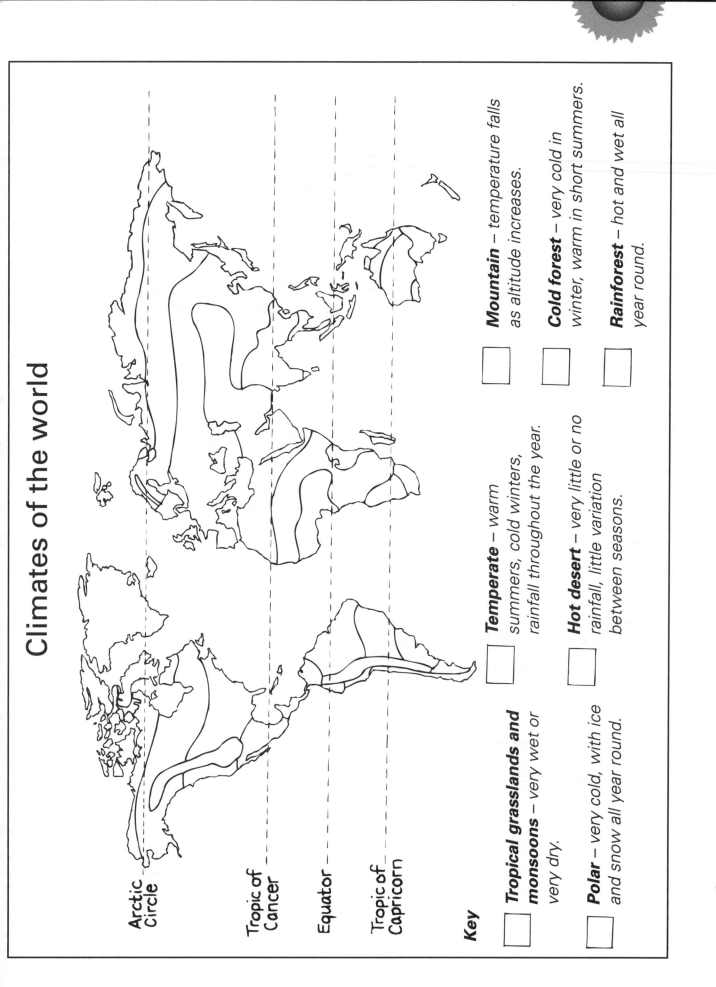

Arctic Circle

Tropic of Cancer

Equator

Tropic of Capricorn

Key

☐ **Tropical grasslands and monsoons** – *very wet or very dry.*

☐ **Polar** – *very cold, with ice and snow all year round.*

☐ **Temperate** – *warm summers, cold winters, rainfall throughout the year.*

☐ **Hot desert** – *very little or no rainfall, little variation between seasons.*

☐ **Mountain** – *temperature falls as altitude increases.*

☐ **Cold forest** – *very cold in winter, warm in short summers.*

☐ **Rainforest** – *hot and wet all year round.*

WEATHER AND TRAVEL: **Weather around the world**
Going on holiday. Page 35
PHOTOCOPIABLE

Come fly with me

Airbus A300–600R
Cruising speed 850km/h
Maximum range 8200km
Seating capacity 361

Boeing B757–200
Cruising speed 860km/h
Maximum range 5630km
Seating capacity 235

Airbus A320
Cruising speed 850km/h
Maximum range 4330km
Seating capacity 179

Boeing B737–300
Cruising speed 805km/h
Maximum range 3862km
Seating capacity 148

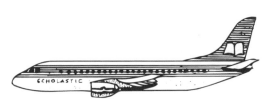

⊠ MPU SOFTWARE INC. eMAIL WIZARD 2000 v.2.03

to:	willy.gofar@flightsrus.com
cc:	
from:	a.manutdfan@southeastengland.co.uk

Willy Gofar Holidays:
Please supply
1. An aeroplane to Madrid for a group of 120 Manchester United supporters.
2. An aeroplane to Bangalore for 350 people from London Heathrow.
3. A short trip to New York for 200 people from London Gatwick.
4. A flight to Moscow for 175 business people from Glasgow.

● Try to find an aeroplane for each group of travellers. Choosing the right aeroplane for the right job saves the company a lot of money. You will find an atlas useful.
● Write an e-mail response from the travel agent.

WEATHER AND TRAVEL: **Weather around the world**
What will I need to take? Page 36

PHOTOCOPIABLE

Where to go? What to take?

● Help Tom to pack a suitcase. Decide whether he should go on holiday to a hot country or a cold country. Draw either red or blue lines from the clothes and equipment he should take with him to his suitcase.

● Collect magazine pictures of hot-weather and cold-weather clothes.

There are lots of things to do in this holiday village, whatever the weather is like.

● Make a list of things to do when the weather is bad, and a list for when the weather is good.

⛈ Bad weather

☀ Good weather

Easy Days Holiday Village

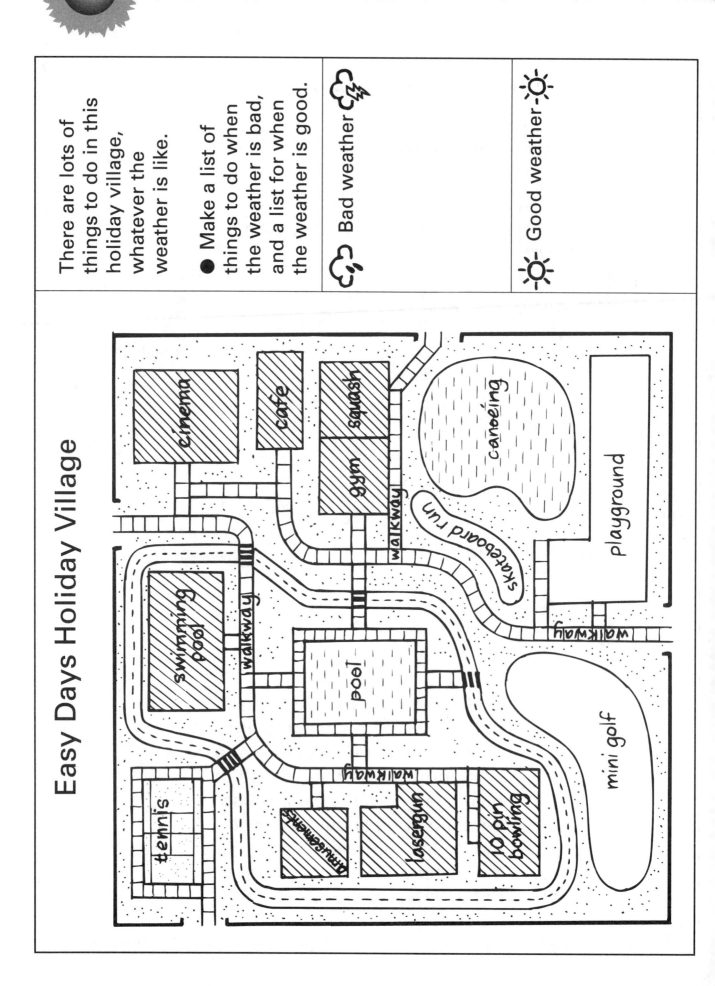

cinema

cafe

gym squash

canoeing

skateboard run

playground

walkway

swimming pool

walkway

pool

walkway

mini golf

tennis

drums&music

lasergun

10 pin bowling

walkway

WEATHER AND TRAVEL: **Weather around the world**
Where have you been? Page 39
PHOTOCOPIABLE

Passport

● Cut out and make a passport. You may need more inside pages.

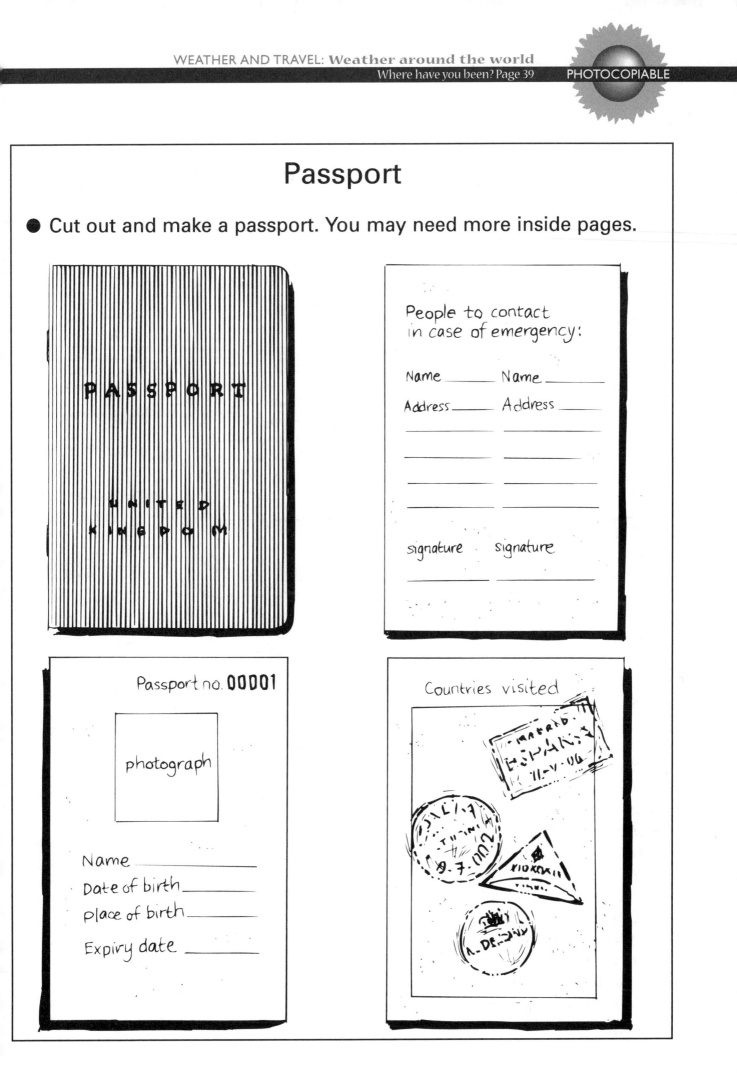

People to contact
in case of emergency:

Name _____   Name _____

Address _____   Address _____

_____   _____

_____   _____

_____   _____

_____   _____

signature   signature

_____   _____

Passport no. **00001**

photograph

Name _____
Date of birth _____
place of birth _____

Expiry date _____

Countries visited

Weatherley Primary School

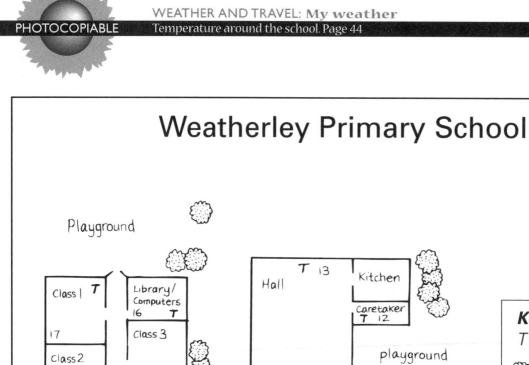

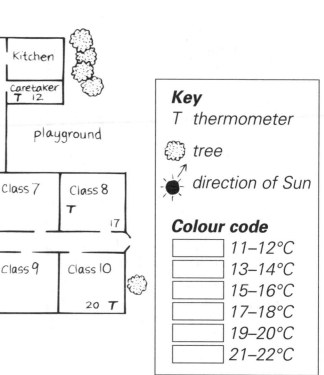

Key

T thermometer

tree

direction of Sun

Colour code

	11–12°C
	13–14°C
	15–16°C
	17–18°C
	19–20°C
	21–22°C

● Colour in the colour code. Use blues, greens, oranges and reds.

● Make a temperature map of the school.

● Where are the warmest places?

● Where are the coolest places?

● Why do you think they are warm or cool?

● Estimate the temperatures of areas that have no thermometers. Colour these in your temperature map.

Temperatures

Entrance	Boys' cloakroom	Class 4
___°C	___°C	___°C

Hall	Head's office	Class 6
___°C	___°C	___°C

Caretaker's office	Main office	Class 8
___°C	___°C	___°C

Library	Class 1	Class 10
___°C	___°C	___°C

Girls' cloakroom		
___°C		

WEATHER AND TRAVEL: **My weather**
Wind speed and direction. Page 45

PHOTOCOPIABLE

The Beaufort Scale

0
0km/h

calm – smoke rises vertically

1
1–5km/h

light air – direction of wind shown by smoke drift

2
6–11km/h

light breeze – wind felt on face, leaves rustle, wind vane moves

3
12–19km/h

gentle breeze – leaves and twigs in constant motion, a light flag extended

4
20–29km/h

moderate breeze – light paper lifted, small branches moved

5
30–39km/h

fresh breeze – small trees in leaf begin to sway

6
40–50km/h

strong breeze – large branches in motion, whistling heard in telegraph wires

7
50–61km/h

near gale – whole trees in motion, walking becomes difficult

8
62–74km/h

gale – twigs broken off trees

9
75–87km/h

severe gale – slight structural damage, slates blown off roofs

10
88–101km/h

storm – trees uprooted, much structural damage

11
103–117km/h

violent storm – widespread damage

12
118kmh +

hurricane – catastrophic damage, roofs ripped from houses, cars overturned

wind speed and direction symbol

wind force

direction wind is coming from

WEATHER AND TRAVEL: My weather
Bring me sunshine. Page 47

PHOTOCOPIABLE

Rainfall map of the UK

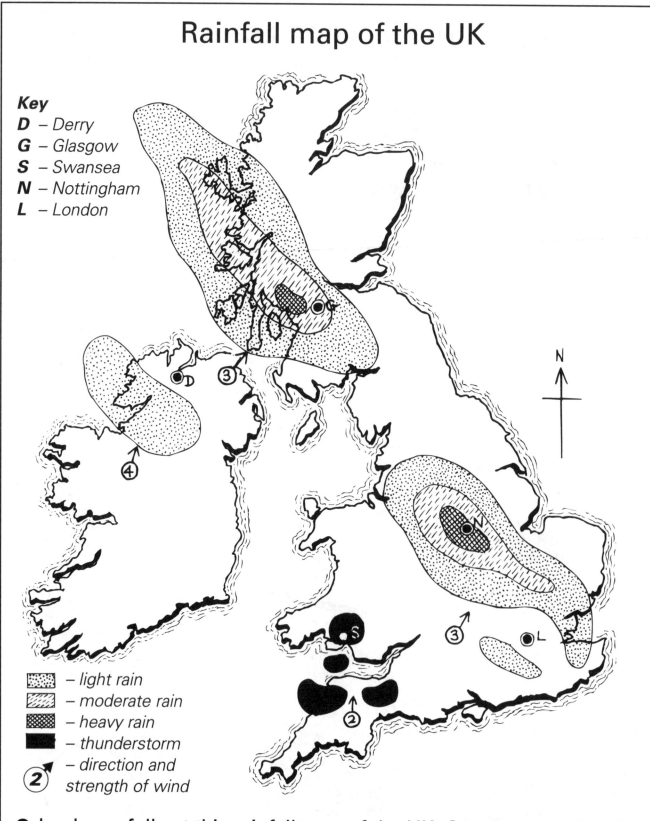

Key
D – Derry
G – Glasgow
S – Swansea
N – Nottingham
L – London

N

– light rain
– moderate rain
– heavy rain
– thunderstorm
– direction and strength of wind

● Look carefully at this rainfall map of the UK. Can you say what the weather has been like, is like now and will be like soon?
● Fill in a weather report for each of the cities marked on the map.

Cloud chart

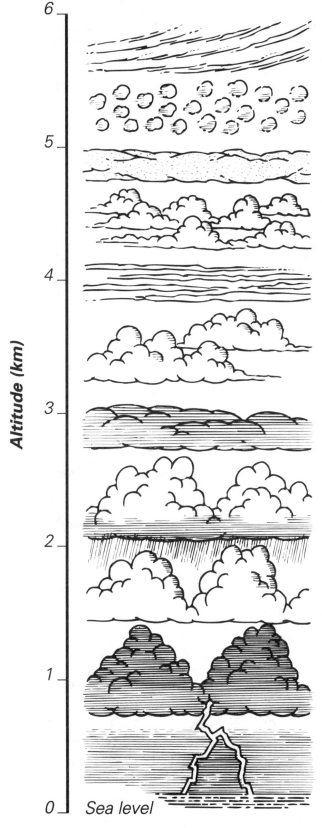

Altitude (km)

6 —

5 —

4 —

3 —

2 —

1 —

0 — Sea level

Cirrus
white filaments

Cirrocumulus
small rippled clouds

Cirrostratus
translucent sheet

Altocumulus
layered, rippled clouds, generally white

Altostratus
thin grey layer, breaks up sunlight

Stratocumulus
layered series of rounded rolls, white or grey

Stratus
layered with uniform base, grey

Nimbostratus
thick layer, dark grey bases, cauliflower-shaped towers, give steady rain

Cumulus
flat bases, cauliflower-shaped towers, white

Cumulonimbus
flat bases, cauliflower-shaped towers, dark grey, give storms

Fog
hovers around valleys, uniform grey, translucent

Weather symbols

sunshine

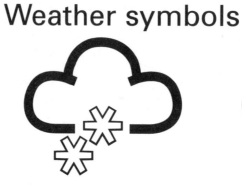

snow

hail

heavy rain

showers

light cloud

heavy cloud

sunny intervals

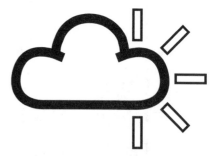

heavy cloud with sunny intervals

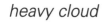

lightning

snow showers

snow showers with sunny intervals

The sounds of school

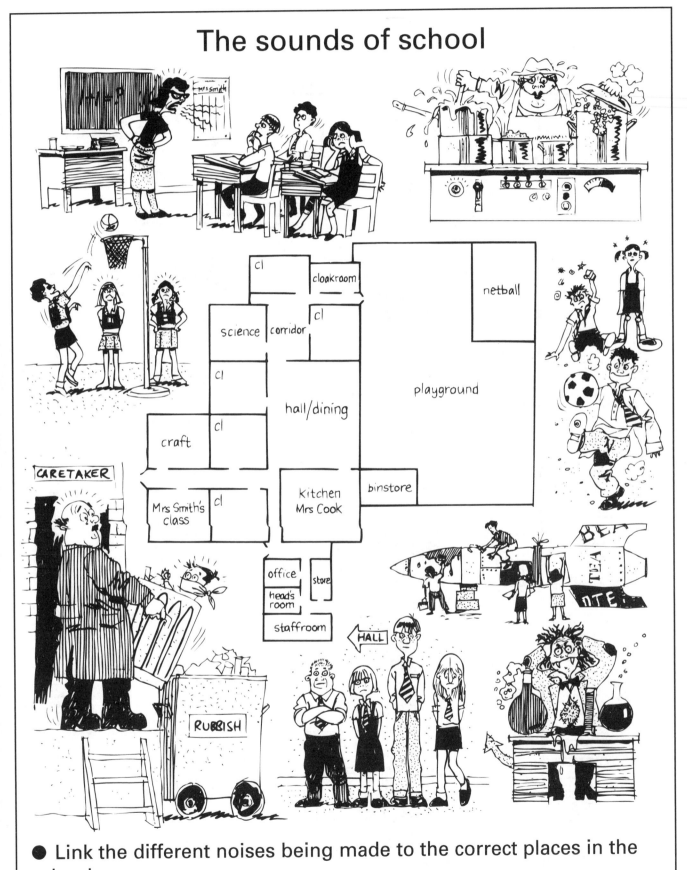

● Link the different noises being made to the correct places in the school.

IMPROVING THE ENVIRONMENT: Improving our school's environment
Don't throw it all away. Page 59

PHOTOCOPIABLE

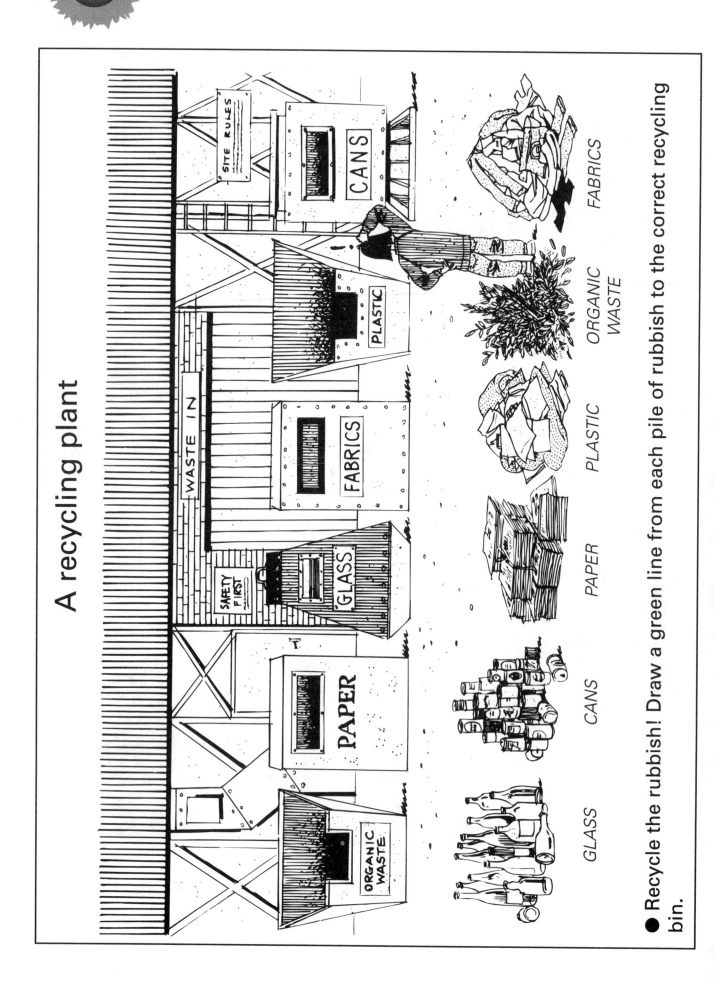

A recycling plant

● Recycle the rubbish! Draw a green line from each pile of rubbish to the correct recycling bin.

Refuse collection

Every year, we spend millions of pounds on collecting and emptying dustbins.

● Can you help the refuse collectors to save money by finding the shortest route around these streets?

● Use string to find the shortest route.
● Write a short description of the shortest route here:

_____

_____

_____

PHOTOCOPIABLE

IMPROVING THE ENVIRONMENT: **Improving our school's environment**
Waste paper and packaging. Page 61

Till receipts

CHEAP-O-MART

+	washing powder	£ 4 - 50
+	chicken nuggets	£ 1 - 50
+	bread sliced	£ 0 - 49
+	1kg margarine	£ 0 - 99
2l	'costalot cola	£ 0 - 35
1l	apple juice	£ 0 - 70
+	stir in sauce	£ 1 - 20
4l	fresh milk	£ 1 - 29
+	spaghetti hoops	£ 0 - 30
+	tomato ketchup	£ 0 - 70
+	furniture polish	£ 1 - 29
+	fresh chicken	£ 3 - 50
+	small tuna	£ 0 - 50
+	mushy peas	£ 0 - 40
+	1kg pasta shells	£ 0 - 89

TOTAL: _____

THANK YOU FOR SHOPPING
AT CHEAP-O-MART

AEROSOL **12P**
DEODOURANT

BREAKFAST FLAKES
LARGE CEREAL BOX **9P**

CELLOPHANE COVER **1P**
BISCUITS

OVEN CHIPS

PLASTIC BAG **1P**

WELCOME TO CHEAP-O-MART

LARGE PLASTIC TUB **7P**

VANILLA TUB ICE CREAM

FRESH Orange juice
LARGE JUICE CARTON **4P**

JAM SMALL GLASS JAR **5P**

medium plastic bottle **10P**
plastic bottle

Shampoo

Sparkling

PIZZA BASE
POLYSTYRENE BOX/TRAY **4P**

SMALL TIN CAN **6P**

LEMONADE

small pineapple chunks

BEANZ medium

MEDIUM TIN CAN **8P**

LARGE PLASTIC BOTTLE **15P**

TOTAL: _____

● Look at the till receipt, then use the chart to work out how much was spent on packaging.

● Fill in the second till receipt to show the packaging costs. How much was spent on packaging?

IMPROVING THE ENVIRONMENT: Improving our school's environment
Reclaiming the wasteland. Page 64

PHOTOCOPIABLE

The wasteland

● Take this sheet into a wasteland area near your school. Answer the questions in the boxes.

PHOTOCOPIABLE

IMPROVING THE ENVIRONMENT: Improving our school's environment
Redevelopment scheme. Page 66

Redevelopment scheme

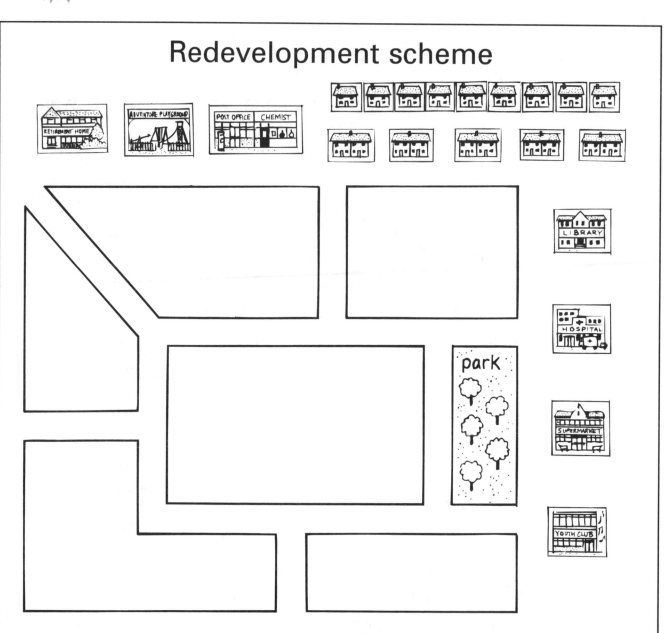

● Colour and cut out each of the new buildings or areas. Place them in what you think are the best positions, then stick them down. Add some trees and gardens, and name the roads.

● Write a brief description of your redevelopment scheme.

IMPROVING THE ENVIRONMENT: A case study: Gretton
Where is Gretton? Page 70

PHOTOCOPIABLE

Find Gretton

● Put these maps in order, starting with the smallest-scale map.

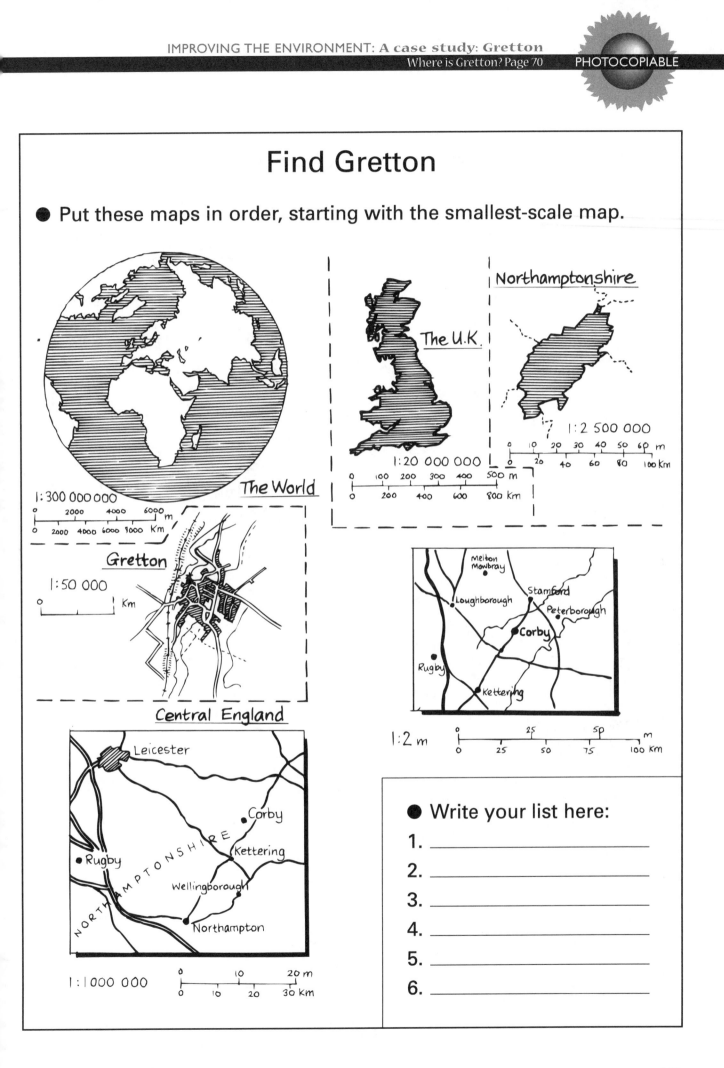

The World
1:300 000 000

Gretton
1:50 000

Central England

The U.K.
1:20 000 000

Northamptonshire
1:2 500 000

Corby
1:2 m

1:1 000 000

● Write your list here:

1. _____
2. _____
3. _____
4. _____
5. _____
6. _____

A map of Gretton

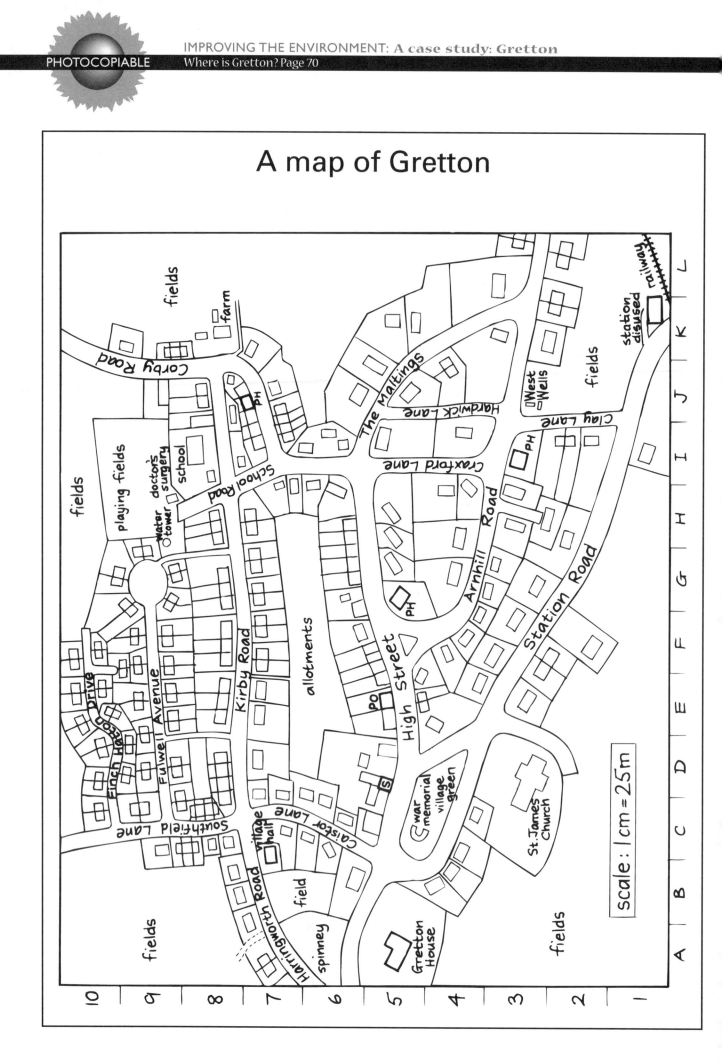

Scale : 1cm = 25m

IMPROVING THE ENVIRONMENT: **A case study: Gretton**
Building the race track. Page 71

PHOTOCOPIABLE

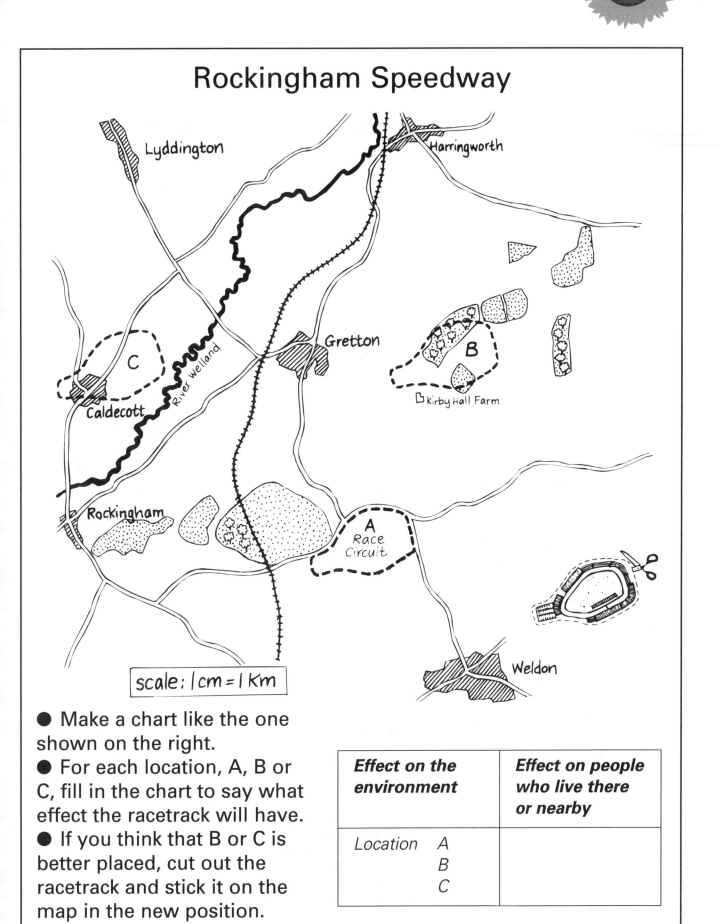

Rockingham Speedway

scale: 1cm = 1 km

Lyddington

Harringworth

C

River Welland

Caldecott

Gretton

B

Kirby Hall Farm

Rockingham

A
Race
Circuit

Weldon

● Make a chart like the one shown on the right.

● For each location, A, B or C, fill in the chart to say what effect the racetrack will have.

● If you think that B or C is better placed, cut out the racetrack and stick it on the map in the new position.

Effect on the environment	*Effect on people who live there or nearby*
Location A B C	

Winners and losers

● Some people will gain from the new racetrack and others will lose. Look carefully at each of these people. Write down whether each person will win or lose, then explain why by filling in each speech bubble.

IMPROVING THE ENVIRONMENT: A case study: Gretton
Track record. Page 74

PHOTOCOPIABLE

The story of the race track

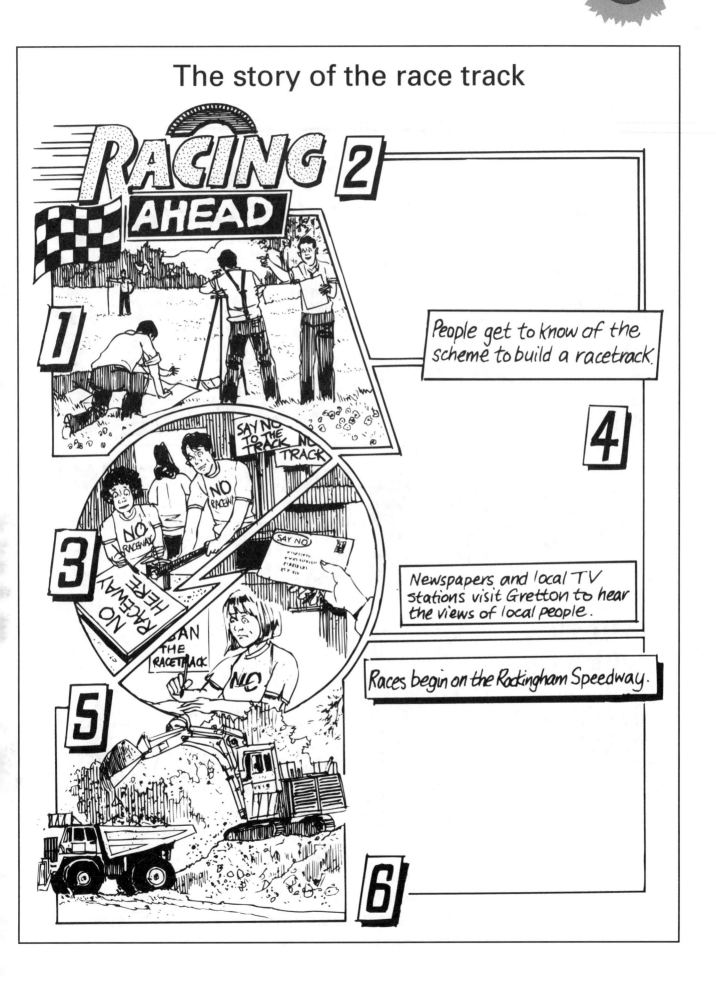

RACING AHEAD

2

1

People get to know of the scheme to build a racetrack.

4

3

Newspapers and local TV stations visit Gretton to hear the views of local people.

Races begin on the Rockingham Speedway.

5

6

Headlines

● Cut out the illustrations and headlines. Arrange them in order, putting each headline with the correct illustration.
● Next to each pair, write a short description of what is happening.

IMPROVING THE ENVIRONMENT: A case study: Gretton
Building a bypass. Page 75

PHOTOCOPIABLE

Building a bypass

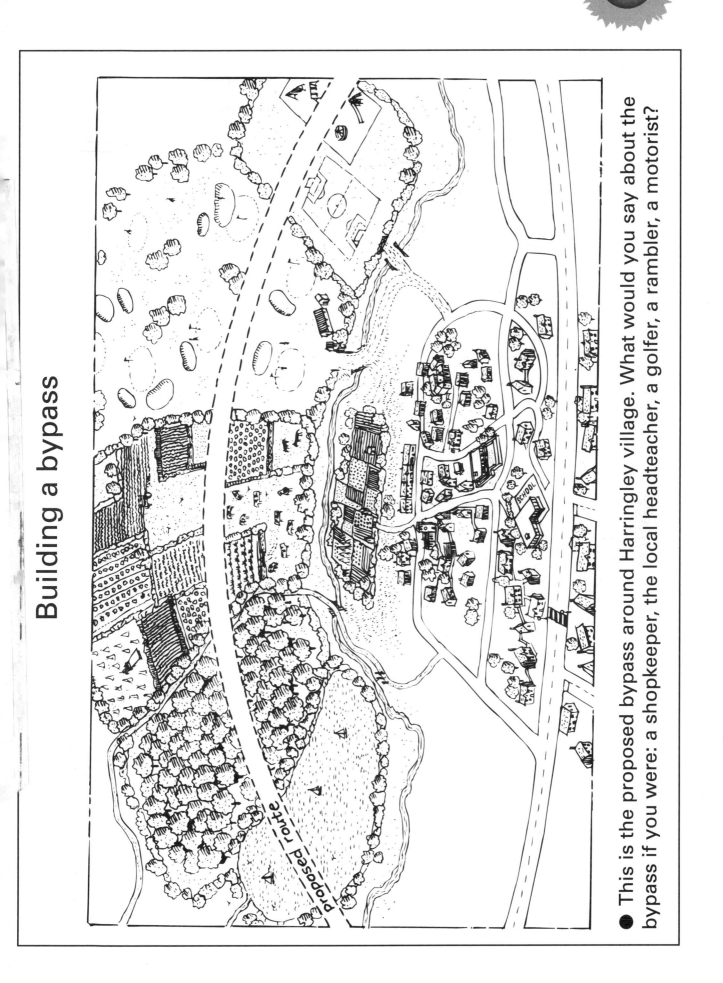

● This is the proposed bypass around Harringley village. What would you say about the bypass if you were: a shopkeeper, the local headteacher, a golfer, a rambler, a motorist?

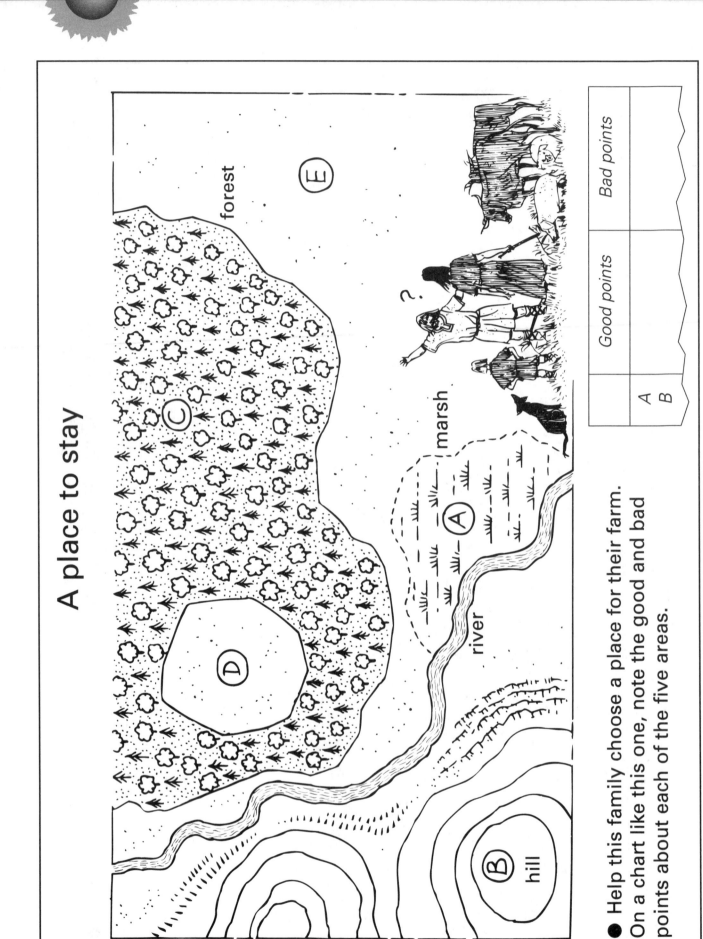

A place to stay

forest

E

C

D

marsh

A

river

hill

B

	Good points	Bad points
A		
B		

● Help this family choose a place for their farm.
On a chart like this one, note the good and bad
points about each of the five areas.

SETTLERS: **Village settlers**
What evidence can we find on maps? Page 82

PHOTOCOPIABLE

A Saxon settlement

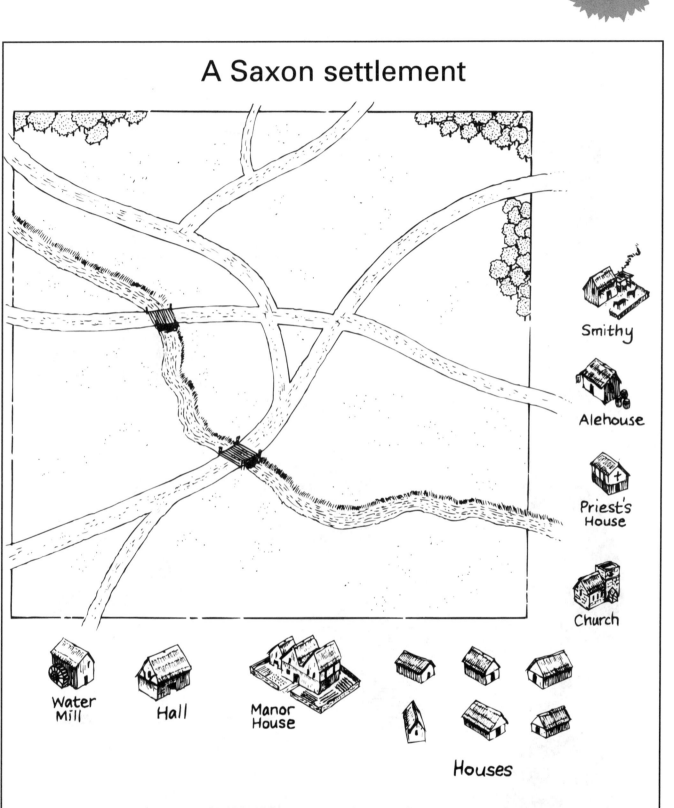

● Cut out these Saxon buildings and use them to make your own village. Colour in the buildings. Add fields divided into strips and common grazing land.
● Give your village a name. Use the place name endings sheet to help you.

Ordnance Survey map symbols

PHOTOCOPIABLE

Isolated farms

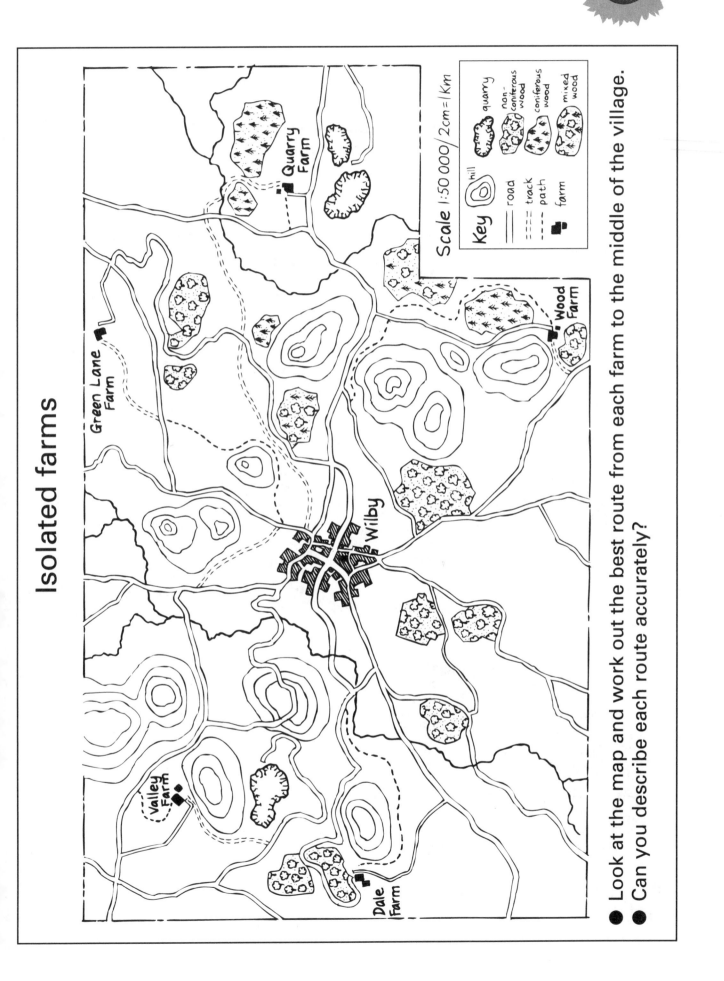

Key Scale 1:50 000/2cm=1Km

- hill
- road
- track
- path
- farm
- quarry
- non-coniferous wood
- coniferous wood
- mixed wood

Quarry Farm

Green Lane Farm

Wood Farm

Wilby

Valley Farm

Dale Farm

● Look at the map and work out the best route from each farm to the middle of the village.
● Can you describe each route accurately?

SETTLERS: **How towns grow**
How did these towns begin? Page 90
PHOTOCOPIABLE

My kind of town

Towns grow because they have different functions that people need.
● Look at these towns and work out which kind of town each one is.
Use the wordbank to help you label each town.

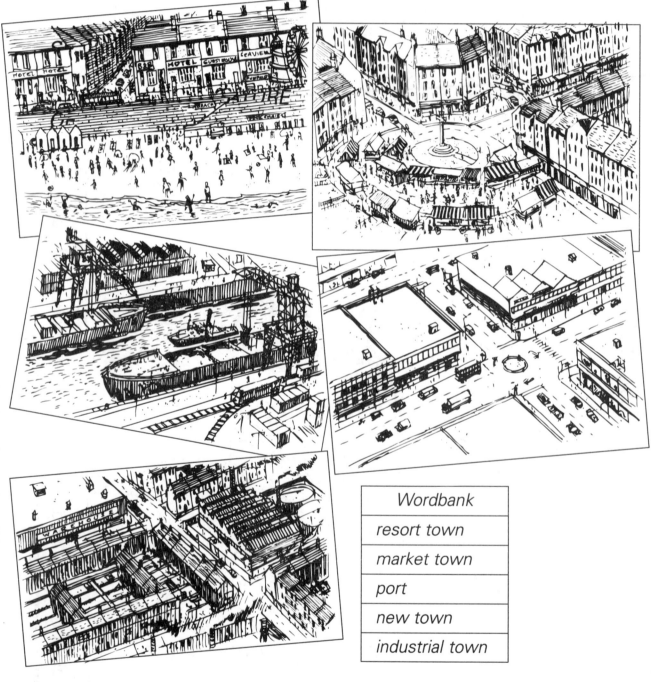

Wordbank
resort town
market town
port
new town
industrial town

● When you have finished, number the towns with the oldest as 1 and the newest as 5.

SETTLERS: How towns grow
In the neighbourhood. Page 96

PHOTOCOPIABLE

Street patterns

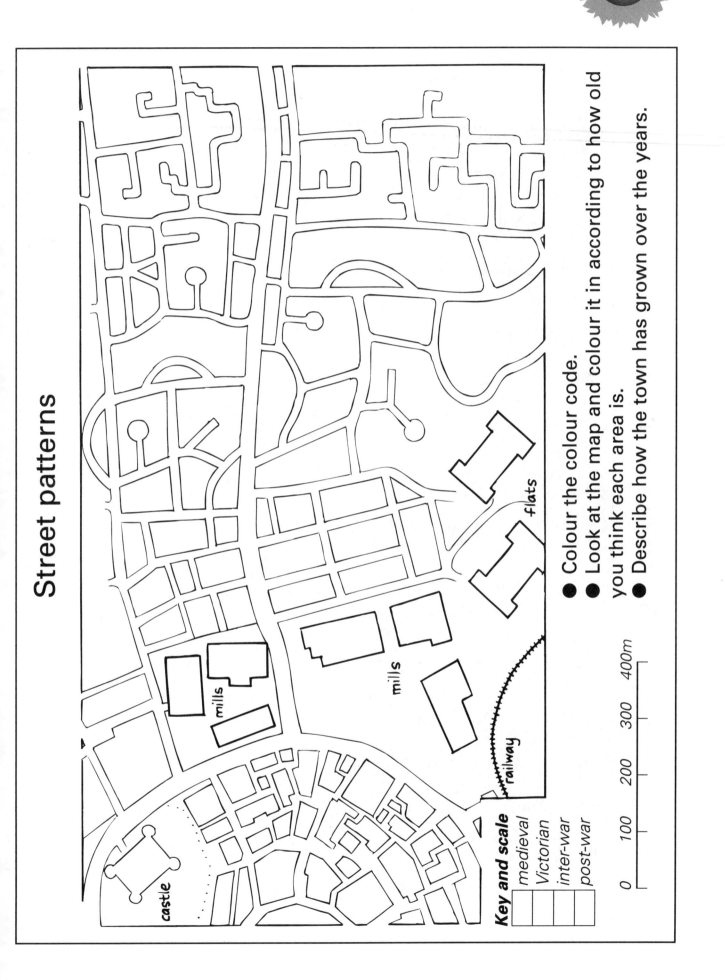

- Colour the colour code.
- Look at the map and colour it in according to how old you think each area is.
- Describe how the town has grown over the years.

flats

mills

mills

railway

castle

Key and scale

	medieval
	Victorian
	inter-war
	post-war

0   100   200   300   400m

Chembakolli village

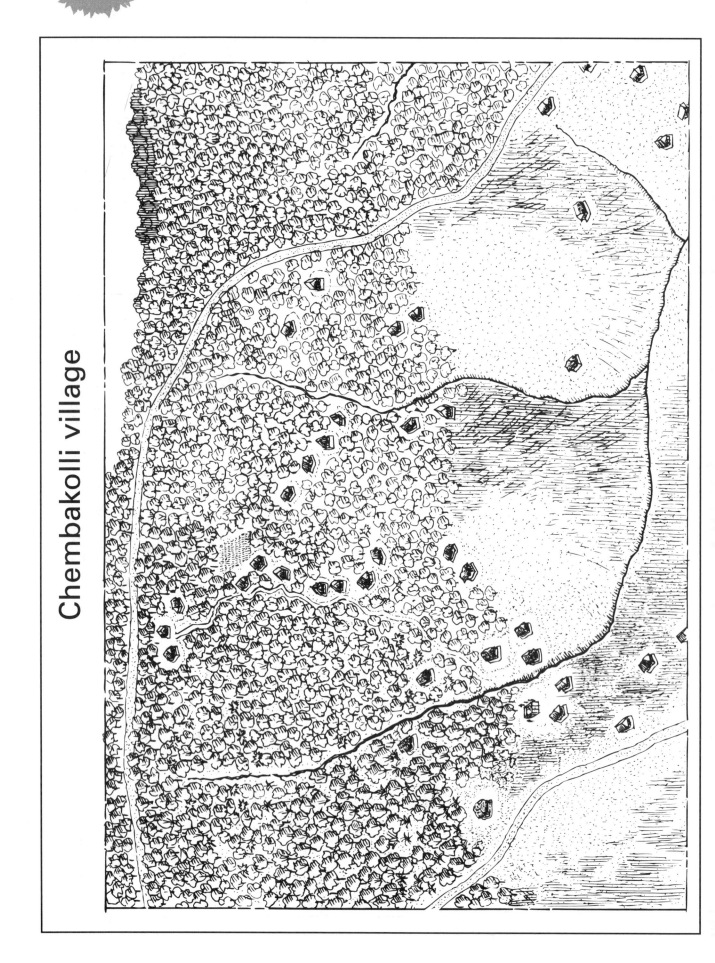

VILLAGE CASE STUDIES: **Chembakolli: village life in India**
The landscape of Chembakolli. Page 104

PHOTOCOPIABLE

A tourist guide

● Make a leaflet for tourists, guiding them around Chembakolli. A plan for a leaflet is shown below. Design yours in a similar way, using a folded sheet of plain A4 paper.

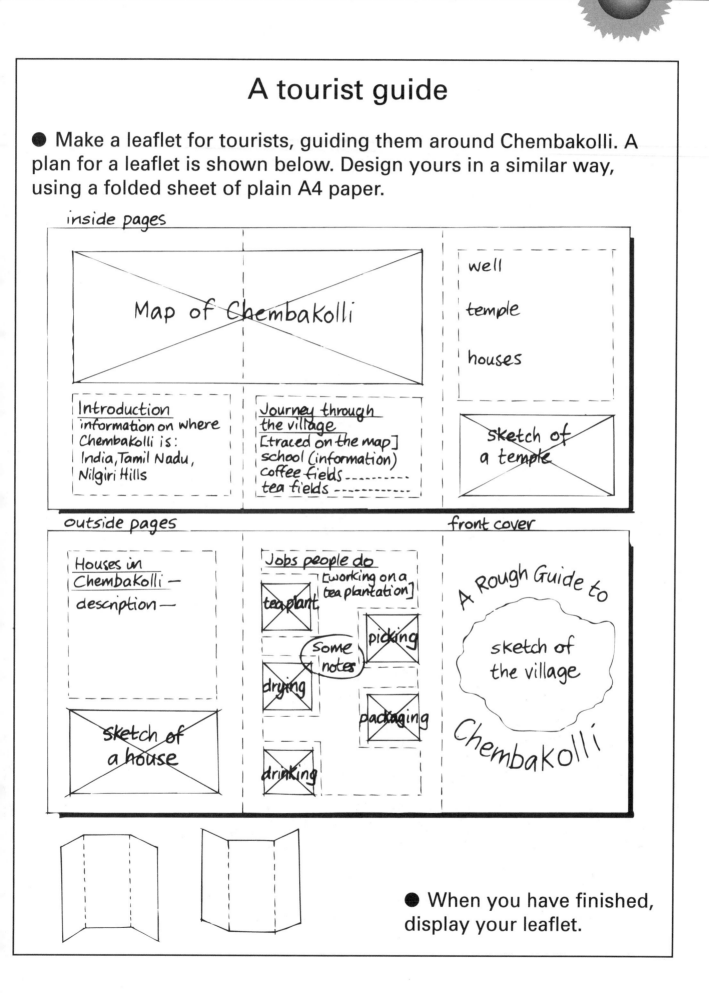

inside pages

Map of Chembakolli

well

temple

houses

sketch of a temple

Introduction
information on where Chembakolli is:
India, Tamil Nadu, Nilgiri Hills

Journey through the village
[traced on the map]
school (information)
coffee fields --------
tea fields --------

outside pages

front cover

Houses in Chembakolli —
description —

sketch of a house

Jobs people do
[working on a tea plantation]
tea plant
Some notes
picking
drying
packaging
drinking

A Rough Guide to
sketch of the village
Chembakolli

● When you have finished, display your leaflet.

PHOTOCOPIABLE

The area around Clapham

● Look carefully at this field sketch of the area around Clapham village. Label the field sketch using the words listed below.

Bypass road, minor road, church, Ingleborough Hall, Clapham Beck, scars, Ingleborough, lowland pastures, highland fells, woodland, reservoir, caves.

VILLAGE CASE STUDIES: **Clapham** – a village in the Yorkshire Dales
The buildings in Clapham. Page 116

PHOTOCOPIABLE

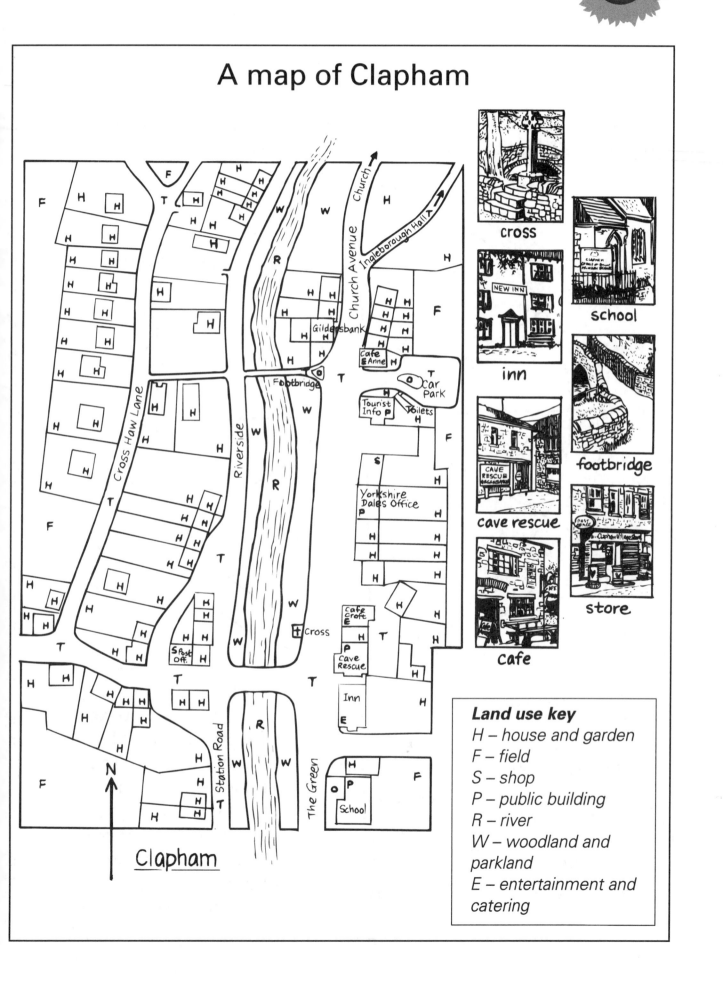

A map of Clapham

cross

school

inn

footbridge

cave rescue

store

cafe

Land use key
H – house and garden
F – field
S – shop
P – public building
R – river
W – woodland and parkland
E – entertainment and catering

Clapham

VILLAGE CASE STUDIES: **Clapham – a village in the Yorkshire Dales**
Making a living in Clapham. Page 117

PHOTOCOPIABLE

Mr Brown's year

Mr Brown lives in a farmhouse in Clapham. His land stretches from the high fells to the rich pastures in the valley.

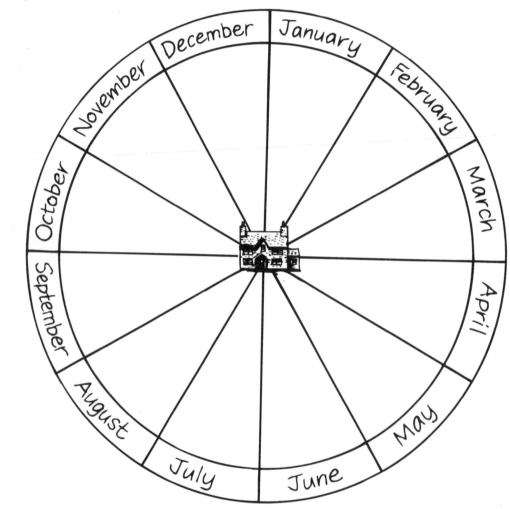

Jan.	– muck spreading
Feb.	– feed sheep
Mar.	– vaccinate cows, calving starts
Apr.	– lambing
May	– lambs tested and marked, last year's calves go to market
June	– sheep dipped, silage and hay made into bales
July	– hay making
Aug.	– dip all lambs
Sept.	– female lambs dipped and sent to market
Oct.	– hogs sent to Cheshire
Nov.	– cows come in for winter
Dec.	– more lambs sent to auction, sheep given hay

Mr Brown keeps animals. This is called **pastoral farming**. Many farmers do this because the soil in their farms is thin and so the land is not good enough to grow crops on.
● Use the information in the box to sketch Mr Brown's farming year.